Kohkumthena's Grandchildren
THE SHAWNEE

Dark Rain Thom

Illustrations by

James Alexander Thom

Guild Press of Indiana, Inc.

Guild Press of Indiana, Inc.
6000 Sunset Lane
Indianapolis, IN 46208
Tel.: (317) 253-0097
FAX: (317) 465-1884

Text design by Sheila Samson

Printed in the United States of America

Library of Congress
Catalog Card Number
94-79098

ISBN 1-878208-53-5 (hardcover)
ISBN 1-878208-29-2 (paperback)

Contents

Appendix (continued)

Dedication

To those who have crossed over to the other side of the Circle of Time
and all of their children, and their children's children,
and their children's grandchildren,
and their grandchildren's grandchildren.

Acknowledgments

Thanks to:

My publisher Nancy Baxter at Guild Press of Indiana, Inc., for asking me to write this book and having the patience to let me do it well. The responsibility of writing a book inspired me to research and validate the information I already had. The process became one of wonderful discovery of information long lost and misfiled concerning the Shawnee People. This book holds less than one percent of the information discovered, with much more still waiting to be utilized. Nancy seems to have been the key to opening these doors. The Shawnee People as a whole should be ever grateful to her for enabling us to rediscover these details of our history, culture and religious information.

Niece Liz Clemons for helping me set up my computer, and getting me started.

Son-in-Law Guy McInnis, who walked me through many a bleak moment, long-distance, as I learned this particular computer system under difficult circumstances.

The kind people of the 'help' department who saved my sanity and works late at night, when I had catastrophes.

Granddaughter Melissa Hewitt who served as my first editor and had excellent suggestions. Author Jack Weatherford for his research's contribution to the story of the Council Oak. And to Tatsii Yazzie for her guidance toward the Newberry resources.

Ayapia, Larry Eveland, Dr. Richard Pape, Rev. Ronald Chrisley, and Carolina Butler for helping me understand the mountain of language information I discovered, and for sharing their own Shawnee language discoveries with me.

A large portion of appreciation goes to my many and various friends, who shall remain nameless, among the Oklahoma Shawnee. A special thank you for their kindness and encouragement to the members of the Eastern Shawnee Tribe of Oklahoma, their beloved Chief George "Buck" Captain, their second Chief Nelis Captain, Laurie Van Pelt, and SuZanna Prophet.

Chief Hawk Pope, United Remnant Band of the Shawnee Nation in Ohio, has always been helpful and an accurate source of information on all questions asked of him. I have endeavored not to ask him many questions, as I know he too is working on a book concerning the history of Shawnee, especially that of the United Remnant

Band, and I did not want to steal any choice information he will be including in his own work. His knowledge of Tecumseh and his followers has proven richly extensive and accurate. I personally attempted to validate many of the oral traditions that Hawk teaches. I have found unbelievable amounts of them have been validated in anthropological and historical works. I am certain this will continue as I resume my research. It is through his generosity that I used his chronology list of prehistoric events which to some degree corresponds with information in the Walam Olum, Megwich.

Several other members of the Shawnee Nation, United Remnant Band, contributed to the oral traditions portion of this book. They include Wakwashbosha Lesa Greene, Sun Spirit Marlene Lowe, Yahma Walter Shepherd, and Black Wolf Paul Harmon.

Rich resource centers for this book include the Newberry Library, the American Philosophical Society, Library of Congress, Lilly Library, Indiana University Library, Archives of Traditional Music Library at Indiana University, and Smithsonian Institute, made possible by their supporters. The National Endowment for the Humanities made possible such resources as the *Atlas of the Great Lakes Indians* by Helen Hornbeck Tanner. Susan Gray and Toni Siler, experts on Greeneville, Prophet's Town I, and Ohio battles, shared their research materials.

The joint project between the Smithsonian Institute and Japan Public Broadcasting-NHK for Japan's Golden Week special on American Heroes, enabled me to visit places special to Tecumseh, and to hold in my hands his personal war clubs which are housed at Fort Malden, Ontario, Canada. The project's interest, generosity, and clout enabled me to envision the war clubs' story of Tecumseh's death, and enrich this book. Thanks to Bob Garcia at Fort Malden for his kind assistance as well.

There must be special thanks to linguist Charles Carl Voegelin, who studied the Shawnee language and saved much of it on wax cylinders, as well as developing the syntax and grammatical structure so at this time, with a little work, the Shawnee language may again be fully conversational, not merely a list of nouns, verbs, and modifiers. The material with which he chose to work included the Great Laws, which have been found nowhere else in print.

Anthropologist Erminie Wheeler Voegelin studied the Shawnee over forty-five years. She, too, recorded interviews in various manners including handwritten field notebooks that show phonetic Shawnee, literal English translations, and then correctly-punctuated English translations. Most of the rediscovered cultural and religious information came from this source. She was a meticulous and tireless researcher intent on writing the ultimate book on the Shawnee, but was always trying to pinpoint just one more detail, and so never did write it. I was privileged to meet and speak with Mrs. Voegelin in 1976, when she agreed to assist Chief Hawk Pope and me on a tribal project. It was twenty-five years before I used her material. She passed away in the 1980s. I pray she knows the treasure she left for the Shawnee People as a whole, and that it is being used as she would have wanted, for their benefit.

An extremely important person to this whole project is Helen Hornbeck Tanner of the Newberry Library. She was a close friend of Erminie Voegelin, and upon Erminie's death saved all the field notes from being carted off and dumped in the landfill. They were instead preserved in a vault at the Newberry, and although they are still mostly uncataloged, not preserved on film, and deteriorating rather quickly, for the time being they do still exist. Helen Tanner was an excellent guide when I was at a loss at finding particular types of material. Her friendship, encouragement, and direction have been a gift from Creator, for at times I felt totally overwhelmed by the requirements for doing this book well. Thank you, Helen.

As this is my first, and possibly only book, I want to thank the people who helped me become the person I am today: my parents Naomi and Sonny Cahill; my father's parents, who taught me what they knew of our Native American heritage, taught Shawnee and Wyandotte ways, cautiously retained much of the culture, and maintained contact with others of like ancestry. The other grandfather avoided his red culture (Cherokee), but kept many of the ways, and the grandmother, who was Welsh, taught me dignity. Also, my Aunt Irma, who enabled me to grow, and exposed me to and taught me of the outside world and the inner sanctum of the red world. She sought out the information her father refused to acknowledge and more. Truly she was a traditional teaching aunt. I attribute to her and my father any objective perspective I have of life, including that which is unseen and spiritual in nature.

I had three teachers in school who affected my life. Mrs. Marie Andrews awakened in me a love of learning, literature and life. Mr. Rodney Senseman took a sensitive, sick, teenager who was losing intellectual ground, and stimulated and challenged her mind. He gave me my first dose of teamwork and pride in works accomplished, and patiently understood that my scrawly handwriting was reflective of great illness and nervousness, not a reflection of my IQ. Had he not taken the interest in my learning process when he did, I would have forever been an underachiever. As a sophomore in high school I had a teacher of English named Mrs. Sharon Sarber who was the first to encourage me to write, and who believed I was talented in that area. She did another thing that made a life-changing impression on me: when I filled out the statistics area of a national test, she brought my paper back to me and, after a lecture, erased the check mark I had put in the "American Indian" box, because I had not been born on a reservation. I never forgot that, and it has prodded me to continue educating others for the last thirty years. I have tried not to use worn out expressions in this book, but one pops into my mind, "You don't have to be born in a garage to be a car."

Reservations are not now, nor have they ever been, the only areas of residence of American Indians. The American Indians living on reservations are the ones who signed peace treaties with the United States government, and thus accepted the reservations and entitlements. This often did not include all divisions of any particular nation of Indians, only the divisions who chose to sign the treaties. Remember, it is the practice of the government to limit recognition to those they can control, or from whom they have something to gain. The United States government spent decades *not recognizing* mainland China and its hundreds of millions of citizens, simply because it was not to the government's financial or political advantage to do so. In no way did the lack of American recognition invalidate the fact that the land China existed, nor did it keep the hundreds of millions of Chinese citizens from existing; it merely enabled the United States government to ignore the Chinese, to not send foreign aid, and to not allow commerce between the countries. This lack of recognition meant less than nothing to the hundreds of millions of Chinese citizens. The fact that my ancestors chose to not sign any peace treaty with the United States government does not invalidate my being a Shawnee citizen, nor does it invalidate the teachings given to me by my grandparents, aunt, and father. Thank you, Mrs. Sarber, for humiliating me that day and causing me to think these things through, and for triggering my defiance button, which had been dormant until that point. But in spite of that event, you have remained one of my favorite teachers.

My beloved husband, James Alexander Thom is many things. He, too, is an author who is meticulous in his research, and he enabled me to write this book. Jim has shared his knowledge of archives and resource centers, his office, the contents of his wallet — as this project has now cost four times the amount of the author's fee. He had set a great example of working diligently under pressure, and enabled me to keep at the task at hand by not booby-trapping my efforts nor by demanding attention. Jim edited my galley proofs as a favor; with his twenty-nine years' experience as an editor, I trusted his suggestions and criticisms, which were very few. At the last moment I asked him and he agreed to be the artist for the book cover and two other pictures, and then became the artist for the entire book. At this point I think his self-interest in getting the book finished and getting me back in the kitchen helped. He has been totally unselfish in all his support. His pride in me forced me to work hard to try to live up to his wonderful opinion of me and my capabilities. Jim has been totally nonintrusive in this work, and I will be forever grateful for his self-discipline in not doing any of it for me, although we both know it would have been much quicker and less painful for him than sitting and watching my inexperienced efforts at muddling through the massive amounts of information. Thank you, Darling, for all you are and all you are allowing me to finally be.

With deepest gratitude to all, including the dozens of generous helpers unnamed because of space limitations.

Dark Rain Thom
October, 1994

Author's Notes and Foreword

This book contains perhaps one thousandth of the knowledge available concerning the great Shawnee People. I have tried to fill every space I could with good, solid information about the People. It is painful to re-read this and realize all I have left unsaid, untold, and unexplained. I have tried to be fair and make it a book about the entire Nation, not a particular division.

In an effort to be fair I contacted each of the Oklahoma divisions of the Shawnee Nation personally. Each was given the opportunity to have me add, delete, modify, change, and explain anything they considered inappropriate or incorrect, or that needed clarification. Each division chose to leave it to me to write the Shawnee story. Having had the privilege of meeting each of the leaders in person the fall of 1992, as well as some of their treasured Elders and other members, I felt a special obligation to be accurate when mentioning the Oklahoma divisions and their past. It was the desire of both the publisher and this author to update the reader as to the current status of the different divisions. Every effort to validate the information contained within these pages was taken. It was unfortunate that no current picture was available of the leaders of the Absentee and the Loyal-Cherokee divisions, though for the sake of history, attempts were made to document their leaders for the reader. Each leader is deserving of tribute.

An Oklahoma informant told me of the words of Jim Clark, a Shawnee who was interviewed in 1935. He spoke of medicine bundles and medicine men of old, lamenting that they had all died out and no one knew how to use the sacred bundles anymore. It is a prophecy that I feel is coming true. Jim Clark said, "They (the People) claim they are going to learn this again some day. Something is coming; a man is going to be ruler of this country, who will ruin it; people are going to fight amongst themselves in a war that will last fifteen to twenty-five years. That's the reason why people are divided up today. One party is on the right side; the others on the wrong side; if the right party wins, then everything will come back as it was in the first beginning. But if the wrong party wins, it will destroy this place forever, and there will be another Creation made. Then, if the professors are on the right side, despite this triumph of the wrong side, the life of Indians will be preserved and grow again, from books, languages, these very words these anthropologists are writing down, and things in museums. The Indians themselves will pass away, but this will be for their children."

A sophisticated People were living well here on this continent the last time the Aliens came to visit and stayed. The People knew all about their section of the world, the animals, the green, growing things, the cycles of life and what it took to maintain the balance, to insure their grandchildren would enjoy the benefits Creator provided for them from earth and nature. I believe that perpetuity is the best single word for their way of life, other than reverence and respect. That word explains how they lived, believing that life came around to them, that they rode the circle of time, and that if they were "right-thinking and doing" that circle would come around forever. For a while they lost their way, but signs are showing that they have again found their way and are again becoming the strong fine nation of old. It is hoped this book will be a beginning in the rediscovery of all the ancient ways that can be beneficial for the People of today and tomorrow.

There are many spellings of some words pertaining to the term Shawnee and to the names of their septs or bands. I know this will at first seem confusing. If the reader will verbally sound out the words, he or she will quickly see that they are indeed merely different spelling of the same words. The French, for example, would spell Shawnee with a "Ch," and also have "ou" or "oauo", in place of "aw," reflecting their nation's pronunciation pattern. The Spanish records are not too difficult to understand; however, the Dutch, Danes, and Swedes were challenging.

Sept or band names are subject to the same problem. One of the worst situations exists with the "Thalegiwas." They are called Tallegiwa, Thawakila, and Sptikotha. I have no idea why these variations exist.

I made no effort to settle on single spellings of the various problem words because I used so many different research pieces written by so many different people over a span of five hundred and fifty-five years. Should you decide to study the Shawnee on your own, you will recognize the different sources and eras this book has used. Because I used literally several hundred sources of various types, and mostly because I have never before published a book, I did not keep a complete bibliography, although if questioned I feel confident I can either recite the source or take you to the resource center, floor, shelf, and area where I found the information. Often in the beginning I would read a resource book and be terribly disappointed at its not containing anything I felt was either pertinent or that I did not already know. Still, I apologize for not having an entire bibliography for your use.

The other reason for the lack of a bibliography is that the book has changed in format several times as Creator molded and shaped it. I originally thought it would be a simple book containing what knowledge I already possessed about the Shawnee People, told in a simple direct manner. It then changed to being told in "voices" which turned out to be the those of the Great House Stones and the Council Oak. I subsequently decided to attempt validating all the oral traditions I could find reference to. Then I accidently stumbled onto the treasure trove of language that the People need, in a form that makes the language teachable and continuable, thus necessitating the last major change in the format of the book.

It is the heartfelt belief of this author that Creator has used both my publisher and myself as tools to give the Shawnee People back what is theirs, preserved for them by their ancestors for this moment. While I possibly may never speak fluent Shawnee, I know that shortly there will be many more traditional speakers than there have been in over a hundred years. This is a great thing for all. For me, it has been worth every bit of effort and expense to keep this precious history, culture, and language from perishing.

Kohkumthena's Grandchildren

THE SHAWNEE

As told by the Stones — the Ancients,
and the Trees — the Old People

The boy, frightened but proud, walked from the light into the deepening darkness. The sounds of the camp had changed: children's giggles and the friendly banter of adults had quieted to soft murmurs that escaped from the walls of the lodges. The night had developed a chill which replaced the warmth the sun had showered everywhere all day. Occasionally the flames of the Night Watch's security fire would flash with a bright flare, as those of the People who were on the watch spoke softly of things close to their hearts and of signs that the Ancestors were at the grounds, happily making their presence known.

The community building at Shawandasse, in the heart of Ohio, the traditional homeland of the Shawnee, was full of tired, sleeping people. This was the piece of sacred land the Shawnee had bought back from the conquering Alien invaders, purchased as individuals in the name of the tribe. The site, with trees on all sides hiding it from the view of casual observers, was situated between Tecumseh's last known camp in Ohio, on Deer Creek, and Old Man's Village of the west branch of Buck Creek. It is considered the new beginning of the People, for here they were regaining their old ways and knowledge about how to live in balance and harmony, guided by the old sacred laws. Shawandasse is considered the fulfillment of Tecumseh's dream of a place for his People, standing in the heart of the homeland.

There, in the community building, with the walls quietly basking in the soft echoes of the day's activities, only an occasional visit by the Night Watch to the coffee urn interrupted the stillness. The boy looked toward two other structures, barely discernible in the dark, at the end of a long path outside the community building. One was an old fashioned dome-shaped wigiwa that housed the things used inside the Great House, so they wouldn't have to be carried so far. The wigiwa was about a tenth of a mile from the community building, which isn't far unless you are carrying the heavy stone items that the Temple Woman used in order to make the Great House recognizable to the Ancestors.

The Great House stood a few feet away from the wigiwa. It too was round and looked something like a stockade. Getting closer, the boy could detect a strange roof over part of it. Not solid, it was more of an arbor covering than a true roof. Here in the Great House was the place where the Shawnee held their sacred ceremonies and gave thanks to Creator for all the blessings of life. It was the most important and sacred place in the camp.

The walls of the Great House were made of slender poles and corn stalks. Through the tiny cracks and spaces in the walls, the boy could see the orange glow flickering at the night watch fire back at the community building. Standing outside the Great House, he could also detect a soft glow in the center, close to the ground. This glow was from the sacred ceremonial fire that was lit at the beginning of the encampment and would continue to burn as a witness until the ceremonies and gathering were over.

The boy knew he was nearing sacred ground. He knew that upon stepping into the Great House one was instantly aware of things that cannot be put into words, that can only be known by experiencing them. When entering the Great House you always remove your shoes, because the ground has been purified and is now sacred. Mother Earth sends you knowledge through your bare feet, and it travels throughout your being, preparing you for what is to come. In the Great House your senses are more keen, thoughts more clear and deeper than usual. You find yourself waiting for something, something exciting and good; and you wait. At Shawandasse you learn that wonderful things come to you when you wait.

Inside the Great House the night watch person stands back against the wall, very still and only watching, just out of reach of visual perception. Once the people stop coming in to offer their private prayers, this Watcher may sit, still out of sight. His purpose is to guard the Sacred Bundle of the tribe which contains some of the most ancient treasures the tribe possesses, brought out for each ceremony. Some objects are hundreds of years old and some are said to be over a thousand. At one time there had been threats someone would steal it. Even some tribal members had made jokes and said they could sneak and hide it because the Watchers were so lazy, or they would take some of the sacred objects and sell them to museums. Among the people were many jokesters who would say such things in jest, though no one really believed anyone would show such disrespect to the Bundle. But just in case, the Bundle was always under careful guard. It was an honor to be a Great House Watcher, and a position of great responsibility.

The boy knew all this. He also knew that this night there were to be two Watchers, one old and one young. As children become better capable of understanding, they are given responsibility which is a great honor and recognition of their abilities to handle adult life. The spiritual growth of the children is also considered. When the adults consider the young ones ready, these children are taken under the guidance of the elders and then are taught all that the old ones know about living life in a sacred manner, and how to serve the People as they honor Creator. This night a Young One was standing security watch for the first time. The boy knew the honor that was being given him and accepted his responsibility reverently.

There were no city lights here, only lights on the corner of the community building, too far away to illuminate this area. Walking to the Great House alone to meet the elder Watcher was just the beginning of experiences this Young One would encounter and endure. This night would be the true beginning of the instructions from the Ancestors who lived so long ago, and the Ancients and the Old People who were here even before the Ancestors. It would be years before the Young One would be considered learned enough to be left on his own, and many years before he would be considered an appropriate teacher for another Young One. Then, if he lived to be very old, he would be honored as an elder and be given the utmost respect of the People.

The walk from the Young One's lodge to the Great House was not long. His mother had lit a small lantern so he could gather his clothes and pick up the new stone war club that the men in the warrior's society had taught him to make. She had decorated this set of clothes with a bit of bead work, and his sister had given him some of her beads to decorate the pouch hanging from his belt that held sacred tobacco which he would use for his prayers.

Once he was outside the lodge, the darkness was thick and impenetrable. The sounds of the camp seemed different when not filtered through the lodge walls. There were sounds coming from many directions — skit-

3

tering of small four-leggeds, the rustle of brush as a raccoon or possum shuffled along. The Young One could tell the sound was not from a skunk by the lack of perfume. That was good because skunks are very nearsighted and can even bump into you, or if they see you in a campfire light, they sometimes will play hide-and-seek with you. Everyone still snickered about the time the Night Watcher tried to shoo a little skunk away from camp, but it dodged into the Great House to hide.

A rush of air passed the Young One's cheek and caught him by surprise. It was too dark to tell if it was a night bird or a bat, come to make night watch more tolerable by eating some of the huge mosquitoes that thrived here on the land. Or was it the spirit of an Ancestor come to greet him?

The Young One straightened himself, took a deep breath, swallowed hard and walked on to the Great House. Once at the door he removed his shoes and went in. The dim, soft, orange glow of the sacred fire held a warmth that made his heart glad. He was no longer considered a child! This night his People would begin to treat him like a young man. It was with relief he saw his mentor, the Old Watcher, sitting on a robe, offering small pieces of sage, cedar, and tobacco to the fire.

The Old Watcher was asking the Ancestors for help as he guided this Young One from boyhood to young manhood. He seldom felt especially wise, but contented himself with the thoughts that with "right thinking" and proper prayers, he could become an empty vessel, a hollow tube through which Creator and the Ancestors could send wisdom to this Young One. This he was asking as he softly murmured his prayers, which he punctuated with bits of tobacco.

The Young One sat in silence beside his mentor. This was the time to get one's heart and mind in the proper condition to receive special blessings. One always received special blessings while in the Great House.

After a long while, the Old Watcher acknowledged the presence of his young protégé, saying, "I see, Young One, you have chosen this night to leave your childhood behind. I am proud of you for this display of courage, to leave the warmth of your mother's lodge to come out on this chilly night to help an Old One protect this place and these pitiful scraps, these pieces of our history left over from the days of our ancestors. You will respect the knowledge even though it may sometimes be strange and you won't be able to discuss it with your friends at school. I say this will be a night we will remember fondly, for I feel much strength in the Great House tonight. There will be many blessings bestowed this night."

The Young One was silent with respect. Knowing just what to say to an Old Watcher was something still very new to him. Often his tongue stumbled when he tried to sound wise and eloquent like the Old Ones. It was best to be a listener and not try to speak or raise questions each time the Old Watcher talked to him. Questions had their own time to be asked, and often one had to wait a long time.

The Old Watcher looked intensely at the Young One. Finally, very tiredly, he motioned towards the fire and asked, "Have you not forgotten something? Is this the way our young ones show their respect inside the Great House? Have you nothing inside that new beaded bag hanging on your belt?" Instantly a hot rush of shame flushed the boy's cheeks. How glad he was that it was dark and that no one was there to see him forget something so basic as to make his offering of tobacco to Creator. This of all nights. He got up and made his tobacco offering. " I won't forget again, Creator, I promise." Then he went back to his mentor. Nothing would escape his attention again; he would show the Old Watcher he was worthy of the efforts of being taught the old ways. He would really be a Watcher.

Quietly they moved towards the altar which was against the opposite wall, beyond the fire. Then in a voice so soft the Young One was not sure he was hearing actual words, the Old Watcher began to tell him many things that he would need to know and understand, as an adult Shawnee man and as a Watcher.

There was an interruption as a woman came inside, went to the center and offered tobacco to the sacred fire. It was understood she had come to pray. People were always coming in for private time in the Great House, many of them to offer prayers of thanks or for help. Some came to replenish their weary spirits with strength and wisdom from the Ancestors. The sacred Great House is always a sanctuary for all who come with respect.

Before going to night watch, the Young One had been instructed as to his own protocol upon entering the Great House, the necessary attitude of respect for the Old Watcher, so no offenses would mar the event.

Now, as the Old Watcher positioned him just so, at the outer edge of the inside wall, his lessons for this responsibility began in earnest. "First you must learn to be there, but not be present," the Old Watcher said. "Keep your own spirit close to you so it does not interfere with what is going on here. Practice being 'invisible,' so even if they look for you, you are not seen. There is no place to hide, so this is something sacred that you must learn to do with your spirit and your mind. By being invisible you will not interfere with the prayers and thoughts of those who come to be alone with the Creator and the Ancestors. After all, this is a sacred place, and we Watchers are here to protect that sacredness, not detract from it by calling attention to ourselves."

This will be fun, thought the Young One. Little did the Old Watcher know that this Young One had practiced being invisible ever since an Old One had come after dinner and told marvelous tales of the warriors of old being invisible and accomplishing great surprises on their enemies. He had delighted in disappearing from his mother's scrutiny while being in plain view, close enough to touch her. He had indeed not hidden from her sight, only from her mind. After the Young One had practiced being invisible, he became so good at it that his playmates thought he must surely be half spirit instead of flesh and bone. The Old Watcher continued.

Midnight passed, the progression of time marked only by occasional night sounds and one beautiful falling star, which the Young One saw through one of the larger spaces in the arbored roof. Even the late night wanderers stopped coming into the Great House. When being taught by Old Ones, many times one learns not through words so much as simply experiencing life and being aware of the occurrences. Old Ones often just make sure you have not missed something, and they discuss the significance of what you just experienced, instead of teaching by drawing pictures with words or pens. Often while you are being taught, there are great lengths of silence. At times thoughts come into your mind that are strange and different. These may be the sprouting of thought seeds the Old Ones have planted. Or, sometimes they are new awarenesses that the Spirits "gift" you with as you mature and grow.

Before long the Young One heard heavy breathing next to him. He quickly looked to see who had invaded the sacred invisibility, but found it was only the Old Watcher, whose spirit had drifted outside the Great House, leaving his body to rest in a light slumber. A short time later, as he gazed into the fire pit, the eyes of the Young One became unseeing, and he too drifted into sleep, while his head stayed erect and his eyes open.

The pit was several feet across and several feet deep. Within it the life of the sacred fire and its coals glowed in ever-deepening shades of orange and red. Occasionally a spark would shoot up in a bright white before crackling into a miniature falling ember. The stones around the pit were now hot to the touch, especially the sides closest to the flames.

To say there was a great silence would not be correct, yet one could not discern the nature or the origins of the sounds which now began. At one time they were like a faint distant laughter, and then again like singing. Perhaps the sound was only the soft wind. No — it was more the slow vibration of ground felt when a distant buffalo herd was on the move, as our ancestors heard it long before they could see the dust or the dark forms of the animals. It was impossible to tell if what the Young One heard was truly a sound at all, or merely a half-perceived dream.

The Young One tried to rouse himself into true wakefulness, and he looked around for what had disturbed his unexpected slumber. He peered intensely into the dark and the brilliant flickers and listened with all the keenness he could. Nothing. In spite of himself, he again drifted back into that place where the wisdoms of ages are spoken into your mind's ears, those specific wisdoms you can never recall to repeat when awake, but which mold your spirit in subtle indelible ways.

Again! There was a wafting of merriment, then the low cautious tone of warning, of someone being reminded to be dignified and quiet because of the sleeping camp. The fire no longer flickered: there was only the continually changing glow of the coals and embers. The voices which had begun so faintly were now becoming more distinct, almost separate and understandable in their low mumbling tones.

The ancient stones of the Great House were speaking! "Ah ho, I see we have a Young One who has come to guard us. Look how he sleeps as the Old Watcher snores. At least the Young One has his eyes open; he might fool a frog bent on mischief." With a long sigh the voice lamented, "Oh, how I long for the old days, when we had our grandchildren around us all the time, not just on these special occasions."

The voice was coming from the darkness in back of the fire. A quick spark caused a prism of colors to glint in the dark from the place of the voice. It came from the giant Crystal which functions as the Eye with which Mother Earth watches her children. The People called it the "Seer Stone."

"What delightful and exciting children these Shawnee were in the past. Each generation, though, seems to have less to teach their Young

"Seer" Stone
(copy of mother Smith's)

Ones. The Young Ones of today know so little of the Rules of Life that Creator gave them in the beginning. Even the Old Ones have lost the essence of the rules. When the children were living by the rules of life they were so happy and healthy, and Kohkumthena was happy too." The Seer Stone sighed. "Now, it is just the sad times before the end with the children trying, wishing, wanting to do what is right, and having nowhere to look for that which they have lost." The Eye of Mother Earth lamented for the loss of the heritage of her Shawnee children.

"It would be wonderful if there were some way Creator could give back what has been lost through the centuries," she continued.

Nearer the fire a slow, deep, somber voice slowly began to speak. All the stones of the Great House gasped as they realized the speaker was the ancient Stone Mask, who had been silent for over two hundred years. They all were respectfully quiet as it continued.

"I too lament these losses. I too remember olden and ancient times. The ceremonies were beautiful and lasted for many days and even weeks. Now, a few hours of respect seems too much for some who come. Our Creator, our Grandmother Kohkumthena, told us to pray, that it is good for us, for the grandchildren, and for her. So we must help these grandchildren with our prayers to reclaim their sacred ways.

"Shawnee live four lifetimes before they can return to Creator. There are a few Young Ones who are in their fourth life, so they too remember old and ancient times. Often these memories come in bits and pieces, not complete, and sometimes confuse the Young Ones. These have the respect that is spoken of in the Great Laws. We must teach them what we remember, to help them understand the knowledge they will recover, so there will never again be a sad time. That is all I have to say at this time." With that, saying the ancient words spoken in all great councils, the Stone Mask fell silent.

Again the silence that comes with respect hushed the murmuring sounds of the Great House Stones.

"Yes," said the Eye of Mother Earth, "we do know, we do remember. Because we Stones have one perpetual life, I had forgotten that at Creation, Kohkumthena had given the grandchildren four lives before they return to her, as she did the deer, the dog, the bear, the bison, and others. We must share with our Shawnee grandchildren all that we have experienced throughout the ages with their Ancestors, so they will be able to

9

understand. Their form of speech is much different from ours but we can share our thoughts and memories. It is good to have this Young One on watch tonight. We will begin our sharing with him and then tomorrow we must observe the others. It will require many Young Ones working together to bring back traditions and the happy and healthy times we all miss so much. Do we all agree?"

There was a full sound of affirmation as the Great House Stones decided to perform this unheard-of thing. The Stones would not let their Shawnee grandchildren forever lose their precious and sacred ways, but would teach them all that they knew, would retell the old stories, the old oral traditions. They would recall the laws Kohkumthena gave them all in the beginning, and remind the grandchildren of their rich past that began so long ago in another land.

A raspy sound began to vibrate from an area near the cedar pit. The voice was difficult to understand because the raspiness was coming from a very ancient piece of copper ore, still in its natural, unfinished state. Beside it were some other pieces of copper ore which had been worked and hammered thin into blanks. These were treasured as sample pieces of copper money brought from Mexico with the Ancestors so long ago. Other pieces of ore had been hammered into a copper mask with pierced eye holes and old mysterious etchings all around the edges. This mask had been brought in the belongings of a shaman, who wore it only on the most special ceremonies.

There was also a very thin and frail copper knife, now celadon green with age. It began its reminiscences, but it directed them to the Young One instead of addressing just the other Stones.

"You see," said the Knife, "when I was young, shiny, and new, I was strong and beautiful. It was I who was privileged to cut the sacred tobacco into small pieces so it could be smoked in the grandchildren's pipes, as they prayed to Creator. Polished to a high gleam, I was carried in many medicine bags of the shamans, medicine people, and chiefs. I was not an object the common grandchildren had, but was only for those of authority and responsibility. I was very respected. Now the grandchildren look at me with curiosity and wonder how an old, soft piece of red metal could be of any importance."

The Young One was startled. Surely this was a dream. Strange things always happened at Shawandasse, but speaking stones and pebbles and knives were a strain on his young mind.

"My gleam is now dulled by age," the Copper Knife continued, "and I look all green, my edge pitted and blunt. I am not even kept in a sacred bundle anymore, just placed behind a glass in a cabinet with many brighter colored things standing in front of me. But I, too, remember times in the

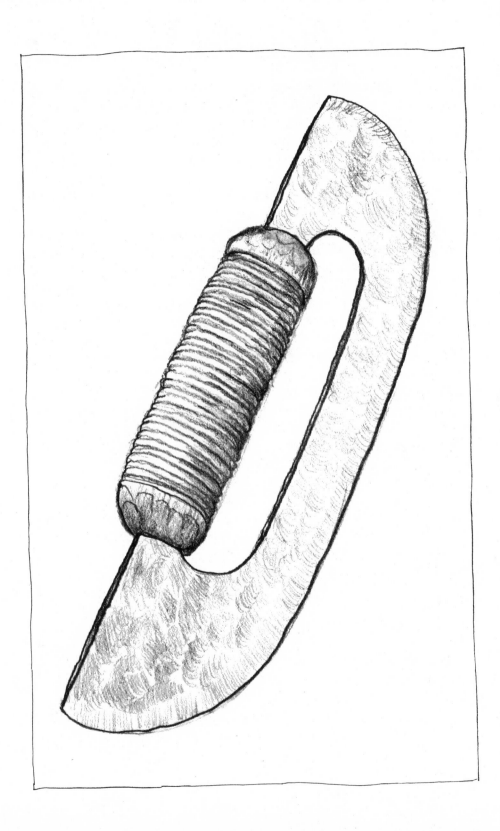

lives of the grandchildren's ancestors, times for which there is no written record. I too, wish to take the Young One on a journey. Let me gather my strength for a moment and I will take him to the south, and later to the Ohio valley where they last traded for my kind."

"Hey!" yelled a confident-sounding voice. "While the old Knife there is getting himself together why not let me teach the Young One a thing or two? After all, my kind and I have always been mighty important to the people too. Just think of all the people who have played games with me!" This came from a round, smooth stone that was slightly flattened on its top and bottom, like a donut with no hole. "Sometimes in the games they would set a mark along a path they had prepared and smoothed, and then shove me towards the mark with a forked pole. Sometimes if they went past the mark they won, other times it was the person who came closest to the mark without crossing it who won. The favorite way was for one person to roll me while another person threw a lance to the point where they thought I would stop. Many a bauble has been lost in wagers on my behavior. They even had teams who would play against one another. I am a *chunkee stone!*" the voice bragged.

The Mask groaned, "Chunkee, be still! You are only a gaming stone. We are teaching the Young One about important things. Things about his ancestors, their history, their ways of life and thinking and worshipping Creator. Hrumph-ph! Time is short enough without your wasting it on your frivolous tales, and about gambling at that. The idea! Hrumph-ph!"

"But I have been everywhere with the grandchildren. They had fun with me; I made them laugh," said Chunkee is a swaggering tone. "They all loved me because I brought them pleasure and diversion from their hard lives, and camaraderie as they bantered and wagered back and forth. These grandchildren were happy people, always looking to have some sport and to pull jokes and tricks on one another.

"I taught them about sharing with one another when one of them lost all to the game. Our grandchildren's ancestors' form of gambling and handling losses was not the same as that of the Aliens of today, and they always held rematches so they could gain most of their things back. The whole tribe would sometimes be cheering. We gaming pieces have always been important in developing character and managing the wealth. Ple-e-e-ease? Let me speak?" asked the Chunkee Stone once more, still proud but now wheedling.

13

The Chunky Stone
(ball & games)

There was a sound of stone grating stone as the Mask expressed itself once more, in a very negative tone. "No! I have decided!" stated the Mask. The Chunkee Stone fell silent with a heavy, thunking, sulky sound, and the others began to mutter.

Finally as all the hissing, crunching, and crackling subsided, the quavery voice of the Copper Knife could be heard saying, " Yes, I believe I have myself ready now." And with that the voice began to move in the direction of the slumbering Young One.

"You see, Young One," it said. "While to your eye I am only a piece of worn and tarnished metal, I have always had a place of honor among your people because of my usefulness. Let me tell you about the ancestors who used me and you will understand your people's deepest roots and my part in their lives.

"It is said that your people's ancestors lived in Mexico at the foothills of the mountains south of beautiful Lake Chapala for untold generations. They had been there so long they did not remember having been elsewhere, and had buried many hundreds of generations there. For several centuries your people had lived with the Mayan rulers who were in control of their area. There were hundreds of small nations that were under the Mayans' protection, and it was not a bad situation even though it was not perfect. Because your ancestors lived so far from the heart of the government they were pretty much left to themselves. As happens in life, this came to an end when a violent change took place and people known as the Aztecs replaced the Mayans as the rulers. The Aztecs were human-flesh eaters. They treated your ancestors with cruelty and meanness. They demanded tribute, or taxes, which deprived your ancestors of some of the necessities they had enjoyed before, and also put them in a constant state of fear concerning their future.

"The ancestors thus sadly came to the conclusion that they would need to leave their beautiful Lake Chapala and the mountains to go somewhere safer and better to live. But where? In their oral traditions there were stories of their ancestors having traveled across a large body of water to the north and east of them, landing in a wonderful land that had many animals, much food, and few people. Their ancestors had made this journey at least twice before, and some had returned to tell them of this land to the north and the routes to take to get there. One of these groups became known as the Fort Ancient people, mound builders whose mounds are seen even today in the Ohio Valley. Your people have loved and defended this homeland so fiercely because their connections go back so far. The soil is made of the Ancestors' disintegrated bones. Another group of Ancestors was called the Leni Lanape who were all Algonquian-speaking people. After your ancestors arrived, some tribes referred to them as the people of unutterable speech, but they called themselves Shawandasse, 'People From Where the South Wind Begins.'

"As your ancestors made their decision to leave the Lake Chapala area, they decided to retrace their ancestors' journeys," the Knife said. "Many of the other nearby villages decided to travel with your ancestors to this beautiful land to the north and the east across the large water which you refer to as the Gulf of Mexico. By the time their neighbors joined them there were indeed several tens of thousands. Your ancestors were going to look for their relatives in the northland, whom they would recognize by their song, or language, and by the way they worshipped Creator. The other tribes were just going to come and start their lives over, because the old oral traditions stated there was much land and few people, with plenty of room for all.

"During the planning meetings they all shared all the information they had with the people of many nations who would be accompanying them about the area they would be coming into. It was already known that this land could also be reached by going east to the shore of the Gulf of Mexico, then northeast along the shoreline, as well as going to the tip of the Yucatan where the Caribbean currents that flow between Mexico and Cuba would take you across the large water to the new land.

"It was decided by the okimas, chieftains, and leaders, that they would risk only half of their people on boats on the water; the other half would go by land. Either way was fearsome, Young One, because either by land or sea they could meet with dreaded flesh-eating tribes. Each people had to decide how to separate, who would go by land, who by sea. Even some families decided they would separate and a mother would take part of her children by land, while her husband would take the rest of the children by sea. It was truly a hard, sad time, but it had to be done.

"Whatever they carried would be on someone's back or the back of a dog, so they had to travel light. There were no wheels for wagons, no horses. Remember, this journey was one thousand years ago, Young One.

The roads in Mexico were wide and smooth from the centuries of foot travel, but your people were not sure what the roads would be like here in the north.

"Now we come to the story of my nation," said the Copper Knife. "The people had good copper mines in Mexico. These mines were not at Lake Chapala, but near enough that they traded for it. The craftsmen would take us pieces of ore and pound us until we were very thin and pliable, or they would make a mold and pound us into that shape. We could be pounded so thin they would use us to plate over precious objects carved of wood or stone. Village chiefs and the medicine people used our thin copper blades to cut herbs for healing and the tobacco for ceremonies. In fact, one of our most important jobs was cutting the tobacco which is so important to you all.

"Young One, how much do you know about this sacred herb which we copper knives cut? Do you remember the legend of why tobacco is used the way it is?" asked the Knife. "No? Well, when Creator was giving us all instructions as to how we were to help you, first the animals, then the trees were asked for their suggestions and given their responsibilities, and then it came time for the plants. As you know tobacco is one of the last plants to be ready, and by the time Creator got to it, all the food and medicine roles had been spoken for by the other plants. The tobacco plant was very downhearted and finally said, 'I guess I won't be able to contribute anything to the grandchildren. I am just a weed that they will gather when they clean off their gardens, and they will burn me. I have nothing else to offer them. I will just be a weed, and then smoke and ashes.' The little tobacco plant was disgraced at having nothing to offer.

"Finally, our Creator Kohkumthena said, 'The grandchildren will always be praying to me. Sometimes I might be busy far above Turtle Island and won't know when they need me. Little tobacco plant, when they have need of me in prayer, I will have them gather you and burn you and then I will see your smoke which will carry their words up here to me. They will always have need to pray. You will always be useful, treasured and sacred to them.' And so it is," said the Copper Knife.

"So, Young One, as they traveled they had to bring tobacco, because even the most foolish knew this would be a journey of many prayers. Tobacco seed was brought and stored in little clay vessels and gourd containers. These gourds proved too fragile, but the seed savers made of clay were

17

dry and much sturdier, for the women had tempered them with crushed shells before the clay was fired so they were less brittle.

"Young One, you are to have very special privileges on this sacred teaching night. Your mind and spirit will travel, yet your body will remain here guarding the Great House treasures. Come with me, Young One, back to the shores of the Yucatan about a thousand years ago, as your people prepare to leave."

It seemed to the Young One that instantly he was among the Ancestors as they milled around near the beach. He could smell the sharp sea water, the salt, the natural iodine, the fish, the sea winds, the smell of the many campfires. There were remnant aromas of the celebration feasts of the travelers, honoring Creator for having provided them a place to escape to sanctuary, and especially for providing the Cunas, the fine people of the shoreland who made the boats and rafts the sea travelers would need. There was excitement in the air, as well as trepidation. The chiefs were calling the people to gather close now.

It was not difficult for the Young One to find his own ancestors among the throng of people, and he was fascinated by the appearance of his ancestors. They were good-looking people, unusually tall, wearing beautiful jewelry that gleamed and glistened in the light. Their colorful clothes seemed to be of woven fabric and of deer skins. This amazed the Young One who had only thought of his ancestors as wretched, ill-clothed people struggling to march under heavy burdens. Instead, the ancestors looked similar to the People today, with pale olive complexions and hazel or grey eyes. The Young One remembered that before the People now called Mexicans intermarried with the dark and swarthy Spaniards, most of them were also more fair-skinned, with lighter-colored eyes and hair. By that time in history the Spaniards themselves had changed in appearance, their darker skin and hair the result of over four hundred years of intermarriage with the Moors.

He remembered the oral tradition of his people of carrying a perpetual fire with them which would never burn out. So he looked for people carrying a long stone-lidded container, suspended on a long pole. There it was! The gray stone container looked plain, but the Young One could tell it was separated into two parts. It was small, only five inches wide and a foot long, with no decorations, except for several eagle feathers on the poles. Two men carried it and two other men guarded it. Heat squiggles rose in the air from the fire inside. Tradition said it did not need to be fed, but mysteriously burned, leaving no smoke. This fire was always carried from place to place by the ancestors. No one came near it except those men who were responsible for it. The container with the sacred fire was in a large, cleared, open area, as if the people feared it might reach out to destroy them. Upon arrival at a new home it would have its own wigiwa built.

Some of the antics and noise of the shamans and medicine people looked very strange indeed, but Young One knew that each movement and sound had a specific purpose and meaning intended to help the people as they went through this historic and heartbreaking change.

The Young One watched the people packing as the camp began breaking into separate clusters of tribes as they prepared to leave. Each family and group of friends was beginning to band close together as they collected their traveling bundles of necessities. As sleeping shelters disappeared the landscape returned to its natural state, no longer showing evidence of the large encampment.

All the tribal leaders apparently had agreed among themselves on a spokesperson who would explain to the people what was going on. Meetings of all the leaders had been held at the end of each evening meal. The cross-country march required much planning ahead. Hunters were sent out to procure food and bring it to the next day's camp site which the scouts would have already picked out, as they worked several days in advance of the arrival of the people. Wood for cooking would be gathered and stacked so time and energy would not be wasted on the mundane details of a camp.

If someone became too sick to continue the journey, the medicine person or his assistant would stay with the patient, sometimes with a protector, until they all could travel on and catch up with the group. All the tribal leaders and people cooperated; they knew what they were doing was necessary and right and that the visions that had inspired all the shamans were really a message from Creator.

Young One was in awe of what he now saw on this last day. A tall muscular man who possessed such an air of great dignity that he must be a great chief indeed, climbed on top of a small mound at the edge of camp nearest the Big Water and began to speak to the people. He cast his eyes all around, from left to right, from the old ones and the babies up front, to the warriors protecting the rear. In back of him were at least three hundred shamans and medicine people of various tribes and degrees. Their clothes and sacred staffs and rattles were all strange and wonderful for the Young One to see. They were chanting and dancing, and some were burning sacred herbs in strange containers of all sorts. He wanted to get closer so he could see in more detail, but the leader chief was now talking to the people and he listened.

A shaman stood near the speaker. As he danced it seemed the air around him was filled with glittering stardust which sometimes changed colors. He held a bright blue parrot wing, each feather layered over with smaller vibrant yellow pointed feathers, interlaced with stones of green and yellow. Seed pods resembling animal heads rattled on one of his wands when the shaman shook his hand. Streamers hung from bands around his biceps, and his forearm bracelets were adorned with cream-colored and rich blue stones which tinkled like chimes as he danced. The shaman's ankles and wrists were covered with the blue beaks of birds strung on leather bracelets and anklets, and multicolored metal tinklers, like bells, were interwoven through the beaks.

The brow band of his headdress was a glitter of silver dangles of every shape which hung down past the nose of the shaman. The back of the shaman's head was covered by a giant bouquet of two and three foot long feathers of all colors and description, radiating from a rich blue carving of lapis lazuli. The feathers of the headdress were lush red plumes, layered black and green iridescent feathers that were cut into unique designs and patterns against the red, diminishing to smaller feathers of intense yellow, pale blue and green.

Across the shaman's shoulders was the skin of a magnificent panther. In his left hand was a spear with a foot-long crystal point and white, black, red, blue, green, yellow feathers trailing down the shaft. Some of these feathers were cut into geometric designs of some mysterious significance, one of which the Young One recognized as representing the six directions that are honored by his people. A strange combination of small gem stones separated the feathers. Some of the stones were polished, some were carved, some were cut with prisms that cast brilliant rainbow patterns. In his right hand the shaman held a long-handled gourd decorated with intricate designs which seemed to cast beautiful stardust, but the Young One could not be sure, even though he watched so intensely he did not think he even blinked.

This must surely be the most important shaman, the shaman of the head chief, Young One thought to himself. Apprentices to the shamans were working in teams. Some danced very fast and their songs were very aggressive, so much so that once he thought the shamans were trying to encourage the people into a warlike state of mind. Thinking on that, the Young One decided this journey was every bit as dangerous as going to war. No one knew the outcome in advance and none knew if he would be the one to survive.

The Young Watcher leaned forward now to try to hear the words of the head chief on this day of the people's departure from Mexico. The man's voice was strong and full of deliberate confidence. The Young One could tell this was serious talk even though he could not understand the speaker's words. The crowd seemed to hold its breath as the tall man finished speaking.

Very slowly the head chief reached into a pouch at his side. He withdrew a small, flat sharp object that glowed soft orange in the light. He then took four quick strokes across his upper arm and blood came forth, making slender ribbons to the ground. The people all gave a hushed gasp at this unexpected move. They all stood with solemn faces, watching, as the sacred blood seeped into the breast of Mother Earth, this place on Turtle Island of all their beginnings. Each tribe's leaders came forward. Each chief, shaman, medicine person, and apprentice then followed suit and they, too, took this sacred copper blade and caused their blood to run to the ground, joining their leader's. The last of them had done this unusual thing before the leader said anything more.

It seemed this act was their silent statement that they would always be a part of this sacred land on the shore of these waters. While they could not stay to become part of the soil, as their ancestors had, this small portion of themselves they could leave to Mother Earth, who had given them so much. This tiny red part could blend with the dust of their ancestors. This small part of them would always be here. The rest would be going on to a strange land.

When the last of them had finished watching their blood sink into the white sand of the shore, the main speaker held a large staff cascading with eagle feathers high over his head and gave a cry. The people then walked forward towards him, using his body to divide them as if he were a razor's edge, half going to the left of him, the others going to the right. This was a sharp cut, and it made their hearts bleed inside. Although there were thousands it seemed to take no time at all to accomplish the division of the people.

An immense sound resonated as the speaker's cry died down, a sound so intense that the Young One felt it came from the very marrow of his own bones. It so permeated the whole environment that he could neither distinguish its identity nor its origination point. There was no letup in the sound; never did it vary in its pitch, tone, or volume. The Young One looked in every direction, but could not tell where the sound was coming from. Every hair on his body prickled and stood on end, and his teeth grated. Sweat began to trickle down the backs of his legs. Never before had he heard such a sound, and nothing, not even thunder, had ever caused this feeling. His emotions welled up, intensified, and tears stung his eyes as the sound continued, still without pause. It became a part of him, vibrating throughout his total being.

Suddenly Young One noticed that the two groups of people were moving away from one another. One group was heading west, the other to the east. Then . . . then he became aware of another sound. He heard the soft weeping and the distraught wailings of the people as they turned their backs on half their families, half their friends and neighbors, and their tribes and set off in the directions away from all that was familiar and sacred. The Young One felt himself caught up in their sorrow and their losses, and as his eyes leaked sympathetic tears, he let out a sob. As he watched the scene, having withdrawn to a place of observation now, he finally understood the first sound. It was caused by the men who blew the conchs to start the people on their journeys, covering the sounds of the people's heartbreak with the sacred sound from these shells.

The sound of the conch would become a sound that would forever cause a catch in the throats of the people's children and grandchildren, and their grandchildren's grandchildren. Now, only the Young One understood why.

As the people began to disappear in their two directions, a few of the assistants to the shamans milled around the former camp site, picking up pieces of unburned wood from the various fires, packing slender twigs and scooping handfuls of ashes into small containers which they then gently stored away in their packs. This was a form of carrying the fire from one place to another, a continuity. They then collected stones polished by the sea waters and sand, common stones as well as unusual ones with designs in various sizes, and these they tucked into their packs. These simple things would be added to the sacred items and stones they already had in their bundles, and these all would become the bases for new tribal bundles, reminding the people of their origins. Indeed, one of the larger stones already part of a sacred bundle had strange markings, like a stick figure of a man holding a staff with legs, as though it was walking. It was told that in ancient times this stone had been brought from the land to the north.

With tears in their own eyes they then started after the last of their own people, headed for new life. They would never forget the old life they had enjoyed here in the land where the warm South Wind begins.

The Young One could feel the sensation of traveling rapidly back to the Great House. He understood that the Copper Knife, which had been speaking to him and carrying him with it in vision, was not strong. It was almost spent and needed to get back quickly. The Young One realized there were more stories that the piece of copper could have told, for as he returned to the Great House he had visions of flat pieces of copper used as money: as the ancestors had traveled in the strange new land and met new people, the copper sheets they had brought had been readily acceptable as barter. He had visions of beautiful copper masks, and headdresses of copper. But of all the things the Young One saw made of copper, he was most impressed with the feathers made of the metal. There were some items made that were too precious to be worn and so they were only used as burial adornments. To the practical mind of the Young One, this seemed like a dreadful waste. But now, he was back on the grounds, sitting propped up near the back wall, watching the fire glow.

The Old Watcher seemed to be awake, though he was not moving. Finally he spoke to the Young One: "The fire needs more wood now. Once you have tended to that come sit by me and we will talk of ancient times."

The Young One promptly got up from his cramped position and went outside to where the men had earlier stacked a considerable amount of wood nearby, so the night watch people would not have to go far from the Great House and leave it unprotected. He chose several pieces of cedar. It is forbidden to poke the fire with a stick, so Young One had to rearrange the wood without becoming impatient or seeming disrespectful in his attitude and movements. This was sometimes difficult to try to explain to his friends, this thing about fire. The Shawnee consider fire a living thing and always treat it with respect. It is one of the witnesses and messengers to Creator for the Shawnee.

"Your treatment of *skota*, our witness fire, is good," said the Old Watcher. "There are only a few acceptable ways for a Shawnee to make a fire. The most sacred way is with a bow drill, using wood on wood. The second best way is with a flint and stone. The ancestors who moved to Oklahoma used flint and steel. Matches and lighters were not allowed. For cooking fires the women had to lay their logs out in a specific pattern with each of four logs pointing in one of the cardinal directions of the compass. They were then lit starting with the east and going in a clockwise direction, one at a time. The Shawnee seemed to have rules about everything."

The Young One finished his fire duties and sat back down with the Old Watcher, who said, "Each of the things in this Great House has a long history, except for you and me. We two-leggeds are some of Creator's most temporary beings. You will learn that we have the biggest egos and must constantly pray for help with them. Sometimes we forget that this Turtle Island, Mother Earth, and all the nations of beings in it, were created just to support our lives, because we are pitiful creatures and can't take care of ourselves. Always, we must depend on our Mother for our very lives. We would have no homes to live in if she did not provide us material from herself with which to build.

"You look at me as if I am forgetting which century we are now in, but I am not lost in time. The bricks and blocks we use today are made of sand and dirt and clay from Mother. The energy to bake them comes from her coal mines and oil-filled veins. The glass for windows comes from her sand. The metal is refined from her ore mines, and the frameworks of wood are from the wonderful trees with which she covers herself. What would we eat if the animals should suddenly hide themselves and not allow us to find them and kill them for their meat? Our medicines and the other foods that come from the plant people, there is no replacement for them. The alternatives that people try from time to time, even they have their beginnings with Mother Earth. That is the way things are.

"The Great Laws of Kohkumthena* tell us that all these other nations take pity on us, so we can survive. I think, Young One, that hurts some

---

* See Appendix for Kohkumthena's Great Laws

people's egos, and they rebel against that thought. Then they spend their lives trying to prove that they can do all in their power to destroy Mother Earth and the other nations, and there will be no consequences. There are always consequences to our actions. Some you can see immediately, some take seven generations. It may seem those foolish people are winning, and usually becoming very rich, as they destroy and sell pieces of the Earth. But consequences do come, and then their children's children, who are blameless, will suffer. Young One, you must always try to live your life so there are only good things that come to your grandchildren's grandchildren from your actions. It is not a hard life, only one filled with right thinking, and respect.

"Young One, have your parents instructed you about the Great Laws of Kohkumthena? Do you know them well enough to tell them back to me, an Old Watcher, who loves to be reminded of the thoughtfulness, love and care our Grandmother has given to our lives? These are important things, Young One, that will help you make sense of this vast world we live in, and our universe, so you will understand where and how you fit in with the other nations, the four-leggeds, birds, fish, plant people, trees, and the herbs. Without knowing and understanding these things, one can never be a right-thinking person: You must understand why we exist and how, and about the laws that Kohkumthena has given to the other nations and why and how they help us and have pity on us that we do not perish. Come, let us get comfortable, and you tell me of these Great Laws. My ears and heart always love to hear about these things."

The Young One began to reach into his memory for the sacred laws that all right-thinking Shawnee were to live by. "These are laws that Kohkumthena gave to all her creations when she brought us down from her home, so we would not perish. There are two parts to the laws, those for the other nations to follow and the first great law which holds the instructions for two-leggeds, whom she refers to as her grandchildren the Shawnee, to follow. All of the laws are designed around the word 'respect.' They explain how respect is shown to her, and to the two-leggeds, and how the two-leggeds are to respect all the other nations who make her grandchildren's existence possible.

"Kohkumthena first counseled with every other nation she had created. Some she told their purpose, and the rules and laws which they were to live by, for our benefit, so we will not perish. Some of the four-leggeds and plants she asked what they wanted to offer us. Then she counseled with us and informed us of the laws, the rules, the purposes and uses of all the other nations she had created. She spoke to us of the future, how we are to think and speak, as well as how we are to act."

These were not really hard thoughts for the Young One to understand, for his parents, aunts, uncles, and grandparents had always told him of these Great Laws. He had known that someday an elder would ask him about them.

It took a while for the Young One to recite all the Great Laws and explain the rules, feeling proud of himself for having remembered all of them so well. His grandfather had told him those rules would make his life easier. He had doubted it at first, but with each day they seemed clearer as his heart understood their intent more fully. He waited for some response from the Old Watcher, but his wisdom teacher was silent. He had dozed off again!

The Young One bent down and peered closely at the Old Watcher, who at that precise moment emitted a coarse "Snar-r-rk-k-k-k." His head jerked up, and thus rudely awakened, he blinked and peered back at the Young One. Smiling slightly, he said, "Ah, this reminds me of my own youth, when I first told the Great Laws to one of our great elders of that time. You have done a good job remembering the words and have made much progress in understanding their meanings, for we old ones have been watching you. Our people will be strong so long as you remember the rules and the talks. Never be embarrassed to say them, Young One, for we all benefit from hearing them."

The Old Watcher's speech ended, and his old head bobbed downward a couple of times and then stayed down, his chin resting on his chest. His soft snores and occasional snarks punctuated the quiet night, as the Young One settled himself comfortably nearby, wondering at the great amount of sleep these old ones seemed to require.

The night deepened and the Young One himself began to catch up on some long-needed sleep. Just then the Great Mask gave a gruff sigh and said, "The Old Watcher is right. It is very good to hear the ancient Rules of Life spoken again by a Young One. And I say if all the young who are in their fourth life are of the same caliber as this one, our beloved grandchildren the Shawnee will truly be as strong and proud as at any time in their past. Let us not waste our time now. Which of you wants to speak next?"

From within the Tribal Bundle, sounding slightly muffled by a bear skin wrap, piped the small voice of a tiny stone doll. "I think this is a wonderful idea. I want to teach the Young One all about my history and purpose. We Stones in the Tribal Bundle have different ages and different pasts as we have been added to the Bundle through the centuries. We all have something different to contribute. Most think I am just a cute little doll, carved in stone. It seems centuries since anyone did the 'doll dance' and asked my help for rain. Hardly anyone knows I am one of the protectors of the Bundle." By its tone one could tell the little Stone Doll was excited at the thoughts of being useful again.

A sound, smooth and soft, seemed to roll from within a small doeskin bag with a drawstring. "Young One, listen," it said. "Let your spirit come with me and I will take you on a journey back to when your People were wanderers. Together we will watch your ancestors leave the shore at the tip of the Yucatan and travel with them as they reach northern Florida near the panhandle. Come."

The Young One looked closely at the bag, which someone had placed near the Altar Stone. Inside was an unusual pearl, perfectly round and over an inch in diameter, so amazing a pearl that most who saw it did not realize it was real. Its color was a deep, rich, warm brown with a coral hue, and its history was long, as it had come from Mexico in the deerskin medi-

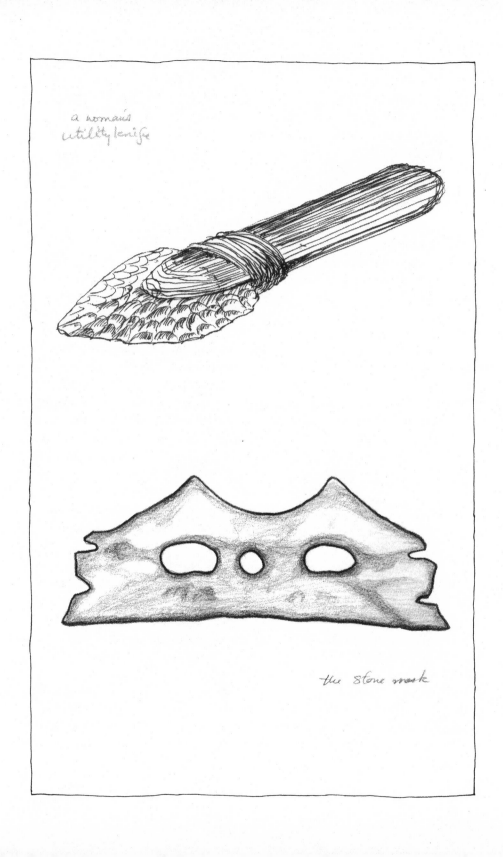

a nomad's
utility knife

the stone mask

cine bag centuries ago. The perfect setting for this perfect pearl had never been found, so it remained in its bag, waiting to be useful. It was delighted to be one of the teachers of the Young One.

"Today hardly anyone remembers that pearls were used so much by the ancestors," the soft voice continued. "They decorated pipes, bowls, tools, clothes, almost everything with pearls. There were even blankets decorated with the soft sheen of pearls. Some were round while others were exotic baroques. Once the grandchildren moved inland it became difficult to trade for the more perfect round ones from the ocean so they resorted to using the river pearls from mussels."

As the Young One realized someone was communicating with him, he struggled for wakefulness, but was unsuccessful. After a minute or so he felt himself begin to drift and the air rushed about him, displacing darkness with the brilliant colors of lush trees and foliage. Colorful birds were calling and the air smelled moist and sweet. Splash! He looked and saw a huge alligator enter the water and swim lazily, its eye on a distant waterbird that was too carelessly intent on fishing to notice the reptile's approach.

The Young One saw the People moving quietly along a path through the forest. There were thousands of people: all kinds and ages and many tribes were there, all dressed in daily village clothes as colorful as the birds and flowers themselves. But for all the noise they made, there might as well have been only a dozen, for they moved in almost complete silence, furtively looking behind them from time to time, as if some enemy might be gaining on them. The Young One knew they must be afraid; his own heart was racing as he experienced their feelings. He could sense how tired these people were, for they had been moving for weeks through the forests towards the water.

The Young One realized he was seeing the ancestors, who traveled east and north after they had been separated by the grand chief at the seashore. In his heart he hoped he would not have to witness again the painful parting of the families.

Soon the people would be at the northern tip of this land called the Yucatan. If all went well, before long there would be boats and rafts made so their journey could continue to the great land on the other side of the water that the ancestors, whose names had been forgotten in antiquity, and the last migrating ancestors, the Lennape, had told them of. That across-the-water land was full of wondrous foods and plenty of animals, but few people. Here would be a place where they could live without fear — at least without fear of becoming someone's dinner. The new Mexican rulers did things that were dreadful and against the laws given by Kohkumthena.

The Pearl began its story: "The people called the Cunas helped make the needed vessels for the half of your people who would cross the waters you call the Gulf of Mexico, while the other half trudged around the curve of the land past what is now called Texas. How did they achieve such long journeys by land and by water without getting lost? By following the stars, celestial navigation. Study of the stars and how to use them for night traveling was part of everyone's basic learning, especially the children. The currents in the gulf were strong and took them easily to the land the ancestors had spoken of. Water was stored and carried in large gourds and even in some tightly sewn skins. It was good that the journey took only a few days because the water began to taste peculiar from the constant heat and sun, even though a couple of wise women had put a few herbs in the water to keep it sweet."

The Young One watched the unfolding scene. The people had finally arrived in their boats, to a land that was very inhospitable, in what is now called the panhandle of Florida near what is now known as Appalachicola. It was marshy and the mosquitoes were so large — they were inches across. No one spoke now, and many kept their hands over their mouths and noses to keep from inhaling the gnats that swarmed so thick you could scoop a handful at a time from the air in one quick grab. Alligators and panthers bellowed, squalled, and screeched, reminding the people of the many dangers awaiting them should they stray outside the safety of the campfire light. They had no choice but to keep moving towards the northeast, so they plodded on.

The voice of the Pearl continued: "It was the reasoning of the people that eventually they would run into their relatives, descendants of their ancestors. They looked forward to meeting their relatives. They would recognize them by their 'song' — language — and by the songs they sang, and the way they worshipped Creator. There were many tales of this land in their old oral traditions. It was a comfort in their minds to think they would not be friendless in this strange new place.

"This journey took many months. There had been plenty of foods to eat along the way for a few weeks. Some they were familiar with, and others the medicine men had performed ceremonies and held prayers over so the unfamiliar roots, berries, and fruits would be nutritious and not harmful. They had found a small yellow squash here that everyone liked, although some liked the cooked flowers best. There were plenty of the papayas they could use in so many ways. Not only was the fruit sweet when it was ripe, but it could also made be cooked when it was unripe to make a tasty dish. There were many types of grapes, cactus fruits, even plums. Many of the palms had fruits or berries that were delectable. The women especially liked the coontie root, which they grated into a fine texture and then soaked and washed several times. Then the women would add all kinds of fruits and vegetables, and meat if they had it, to make the most heavenly and nutritious stew anywhere.

"There was no scarcity of meat and fish. Even when they were far from the beaches, the water seemed to be everywhere, alive with all types of water life, fishes of all sizes, shapes and colors, lizards, 'gators, eels, and snakes. There were plenty of raccoons and deer. Sometimes a hunter would even bring down a panther. The birds were similar to those they had left behind, large and small, colorful and noisy. It was always fun to share in using the feathers of some of these beautiful birds, feathers sometimes longer than a boy's arm or even his leg.

"But after a while the tasty foods began to be scarce, and the effort to glean them from the quicksand-filled marshes seemed too dangerous. Constant watch for the poisonous snakes and dreaded 'gators wore on their nerves. Mosquito sickness caused many to be ill, and the mosquito medicine that they had brought with them was finally all used up. Some became so sick they died. There seemed to be none of the medicine plants they knew in this area, and the medicine men were constantly trying new cures because the old ones were no longer available. As they became more sick and weary from the harsh, soggy land, many of the people wondered if indeed the ancestors had told the truth. Was this land going to be good and full of food and animals and medicine?

"The people were always brave and strong. Still, the ever-booming calls of the alligators, and the swishing and splashing sounds that always happened when they were least expected, wore at the people's nerves. The mothers kept the children closer to themselves, and discouragingly, the scouts were coming back with only words of the sameness of the land up ahead.

"After traveling in this manner for what seemed forever, the people's vitality finally gave out. They lost all heart to go on. Perhaps they had not remembered the stories correctly, perhaps the old tales were just that, stories and tales to amuse them on cold winter nights."

The Young One looked at the people around him. Their faces were drawn, their bodies no longer shone with health, but instead they were tired-looking and spent after having wandered for so many months. And because the Great House Stones also gave the gift of sensation, the Young One himself felt as restless and uncomfortable as the exhausted travelers. The air was humid and hot; his clothes seemed to cling soggily to him. Where his skin wasn't covered by clothing he was scratched and either bleeding or scabby from the coarse leaves of all sorts that sawed into his flesh.

The insects were having a celebration on his blood. There seemed to be bloodsuckers of every size and description. And of course, there were the miserable intense biters called "no-seeums." Some of the flying bugs were as big as his hand, hard-shelled and making a racket when they landed, and there were snakes and lizards here. Although he was used to some of their breed, the ones the Young One was seeing now seemed more colorful, larger, and much more menacing than the ones he knew.

This did not seem like a place of welcome; the Young One felt he could detect animosity in everything he encountered. At times he could even hear the snarly breath of the dreaded panther that lived in these swamps. Some said it was the Underwater Spirit Panther that at night traveled on top of the water. Young One felt a shiver run through his body as he thought about such things.

The people had seen huge clouds of black smoke from forest fires for weeks. Brackish waters replaced the sweet fresh waters, and then foods became harder to find as evidence of the forest fires was seen in the blackened tree trunks, foliage, and plants. Although there was plenty of meat as the animals ran from the pervasive fire that ate at their home land, soon the fruits were scorched and ruined, and the air became heavily flavored with smoke. The stores of food they had dried and brought with them had been consumed months ago. It was a very good thing this was a land that knew no cold, so foods grew all year round.

"If only there had been real land to walk on instead of this perpetual bog! You never knew when you would be sinking chin deep into an unforeseen hole. There was quicksand. There was stinking sand, and there was land that seemed hard under your feet but suddenly gave way leaving you frantically scrambling out of a sink hole. The grass and plant leaves were the most unforgiving of all. Everyone's clothes were shredded from the tangles and thorns and sharp blades, and kept the curers busy making salves and treatments for these wounds. It was comforting to know the curers recognized the healing plants here, besides the true medicines they had brought with them. Still, these rigors were wearing everyone down. Each day it seemed harder to get up and start again, to march towards this sacred place that the ancestors had mentioned so long ago. The tiredness never eased, and sleep was always fitful because of the biting and stinging of the insects.

"This land seemed to have angered the Thunder Beings, because every day it stormed. The rains were sheer torrents that made the air so wet that one almost inhaled the fresh water as it fell to the earth. The lightning was awe inspiring — fierce, brilliant, and profuse. There was no doubt that the Thunder Beings had started the forest fires. The sweet smell of the forest and everglades sometimes turned acrid and thick as the lightning strikes came close to the People. Once the storms had gotten so out of hand that Cyclone Person came whirling overhead. The Shawnee ancestors were not afraid because Cyclone Person, who had originally been Shawnee, had long ago promised that he would not kill them if he knew where they lived. But being constantly in motion, some of them wondered if Cyclone Person would recognize them in this mass of mixed peoples and keep his promise.

"Each morning it became more difficult on the narrow paths. The people groaned louder and moved more slowly. The rests grew longer, and getting started took so much time that the distance of their days' journeys became increasingly shorter. The natural cheerfulness of the people was harder to rouse. The stories at night were short and even though the olimpease, or storyteller, was as good as ever, even the children hardly smiled, so deep was their fatigue. Their little legs ached and cramped. They were covered with festering sores, keeping their mothers and the medicine men busy trying to clear them up and keep them from hurting. The grasses and plants actually seemed to be trying to cut all the people up into pieces or to make them too sick to continue. One almost could believe the area was bewitched by an evil presence which did not want them there.

"Finally, after having progressed many hundreds of miles, they made a camp at the edge of the woods on the banks of a large river. Wearily they decided they might as well stop there and simply prepare for the remaining survivors to cross over to spirit, because they had neither the strength nor the heart to go on. They settled down to sleep after eating bits of berries and little else, trying not to think of their great discomfort and weariness. In the morning their okima would talk with them about what they would do.

"Come, Young One," the Pearl said. "This is something you must see. What happened next is too fantastic to tell, you must experience it with them."

The unseen voice from the doeskin bag surrounded the Young One, and again he was swept along, to a river embankment in the Florida and Georgia area, with the remnants of his people. They had dwindled to perhaps one-tenth of the multitude he had seen preparing to leave the Yucatan.

"Young One," the Pearl said, "this day everyone felt they had spent the very last of their energy, that soon the sicknesses and hardships would surely be the end of them. The only thing the people responded to now was the call for ceasing the day's walk and making camp."

The camp was quieter than any the Young One had ever heard, with no chatter as women quietly prepared the few evening foods. Nominal bedding was prepared, with just a few branches of brush, placed on forks to keep the people off the ground and away from the insects and lizards that were always looking for a free meal and a warm body to sleep with. Even the snakes would sneak into your bed sometimes and curl up close to you. Some of the people longed for the simple torments of mice and pests of their homelands.

Many wondered what would become of them in this tormenting place.

The evening of beautiful stars reminded a few of the people of the legends that the stars are our Ancestors and our songs are the bridges which help them climb from this world to the Milky Way, where they watch over us. The children were taught to read the stars so they would always know how to get home. But now, none of that mattered because to get home one needed a boat, and at home were ferocious and cruel people. No, there was no use in thinking on these things anymore. This was the new home. Sleep descended as quietly and quickly as the fog that arose from everywhere at once, blocking out the stars and the night sky. The night sounds became muffled with only sharp snorts and snuffles and random coughs breaking the damp, velvety spell.

Suddenly they heard voices on the other side of the river. The camp became deathly quiet as they listened, trying to peer through the gathering mist, and trying to get up and hide themselves until they knew who and what they were facing. They did not know the people of this territory. Silent caution became the rule of the camp, as the people tensely peered into the darkness across the river while the fog thickened and gently swirled towards the sky.

Dim hints of dawn came and the Young One suddenly found himself among the People in the dark camp, no longer just an observer, but one of them. He too felt the bone-weariness of the travelers. His stomach ached with the hunger one feels from a long absence of warm, cooked meals, and it growled in protest at the meager rations handed to him to eat. How could one run, or fight with no more than this to fuel his tired legs and body? The people could not plant corn until they found their relatives or a permanent place to live. So this morning of all mornings, with strangers on the other shore, there was no warrior meal, only leftover grapes and cactus fruits, and not many of them.

Finally the Young One saw the glare of the sun penetrate the heavy fog, with all the camp awake. The quiet stillness by which they had gone to sleep continued, broken only by serious whispers as the leaders tried to figure out what they should do next.

By this time the other camp had noticed them and their leaders could be heard shouting for the warriors and people to take defensive measures in preparation for a fight. The air was alive with fear and foreboding. The hair on the Young One's body seemed to be standing at such attention from his neck to his ankles that surely if someone raked across him the brittle hairs would break. Some of his people clutched their medicine bags and pawakas, murmuring quiet earnest prayers for help. Tiny streams of smoke rose as tobacco was frantically offered. The scenes on both sides of the river were similar, mothers giving children instructions, trying to keep them calm and confident, with their own nervous perspiration trickling down their sides. The old men and warriors tried to determine the best defensive positions and escape routes in case the people on the other side had rafts or canoes. The medicine men and shamans made preparations, some dancing, chanting, and gesticulating, trying to intimidate the people on the other side, and each calling for special protection and help from Creator for their own people.

Suddenly the okima stopped and listened. Then with a raised hand he shouted across the river, "Who are you?" A voice on the other side shouted back, "Who are *you?*" Then the okima smiled. He had recognized the words on the other side as being in his own language. With a few more calls back and forth the unexpected wonder was confirmed, and indeed it was a wonder. The people who had traveled by boats across the Big Water had finally caught up with those who had come to North America across the land on foot. They immediately joined together on the northeast side of the river, and many days of celebration began as families and friends were reunited, and the people were together again.

In the midst of them all, with immense relief, Young One felt his knees turn to water, and he sat down quickly on the ground, oblivious to scurrying lizards and bugs. He felt like singing the celebration song. His eyes misted at the sight of the families reuniting. The people's strengths were renewed when the separation ended.

The smooth voice of the Pearl spoke to the Young One again. "It is said that the people lived together at this site for many years. It is one of the last times so many of the People lived together in one place. No one can say at what time this took place.

"Later a large portion of the People began migrating west, but those who were to become your direct ancestors stayed in Florida much longer. Finally, around 990 A.D. your direct ancestors traveled northward and established the mound building cultures responsible for the Etowah and Stone Eagle Mountain mounds of Georgia. Your ancestors were of the Mississippian culture and the Fort Ancient Mound Builders were your first ancestors in the Ohio area. The Kispoko band, or a group who were predominately of that sept, arrived in the southeastern part of Ohio about 1200 A.D. They also had a permanent site near what is now Logan, West Virginia. By 1450 to 1475 you had camps in most of northern Kentucky, towns in southern Ohio, and were as far west as your cousins the Miami.

"In the 1500s you were joined in the North by those who earlier had stayed South: the Hathawakela of Georgia, the Piqua of the East and the Chalgotha of southeastern Ohio and northwestern West Virginia. That is the last time you were all together in such large numbers.

"Remember, Young One, at each place you moved to and lived, some of your ancestors intermarried with other groups, and some simply chose to stay. There was never an instance when every single one of your people left an area. Throughout the Aliens' documents there are mentions of your people having villages or living near other tribes villages, in all the areas you ever lived, even hundreds of years after the main body of your people moved on. What might be termed the glory years was the short time period between 1575 and 1600.

"Trying to trace your people's migrations and moves creates a tangled but fascinating tapestry. I am certain that you will be confused because your ancestors went different directions, at different times, with various combinations of the septs for hundreds of years. It was late in the histories kept by the Alien invaders that some of the details of the People's travels were recorded. The different invaders spelled the names according to their own languages' interpretations. Before the 1700s the People were noted by their sept divisional names instead of the nation's name. Oh, Young One, it wearies my head to even think about all these details. Just be patient as you attempt to sort out the trail of travels."

The voice of the Pearl now began to sound tired and it said to the Young One, "I have started your journey to the heart of your People, to your most ancient beginnings in this part of Turtle Island. We Ancients, the Stones of the Great House, have taken upon ourselves to teach you in many different ways. Listen with your heart, Young One. Trust your spirit.

"We will return to the Great House now, as others there are waiting their turn to teach and show you." With this said, the Pearl was once again in the bag on the altar, and the Young One realized he was back in the safe enclosure of the Great House, seated next to his mentor the Old Watcher. The Young One began to puzzle in his mind about what he had just experienced in this strange dream. A soft sigh came from the little bag on the altar stone, as the beautiful Pearl rested from its adventures. The Old Watcher was still snoring, so there was nothing else for the Young One to do but sit and wonder at the strange things that happen every time in the sacred Great House.

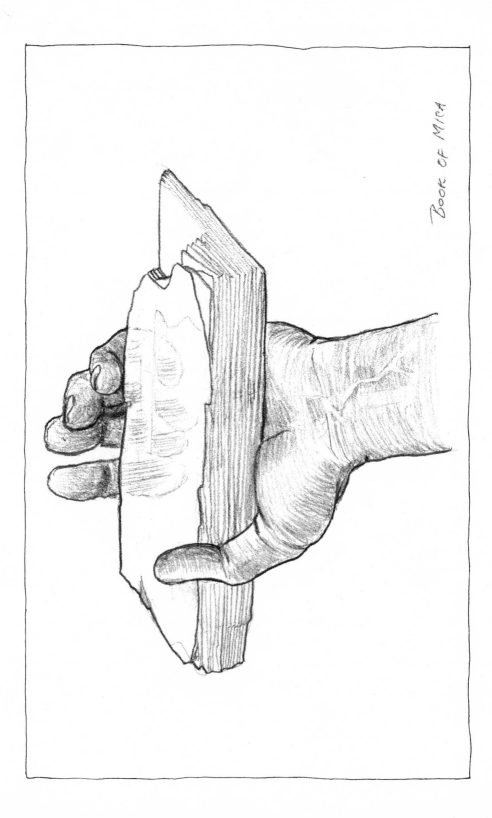

BOOK OF MICA

The Young One sat where he had last noticed the Old Watcher's head dodder down to his chest, savoring his last spirit journey to the Ancestors' time.

It wasn't too long before a thin, high, breathy voice was heard in the Great House. The thinness of the sound caused all the other stones to listen very intently. It was a Book of Mica that leaned against the supporting stones under the altar stone. The little voice said, "It was shortly after the People were reunited that the grandchildren came into the territory where I was formed, in what you call Alabama. Their ancestors, the Fort Ancient people, had been there long before them, and had used many of my mica relatives to make their sacred and ceremonial pieces. Hundreds of years after they and their ancestors left, the Alien conquerors dug into their burial mounds and found the exquisite effigies of hands and birds and other things that Shawnee ancestors had carved and cut from my relatives. The huge sheets of mica that they used to cover the burial floors and their dead are still spoken of with awe, for today it is almost unheard of to find such large pieces of us intact. The sacred items I refer to are known to your archaeologists from the mounds associated with the Hopewell, but your ancestors, the Fort Ancient Mound Builders, also used my nation in these ways.

"We Books of Mica and clear quartz were very highly regarded and usually used only in a very important and sacred manner. Mica is unique. We are mineral like the rest of the Great House Stones but we are ever so fragile. You can peel us like layers of pages from a book, yet we are very useful around fire because we don't conduct heat, and you can see through us. There are very few natural things that one can see through, you know.

"Only we Mica Stones remember what religious purpose those burial pieces of mica served and what they represented. It is sad to say, but it seems better to my mind, that specific information is something we should not retell to the grandchildren. As we Great House Stones help the grandchildren tonight, we must be careful to protect them from unscrupulous ones who would use such information to harm them. So, if you all will agree with me, I shall not tell them the purposes their ancestors put us to, other than decorations that they might want to make and wear today.

"Instead, I will tell about the times the Ancestors lived in my homeland after coming from Mexico and passing through Florida. I will remind them of the wonderful friendships and relationships they enjoyed there in what they now call Mississippi, Alabama, the Carolinas, and Georgia. I will also tell them why they moved on, and about their ancestors who chose to stay in the south. This may help them understand their beloved leader Tecumseh more, because it is said his mother was part Creek, from my creation place, and he spent much time among the people there. Even his style of headwear, a turban adorned with a giant ostrich plume, reflects the Creek influence."

There was a general rumble and squeak as the stones discussed this new thought. Finally the rich voice of the Mask became clear as it said, "Well thought out, little Book of Mica. It is a great responsibility that we Ancient Stones are taking upon ourselves to reeducate our Shawnee grandchildren. We must be careful that all we tell them is useful and in no way harmful. Thank you for reminding us of this, little Mica Book."

The clear Book of Mica then began to address the entranced Young One. "Look south now to the lands of the Temple Mounds. These were created by the ancestors of the people you now call Creek or Muskogee. Look closely and you will recognize some of your ancestors living among these fine people."

The Young One moved eagerly into the spirit vision the Mica Book was creating, as it continued to speak. "The ball game is about to begin — see the thousands of people lined up to watch? And there are hundreds of players. This game is pitting village against village. The players' bodies are gleaming with oil, their hair is slicked down and back so as to not give any hand hold to opponents. This will be an all-day game, until one side or the other reaches a score of one hundred. We will not have time to watch them play. It is like your modern football, soccer, and rugby all in one. The men usually play against the women, with the women allowed to carry, hit, kick, throw, and do anything with the ball, but the men are allowed only to kick and hit it. The women are noted to be formidable opponents, by the way.

"The feast after the game will be a delightful one, for the women have been preparing and cooking for days now. There will be many a broken bone that needs to be set and noses that will need straightening later. This will keep the people busy for at least a week. In spite of the broken bones, those in the villages have great fun with the ball games. They look forward to these events with great anticipation, spending months think-ing of ways to disable and defeat their opponents during the games. When it is all over, the camps will be friendly and full of new tales exchanged over the campfires as they share celebration feasts.

"There were many marriages between the Creeks and Shawnee, whose relationship goes back hundreds of years. Although they were of different language bases, they shared the same attitudes about the Aliens' invasion of Turtle Island and fought together against them. Many songs and dances were similar, and it is impossible to tell where they originated. There are some songs that both the Shawnee and Creek agree came from the Shaw-nee during the last time they lived among the Creek. Both had mound-building ancestors. The Creeks' ancestors had been the Temple Mound People. The ancestors of the Shawnee, who had come before your imme-diate ancestors came from Mexico, were the Fort Ancient Mound People. The ways they celebrated the Green Corn Ceremony, which the Creeks called the *Busk*, were very similar. There was always a great respect and easy affection between the two peoples.

"It would be remiss of me if I did not mention another of the tribes that your ancestors intermarried with, because at this time they were con-sidered a part of the Creeks. The Eyuchies had been conquered by the Creeks after many centuries of war and conflict. After the Creeks won because there were no longer enough Eyuchies left to fight, the Creeks adopted the Eyuchies and they lived both nearby and among the Creeks from then on. The Eyuchies were a beautiful people with a related culture and the Shawnee ancestors got along well with them. The oral tradition of both states that their relationship is very ancient, much older than the relationship with the Creeks. These were happy times for the ancestors, being with these good people in the south.

"Through the decades with the Creeks the Eyuchies had lost most of their own personal songs and dances and when they held celebrations, it was with the Creeks' customs and traditional forms of expression. Your ancestors were such good friends with the Eyuchies that they gave them several songs and dances to have for their own, with which to remember their friends the Shawnee. Hundreds of years later this song-swapping confused the anthropologists, until one of them asked about the oral traditions and found both the Eyuchies and the Shawnee say that these songs and dances originated with the Shawnee, with the Eyuchies just the recipient of these as a gift of friendship.

"It is said that in the early 1700s, when the last large division of the Shawnee was moving away to rejoin their brothers in the northeast, they were still trading with the Spanish in Florida. They made a special trade with the Spaniards at Saint Augustine for a gift for the Creeks. So, at that year's Busk they presented the Creeks with copper plates to remember them by. While years of intermarriage between the tribes had created the atmosphere of a large tolerant family, your Shawnee always held fast to their own identities, culture, religion and ways of doing things.

"Into the 1930s these plates were used by the Creeks once every four years at the Busk feast, by the special members of the ceremonial committees. Even today they are shown to all the People every year, and washed once a year with sand and water to brighten them and remove the verdigris buildup. Even the washers are not allowed to read their inscriptions and writings. Then the plates are tenderly dried and stored at the home of the special custodial guardian until the next year. It was said if the Creeks ever tired of the ceremonial plates, they would give them back to the Shawnee who gave them to them, meaning the Kispoko Shawnee, but they have not tired of them yet.

"It was only after the Alien invaders came and brought their god or gods that Indians ever began to quarrel about there being a 'right way' to worship Creator. I know you have heard that the Alien invaders worship only one god, but they do not all act alike, and each says their god says something different, so we don't know just who they worship. Nor do we know how many gods they really talk about in their little black book; we only know they do not act very civilized or loving towards one another or others. Therefore we encourage you to maintain your ancestors' celebrations and worship the Creator in the ways we know work, from thousands of years of experience.

"But it is a wonderful thing, Young One, to see a friendship between two different Peoples that lasts over so many centuries. Yes, you should remember later to investigate these Creek friends of the Shawnee. They were the only southern tribe that truly joined Tecumseh and the Prophet when the Shawnee were fighting the Aliens. The Creeks and the Eyuchies have many wonderful warriors and chiefs in their own history, and they have wonderful memories of your ancestors, too."

The Book of Mica continued to explain: "While your ancestors were with these southern mound-building people, they held the most elaborate and intricate ceremonies of their history since the days they were in Mexico. Some took weeks of preparation.

"Some of the decorations and items they used were made of the clear crystal we spoke of. Some were elaborate beaten copper and silver, obsidian, even the blood-colored obsidian, and semiprecious jewels. Ah, Young One, sometimes if you hold me in the light just so, I can reflect all those dazzling brilliant colors that the leaders adorned themselves with. And the people too, they were beautifully arrayed and accented with the feathers, copper, pearl, jade, cinnabar, and shells. Then they would paint colorful statues, and their ornaments, and themselves.

"Such beauty we may never again experience," sighed the Mica. "Because most of the things I was involved with were and are sacred, I cannot tell you all I would like to. Continue to be right-thinking, then, another time, I can come to you and teach you of those wonderful things. Now I will take you back to the Great House where others are waiting for you with more to tell," said the Mica Book. The Young One was lost in the images created in his mind by the descriptions of the ancient ceremonial objects, until at last, he recognized the flickering of the fire, as it flashed a distress signal, being almost out of wood.

The Young One could only wonder at what was happening to him. He tried very hard to search his mind to determine if these were real occurrences, like visions, or merely dreams.

Occasionally a farm dog would howl or bark for a few seconds, reminding errant four-leggeds that they were trespassing on its territory. But for the most part the night was quiet, with the air fairly still now.

Young One was watching the deep, inky sky for a telltale hint of the time, when he was startled by a strong voice near the entrance. His eyes could not penetrate that dark corner. As he raised his hand to his eyes to try to concentrate his vision, the voice said, "Young One, I have many things to tell you and show you. I am usually very plain looking, yet I have served your people, men and women, for as long as any of us can remember, everywhere they have ever lived, so I know almost all of their story." Young One's mind raced, trying to figure out what stone would have been with his people always. Suddenly he softly said, "A flint! It has to be. You're a piece of flint!"

"Yes, I am of the flint family, a family that is found all over the world," the strong, smooth voice continued in a kindly manner. "Some call us chert, some flint, and there are other names. But we have always been excellent tools for both women and men. One of the first things you yourself were taught, Young One, was to knap a piece of flint into an arrowhead. We have always been so much more than just points on the arrows and spears, though. The women had wonderful uses for us as tools in their daily life, and used us to make beautiful clothing. Most flint knives did not have a handle and simply lay in the palm of the hand. When the blade became broken or chipped and dull, it took a woman but a minute to chip the edge and make it sharp again.

"Have you ever seen the ancient blanks your people made from me? Has anyone ever told you about the trips to the flint ridge, where your people collected me after they migrated from the lands of the Creeks and elsewhere to the Ohio Valley? Well, let me tell you about one. Once in a while there will be a mountain of flint, or huge seams of our material hundreds of feet wide. Here in Ohio the colors are so different that flint is considered a semiprecious gemstone and they make jewelry of us. Some of us contain unusual prehistoric moss, but many claim our most beautiful form is when we are black with blue lightning streaks.

"The locations of large outcroppings of flint have always been considered sacred ground, made by Creator for friend and foe alike, not just for a special few.

"If a village needed flint for tools, the men who were best at working the flint would pack up, taking a few strong young helpers, some spare bags or rawhide boxes, their chipping and mining tools, and a few days' supplies. Off the group would go to the flint ridge. During times of war they might stay for weeks, preparing for the warriors' needs.

"The most experienced men would walk through and identify the places with the best flint. They would hold the appropriate ceremonies, purifying themselves and the tools and containers, then make the offering to the stones whose lives they were about to use. They would then set about chopping large blocks of the flint from the main vein. Sometimes these would be several feet thick and would require more than one man to move once they were broken free.

"Right on the spot or within a very few feet the experienced knappers would help the strong, young helpers chunk out the large slabs of stone. Once they had a few dozen slabs, the knappers would sit down and chip away and eliminate as much useless stone as they could. While these knappers were paring the slabs down to size, the other men would continue to work creating the slabs until they had many months' supply, and sometimes even a whole year's or more, set aside. When they were finished, the knappers would continue to take away all the irregular stone they could, leaving beautiful smooth, large blanks. This process removed extra weight so the men were not carrying useless waste back to the village. Sometimes they made the actual points and tools on site.

"Perhaps there would be a time of peace and the trip would be just for tools and hunting weapons. At the flint site other tribes would have their people collecting their tribe's needs. Sometimes bitter enemies would meet at the digs, but no matter what, no one ever fought, quarreled, or killed there. It was neutral territory and sacred ground.

"Many times, if there was a battle coming up with an enemy, the medicine man might even go with the men. He would have special blessings he would ask of the Stone People, and plead for their strength and life to be put to the most effective use in protecting the people of his tribe.

"It seems strange that the preparations for war should begin under a truce of peace. You do know, Young One, that your people had a great reputation for using flint under the circumstances of war. Some of that is well deserved, but some is a misconception of what really happened. Let me explain: Flint is usually thought of in connection with warfare, and while your people moved north it is true that they had occasions to use us in this manner.

"Because your people traveled so far trying to find their relatives here in the north, they met many people. Some were friendly, some were shy, and some were very hostile. There were always misunderstandings that came from language difficulties and inaccurate translations. It did not take long before your people had to defend themselves from people trying to run them away. Your people brought with them much knowledge about many things. Very observant and shrewd, they had seen many things concerning war in Mexico. They were also larger in stature than most of the people they came in contact with, which usually gave them an advantage, and they quickly developed a reputation as impressive strategists as well as fierce warriors. They seemed very good at outthinking the enemy, partly because they could look at the battle area and figure the most advantageous positions to take.

"Women sometimes participated in the battles. That was an unheard-of thing for most of their enemies, but there were almost always a few Shawnee women warriors who fought with the men. The sight of women on the battlefield sometimes caused such a disturbance that the other side would quit and flee. Once the enemy warriors were distracted by the women disrobing and walking in front of them, and your men took them by surprise, quickly ending the dispute. That must have been a funny sight.

"But the true women warriors were women who would actually fight alongside the men. These women would usually have received the proper training as they grew up from their uncles. Fathers taught their sons, but the uncles were the teachers of the girls. Usually a woman would not lead in battle unless she had received a powerful vision that she should. She would advise the war chief and the medicine man of her vision. Always, when a woman had had such a vision the men let her lead, and they never lost a battle that a woman led. There were also women who went to war to save their families from disgrace because their husbands were cowards. Your most well-known woman warrior was Cornstalk's sister Nonehelema, also known as the Grenadier Squaw. She lived in the late 1700s and was also a village chief in southern Ohio.

"The war chief was the leader in every sense of the word. He had to have a plan of attack, and he had to convince the men it was a good plan. Then he would have to convince the women's council that it was a good idea to go to war. If the women's council vetoed the idea, then the men did not go to war until they could get their approval. You see, the ancestors realized that it was the women who would suffer if any of the men were lost in battle. It was their fathers, brothers, husbands, and sons who would be going. The women are the life givers and should have some say in situations where life might be lost. In the event a battle was called for over something trivial, or that just involved various egos, as it sometimes did, the women's council was there to point out that the offenses were not serious enough to risk lives over and cause suffering to innocent people.

"Each village had a women's war chief and a women's peace chief. The woman war chief had particular responsibilities and leadership of the majority of the women's activities. At ceremonies she also provided the meat. The women's peace chief spoke for the women when the women's council voted against the men going to war. The women's peace chief's main responsibility was to convince the male war chief to stay home and at peace when the women had so voted. Any incident of failure of the men to respect the women's votes and pleadings was never reported. The women peace chiefs were very good at persuasion.

"Every man was considered a warrior unless he specifically refused to participate. If he declined, the man would still be respected by the people. Your ancestors were very proud of being a free people. No one, not even the chief, told Shawnee people what to do. A chief could ask his warriors, encourage them and try to show them why they should go to war. But no one demanded anything of a Shawnee. Should someone have a bad feeling about a particular battle and decide to stay home, he was respected for paying attention to the messages the spirits had brought him. Even during a battle, if a man decided this was not a good day to die, he was free to turn around, go home, and live to fight another day. The war chief was the leader in every sense of the word, convincing the men the plan would work, then convincing the women's council that it was a good idea to go to war.

"Once the war chief had the permission of women's council to make war and all the preparations were made, then he truly had to lead the men. There were no 'armchair generals' in the Shawnee armies. The war chief had to be the first one on the battlefield, for if he did not have enough confidence in his own plans to lead, why should the other men follow? When it is said that someone was a great war chief and leader, now you understand just what they meant.

"During the time your ancestors were in the south, they were asked for help by a Choctaw chief. His war chief had taken a large group of their tribe, broken off from the main group, and was causing all kinds of problems. So the principal chief asked the Shawnee war chief to fight his war chief who had deserted until he was tired and through making war and would bring his group back to the main body of the tribe. The Shawnee war chief accepted and fought the renegade war chief until he returned to the main tribe. In that instance your ancestors functioned as mercenaries, or hired soldiers.

"There were many wars and battles in which your ancestors participated. Seldom were they the aggressors, but were usually defenders in the situation. Once they fought the Cherokees, and then a few decades later they joined the Cherokees and they fought together. Other than the Catawbas, the only major group that your ancestors just did not get along with, were the Iroquois. The Shawnee ran into groups of Iroquois on the east coast as they worked their way up along there and up through Tennessee. There were many happy years living with the Delaware and Nanticokes and the others, but always the Iroquois caused problems with the Shawnee. When these people were not actually fighting with your ancestors, they were telling falsehoods to the white men about the ownership of pieces of land and spreading rumors of having fought and conquered your ancestors.

"At one point the Iroquois were to have allowed your ancestors and the Delaware into council as full members, but it turned out to be another betrayal and the people were treated with disrespect, as if they were servants or conquered people. Once your ancestors left the 'protective arm' of the Iroquois and resumed their past standard of living, they were deal-

ing with the Alien invaders and trying to live under peaceful circumstances. The Iroquois spread false rumors, and did mischief that was blamed
on your ancestors and continually stirred up troubles.

"About that time in the 1700s another treaty had been broken, and
your ancestors in Pennsylvania were presented with a new one that would
move them from the banks of the Susquehanna and the lands between
there and the Juniata. They received an invitation and request from the
aged Wyandotte and Delaware of the Ohio Valley to come help protect
them from the marauding, invading Iroquois. In return, the Wyandotte
and Delaware would give them a large portion of beautiful, productive,
land for their own home. In the middle 1700s there were so many Aliens
invading the eastern section of the territory that this was a welcome invitation indeed, and thus your ancestors did move into western Virginia,
western Pennsylvania, and eastern Ohio, bringing with them more Delaware, Senecas, Nanticokes, and several other small tribes.

"If you will remember, Young One, some of your ancestors were just
then leaving the south, the Carolinas and Georgia area. There was another group of your ancestors that had already moved up through the interior of Alabama and Georgia into the Cumberland area, on up through
Kentucky and to the mouth of the Scioto River in Ohio. It seemed that
after all those centuries of traveling, the Ohio Valley is where all these
different migrating Shawnee were to find their new home. I must also
point out that a small group had visited west of the Mississippi by then
and returned to the Pennsylvania and Virginia area. But as conflicts and
wars continued to plague the people even in their beautiful Ohio Valley, a
large group moved permanently west to what they called New Spain, but
what you know as the Cape Girardeau area of Missouri.

"Do not feel confused, Young One," the Flint consoled. "It is just that
there were five divisions of your Shawnee people — some say six — and
seldom were they all at one place at one time. They walked all over this
eastern portion of Turtle Island.

"Their traveling, of course, gave them certain advantages. They had
seen many things that other tribes knew nothing of. They became mas-
ters at trading, because they knew all the wonderful things to trade and
where they could be found. There is some evidence that some Shawnee
traders actually went to the northwest across the Rockies and discovered
things like the beautiful dentalium shells.

"They traded for the obsidian they found at Yellowstone. They were familiar with it because they had brought many precious things made of it from Mexico. Obsidian is the only thing that surpasses my family of flint in cutting a fine, thin edge. Today only the exotic laser beam cuts cleaner and finer than obsidian. The people made beautiful points of all sizes from this clear, natural, glass-like stone, which sometimes comes in colors of red, brown, or gray, even mottled and banded. These were certainly beautiful things but they were fragile, for they also broke like glass. It took no time at all for the people to decide to use them mainly for ceremonial and show purposes, so they would last and not be destroyed from too much handling and use.

"Your people knew the animals and their regions, and so could provide pelts to people in distant places that did not have those particular animals living there. Medicines, herbs, paints of different colors or the dry powders to make them, pearls, mica, copper, lapis lazuli, crystal quartz, white quartz, soapstone, jade — these were just some of the things your ancestors traded. They would even trade blanks of flint. Some were very beautifully colored and not just field gray or tan, but looked almost like obsidian or colored quartz.

"The trails that they used were sometimes just animal paths through different areas, but there were indeed some very definite wide roads through the forests that the ancestors' ancestors had made which were still maintained. The brush was cleared out, and sometimes they would burn the trails to keep them from becoming weed-choked. Remember, too, the people did not just walk: most of the time they ran at a reasonable speed, so they could cover considerable distances.

"Until the 1700s there were no horses in the area where your people were, so walking, running, and canoeing were their only forms of transportation. All the people, women and children too, were in good physical condition and had been running since they were old enough to walk. The Shawnee saw and learned more than any other tribe with their migrations and wanderings. Their oral traditions kept the information alive in their memories and their children's children's memories so they would not forget all they had seen and learned, and of course they were taught how to get where they needed to go.

"They learned a quick way to make fire with pieces of my relatives," the Flint said boldly. "That is the contribution to your people that we are most proud of. At first they struck a piece of the right type of flint against another rock, of the kind that would create a spark. This spark would land on some soft dry material underneath, usually cattail fluff or milkweed fiber, which they would then fan or blow until they saw it flicker, and then they added tiny dry twigs, and then sticks until they had their fire going well. Once the Aliens came, they brought bent pieces of steel which the people used to strike the flint with. The ancestors called the flint fire the *sacred fire*. It was considered sacred because it is like a miracle to be able to create fire from a stone which is cold and does not burn itself. Only the men were allowed to make flint fire, and so they would start the cooking fires for the women.

"Occasionally the archaeologists will discover some ancient village site and find hundreds of flint blanks at one homesite. This would have been the home of the best knapper of the village, who might stay there and make the points needed by the warriors while they went hunting for food. Not all people were good at all the things they needed to be able to do, and just as today there were some people who were more talented than others in certain ways. Some of the ancestors were even what you would call experts in their fields of endeavor. The knapper who could read a block of raw flint, cut it into the slabs and then refine it into the blanks to be brought back to the village, was highly valued by his people. Because the knapper was busy procuring the flint, someone else probably had to hunt to provide for his family. When the knapper got back to the village he would offer this hunter part of the blanks or even offer to make a certain number of points for him to repay the kindness. This sort of generous sharing was typical of Shawnee custom. Giving is a blessing that always brings the giver happiness. I am glad to see that this custom has not died out among the Shawnee. Just yesterday did not your village knapper share his flint with you and several others? Then did they not find ways to gift him for his generosity? One with deer antlers to use for tools and another with thick deerskin to cushion his strokes? Communities are better and much happier places to live when everyone adheres to this philosophy of giving and sharing. It is said to be an insult to Kohkumthena to be stingy with anything, for Creator made all things for all the people to use.

"I must return you, Young One," the Flint said. "There is so much you need to learn and our time to teach you is very limited. I hope you are able to understand some of the things we are trying to teach you that we have not expressed in your words. You must be able to think on these things and realize the importance of each small thing that Creator has put here for you. We hope you will be able to see what is wrong with the way the People have lived the past hundred and eighty years. We know it was not the fault of your ancestors, that they did not want to give up their way of life, but that it was forced on them after they lost all their wars, battles, and treaties. But if you can understand what is wrong, there is a chance that the society you now live in can recapture the important, good, and precious things.

"You are living in a great time. The common citizen is allowed more and more freedom to live in the sacred manner of his choice. Though it was spoken of and even written into the words of the Aliens' Constitution, the reality of this freedom was not there. As you are learning from us Great House Stones, there are people fighting the great war of words, to make sure you can practice the ancient religion in the old, sacred ways using the things Creator instructed your people to use, such as eagle feathers. Be strong in your heart, Young One. It is a great time to be Shawnee. You must return now so the others can continue, but I may add to your understanding later," said the Flint, and with that the Young One again found himself gazing at the fire in the center of the Great House.

Now that he was sitting back inside the Great House listening to the Old Watcher snore in the firelight, the tiredness that comes after a full day's activities and sitting up half the night began to catch up with the Young One's slender body. It was difficult to think. Between all these strange thoughts and visions and the tiredness he felt, the Young One was beginning to wish he were back in his mother's lodge. No one was ever going to understand all the strange things he was experiencing. Who could he ever tell or ask? Certainly not the Old Watcher, who had slept the night away oblivious to the goings-on. They would think he had gone silly in the head if he told them the Great House Stones had been teaching him.

A soft voice came from the cluster of items near the drum and the war pole. While the voice was soft, there was a strength in it that caused the Young One to look around to see if someone was playing a trick on him. The darkness in that area was the darkest of the Great House, so his eyes perceived only inky black space.

The voice continued: "Young One, I want to show you about the women of your ancestors. There is so much misunderstanding about their role in the tribal life that you need to know how it truly was. I am a Woman's Button. Oh, I'm not the kind of button you know about today. I do not fasten clothing. I am egg-shaped, large, and covered in leather and attached to a three or four-foot length of braided leather. A woman would tuck two or three of me into the belt or sash at her waist. I was one of the original 'attitude adjusters.' Let me explain how the women used me.

"It was the place of the men, you know, to go hunt large animals for food, and they went to war when necessary. These battles were always held as far away from the village as possible so the women and children would be safe. While the men were gone, the women would work around the village as usual with their skins and hides, mending, sewing, cooking,

The "Woman's Button"
self-defense weapon

tending to the children, and cultivating the gardens so there would be many good flavors and nutrition in the meals, not just meat.

"Simply because the men might be gone did not mean that the women were left defenseless. There would always be a few men around, some old ones who no longer hunted, and some young ones not yet good enough to go with the rest. But the women themselves were good at defending the village, for they would have played the same games and learned the same lessons the boys did while they were growing up. They would have been instructed to run, not walk, when they needed to go somewhere. They would know how to shoot a bow and arrow, even if their arrows did not fly as far as the men's. They all could swim. The women would have participated in the good-humored competitions with the men, throwing knives and the tomahawk after these items were made with steel heads. The women were proficient in using the sling with which they hurled stones at small game. They knew how to use spears for fishing, and they were strong from all the hard physical work they did all their lives.

"When the men went to war with an enemy, that did not mean that all danger from other tribes was gone. Other tribesmen visited, perhaps even in a friendly situation. Your people were very cautious not to inter-marry within their clans, because they were like large families and incest was forbidden. This was true of most of the People. Occasionally someone of another village or tribe would need a wife and not find anyone suitable in his own tribe. Men would go visiting other nearby tribes, even if they did not speak the same language.

"While a woman was tending the gardens or picking berries, a man from another tribe might try to kidnap her because she was attractive to him. He had no way of knowing if she was already married, engaged, or too attached to her own family to leave home. So then the woman would reach down and grab the leather thong of her button, give it a swing, bonk the fellow on the head and 'change his attitude' about taking her away.

"All manner of other stones were used by the women in their daily lives. The women had many forms of grinding stones. They had the very small ones to grind medicines and seasonings like pepper weed, mustard, and spices. They kept the metate and manos for grinding corn and they even ground the things they used for their facial paint. Some grinding stones were very small, just a couple inches across, while others like the metate and manos were large and heavy, as big as two feet long. The small ones were often very smooth, even shiny. They were used for special things so they did not wear out very quickly. Actually, few Shawnee women used the manos and metates, and it is thought that they were actually women from other tribes who brought them with them when they married Shawnee men. Shawnee women customarily used wooden mortar and pestles. They would hollow out a large piece of tree trunk so they could pour in dried corn, then they would use another piece of wood about three and a half feet long and about six to eight inches in diameter to pound the corn into small pieces and create their meal and flour.

"There were many kinds of cooking stones. The women would heat some rounds or ovals about the size of a fist over the coals and then place them into the vat of soup or stew. It sounds strange, but placing hot stones in soup or stew was a very effective method of cooking. It took only eight or ten stones to make the food come to a boil. Usually only a small time was needed to cook the stew, perhaps twenty minutes or a little longer. The stones would last for several weeks and often even months if care was taken not to let them heat too long in direct flames.

"Eventually the stones were replaced by ones the women made from clay when they were throwing pottery. Making clay cooking stones was a perfect way to use up the leftover clay when they were finished creating pots. Every couple of months they would make a batch of pots and cooking stones, because they would wear out from use, finally breaking. Since it took several days to create these clay stones, you just insured you never went too long without replenishing them. The women would decorate the clay stones just as they did their pots, with their own particular designs."

The Young Watcher could hardly keep up with the fast, soft-talking Woman's Button. He could tell she had been waiting for a long time to speak and had thought about all the things she thought he should know. Everyone had said there was only a little time in which they could teach him, so perhaps the time was growing shorter than he realized.

The Button continued at its breathless pace. "There were cooking slabs that were used like our modern griddles. When placed over cooking pits they created a natural oven as well as a griddle. Shawnee women were excellent cooks, Young One. The foods they cooked were indeed the tastiest of any of the tribal peoples around. They would pound dried pumpkins to make thickener for their stews, or use what your mother calls cornstarch. Then they would add oil of bear, or fat from some other animal, or nuts, and when it was all just right they sprinkled in their herbs and spices. It is not true that the diet was coarse and plain. The Shawnee women had wonderful recipes. There were even forms of candy and cakes for the children to enjoy, and they dearly loved the dried persimmon and pawpaws. They would just break off small pieces and eat them like candy. Some of the breads were filled with fruits and nuts and were very like today's cakes, but without all the air bubbles.

"When the first Aliens came and shared meals with the People they were always delightfully surprised with the flavors of the food. They had expected to find nasty, half-cooked dishes, but found that the meats were well cleaned and trimmed, well cooked, and enticingly seasoned. Your ancestors were very particular and clean in the manner in which they cooked and the way they stored their dried foods. Meals were served in clean bowls, with clean utensils and clean cups to drink from. They even used some of the Aliens' nice things in their kitchens when they could, because there were items that made the work easier. Some were just pretty. Before that they used natural materials.

"Would you like to see what a Shawnee woman's life was like before the People were moved from the Ohio Valley?" asked the Button. "Wonderful! Let me take you to a Chalagawtha village on the Little Miami. This is a place that the famous Shawnee leader Tecumseh knew well; in fact he was born at the edge of this village. It seems he was in such a hurry to be born that he did not wait until his mother reached the Piqua town where they were going to live."

The Young Watcher became aware that he was no longer looking into a campfire but into a fast-running stream. He heard the voices of children running and playing and mothers calling after them, some sort of instructions that they were too far away to hear. He directed his gaze towards the sounds of the children and saw them dashing and jumping into the water, giggling and splashing silvery sprays of water at each other. He then looked toward where he had heard the mothers' voices and saw the women standing at the edge of a field. Then he was sure he heard them singing a song of some sort; he thought he recognized some of the words as being part of a prayer. On a signal from the head woman, they began to work the field with strange-looking hoes, in ground which was rich, dark, and well-prepared. The hoes seemed to be made of the big shoulder bones of deer. A few hoes were made of very large mussel shells. They had short handles, and that made the Young Watcher wonder why they did not use long ones like people do today. Did these people not get backaches? It was a puzzle to him.

The many women worked together to get the garden quickly planted. They began at the southeastern corner of the garden and moved north and west making the rows. The corn seeds seemed to shine, so the Young Watcher asked the Woman's Button, "Why do those seeds look so shiny? Are they wet?"

"No," said the Button. "They have been greased with fish oil and deer grease so the corn crop will be able to withstand any dry times without wilting."

"Oh," said the Young One. "Does that work?"

"I can only tell you that the women believed it truly worked and never planted their corn without preparing it in this manner," the Button replied.

The children had finished swimming and had gone on to other delights. They played well together and did not seem to be chaperoned, although the Young One had seen several teenagers watching nearby, sometimes playing with them.

Lunch time had come and the women took a short break to eat and refresh themselves, but they quickly returned to their planting. It was nearing the new moon when it was good to plant the things that grew up from the earth. Soon, when it was the dark of the moon, it would be time to plant the things that grew down inside the earth, such as the root vegetables and peanuts.

By the time the women had finished planting the field, it was the middle of the afternoon. They were in the farthest corner of the field now. Then as the Young Watcher was admiring their work, they did a strange thing, taking off their dresses and dragging them behind them while they sang more songs and marched around the edges of the field.

The Young One was bursting with curiosity now. "Woman's Button, please tell me why they are doing that? What a strange and curious thing to do after planting a garden."

"Well, Young One, it is not as strange as you think. Remember, your ancestors lived very close to the natural world and interacted with the animals in ways that your generation has forgotten. This parade of dragging the women's dresses has a very good purpose. They have perspired all day long and their dresses are impregnated with their smell, so now they are telling the animals in the neighborhood that the plants in this garden belong to them and the animals must stay out. It was a form of territorial 'marking,' such as animals do by spraying musk or urine. Animals have a keen sense of smell and try to avoid humans if they can, so when they came to the garden area and smelled the human scent, they would leave."

As the Button finished explaining about the women's gardening tactics, the Young One noticed they were leaving the field and heading towards the water. They all jumped in, kicking, spraying, and giggling just as the children had earlier in the day. This was rather amazing to the Young Watcher, because like all youths it never struck his mind that adults liked to laugh and have fun just as children do. It made his heart feel warm to see the women playing and enjoying the refreshing swim together.

Once the women finished their swim, they dried off and went back to the village. There they went to their individual homes and began warming up the evening meal. Some had left a pot cooking all day; some were quickly preparing something new. It took a short time for the meal to be ready and the women to call their families to come eat. It was now about four in the afternoon.

The Young One noted with interest the way the wigiwa to which the Woman's Button had brought him was constructed. Saplings about two inches in diameter were trimmed of their branches, stuck into the ground several feet deep, and spaced one-and-a-half to two feet apart, thereby creating a circle of about sixteen to twenty feet in diameter. The tops were bent over toward the middle, where they were tied with stout, almost unbreakable twine made of inner pawpaw bark, creating a dome. The top of the dome was about seven or so feet high. The sides were reinforced with a row of saplings, lashed to the uprights, about every foot to foot-and-a-half from top to bottom. The winter homes were always covered with slabs of bark which were cut in spring. The women preferred elm but used other trees as well. There were small holes in the bark panels that allowed them to be lashed to the support poles and cross pieces. The bark, still full of sap when it was placed, gently shaped itself to the curved framework of the wigiwa. The piece of bark on the very top of the wigiwa would be left maneuverable, as it covered and uncovered the smoke exit.

It was warm weather now, so some of the panels had been replaced by cattail reed mats that could be rolled up when privacy was not needed but fresh cool air was. In winter the bark mats would be secured in place and then a second layer of bark mats would be lashed on over the first layer. Dried leaves, corn shucks and many other things would be stuffed into the space in between to act as insulation. That area would also serve as extra storage space for the family. A bark wigiwa such as this would survive twelve to fifteen winters before it would need replacement.

Inside the wigiwa the Young One saw sleeping racks. Made of short, forked sticks stuck into the ground, with long poles resting in the forks, they were covered with soft boughs, usually of pine or cedar which were replaced periodically to maintain their softness and insect repellent qualities. These were then covered with a soft skins or hides with the fur intact in the winter.

The Young One was amazed at the variety of baskets lashed to the wigiwa framework intersections. Large, covered ones were also sitting out of the way. Some were filled with left over cattail fluff and milkweed fluff that had been used for insulation and for stuffing moccasins for warmth. Sometimes the mother also used the fluff for tinder. There was the hominy sifter that looked like the top to a very wide basket, with holes in the weave about a half inch wide. Although most of the larger baskets were woven of oak or ash splits, some were of maple, with the splints all from three-fourths to one inch wide. There were berry baskets of honeysuckle or other vines and splint baskets that were very long and slender for catching eels.

The Woman's Button spoke to him saying, "Young One, each woman makes the home, and then fills it with the tools she needs to run her household." The Young One's admiration for the women was growing. The Button continued, "A woman must be able repair her tools, weave cloth and baskets, make fire, and make and decorate pots from raw clay. She must be able to plant, harvest, preserve, cook, medicate, butcher, tan, sew, decorate, build, repair, and be a considerate daughter to her parents, loving wife, and good mother, teaching grandmother, and voice in council. A woman's life is full to overflowing. She deserves the respect that she is given, for her life is not an easy one. She gives life and is usually the one who buries her loved ones. It is for her laughter that she is loved, and her love of life and love of Creator that guides her children and strengthens her husband. Many women feel that even though it is a hard thing, it is a great honor to be a woman. Enjoy the rest of your visit with this family, Young One, and I will take you back in a little while." With this said, the voice of the Button left the ear of the Young One, and once again, he was mingling with this family, seeing, smelling, tasting, touching, and hearing but not being seen or acknowledged by these Shawnee ancestors of this old Ohio village.

It was amazing just how many things there were inside the wigiwa, even though it looked very neat and almost spacious. There were gourds of every size and shape present, some decorated beautifully, and various clay pots sat about the area. These were used to store water and dozens of other things. There were legless chairs or rest supports of cattail reeds. A large, decorated rawhide trunk sat near the back of the lodge. Thick deer-skins with the hair still on them covered a stack of parfleche bags that were empty now, just waiting for a new batch of jerky.

Bundles of herbs tied to some of the poles made the wigiwa smell fresh and interesting. Small buckskin bags of various sizes and degrees of deco-ration hung in the far areas of the home. Spare spoons made of gourds hung ready for any weary, traveling guest to join the family at the cooking fire. The fire pit was dark because it was summer; unless it rained, the pit out in front of the wigiwa would be used, in order to keep the home cool. Each bed had a stack of hides and rawhide containers, parfleche bags and gourds beside it, with each person in the family having a container of some sort for his personal belongings.

The floor of the wigiwa seemed to shine as though modern floor wax had been used on it. On closer inspection the Young One could tell that it was still just a dirt floor, but the women knew how to treat the dirt in a special way of some sort. The outside yard around the wigiwa had been swept so much that the dirt had a sheen that almost rivaled the shine of the wigiwa floor.

Suddenly the Young Watcher smelled the most delicious aroma, and it reminded him that he was hungry. Allowed as a special favor of the Great House Stones to participate in some of the night's visions, he was handed a gourd bowl full of steaming stew. It was filled with all manner of veg-etables, some deer meat, dried plums and berries, green onions, and other tasty things he couldn't identify. He was also given a small piece of round bread which had a crunchy crust with herbs, currants, and nuts inside the

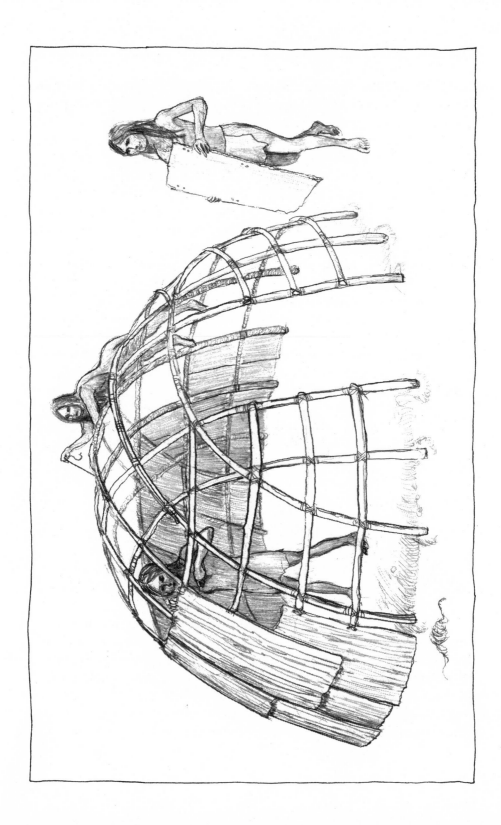

soft, moist middle. It smelled so good his mouth began to water. He had his traditional spoon tied to his waist so as the small family sat around and began to eat, he untied it and sampled this unbelievable treat.

The family consisted of a man, a woman, a girl, and a boy about his age. The woman was saying to her husband, "You have reason to be proud of your son today. I saw him racing, and he beat the other boys at running by at least the length of the wigiwa, and they were all older than he."

The husband nodded. "Someday I believe he will be a fine hunter and provide for us well in our old age. Thank you for telling me this good thing about our son."

There was a slight silence as everyone ate. "Did not our daughter do anything special this day?" the father asked.

"Oh yes. I was just going to tell you that she helped to prepare our dinner tonight because I was so long in the field. I also saw her swimming with the other young girls today, and she is very strong. I do think she is getting old enough to start thinking of young men now. She is no longer so young but almost a teenager. Soon we will be overrun with young men, all suffering from moon eyes for her."

The father laughed, "She had best get over her squeamishness when it comes to tanning the hides and dressing the skins then, for no young man will want a wife who can't keep him clothed." The young girl just blushed.

The Young One observed that the meal was finally finished, and the family members drifted off in their different directions, leaving the mother to tidy up. She took the eating utensils to an open area and washed them with water from a large gourd container about the size of a half bushel basket. She then set them in the sun to dry so they would be ready to put away before nightfall. The main food pot was left near enough to the fire that it stayed hot but did not continue to cook. Anyone who wanted to was free to eat what was left, whether they were of this woman's family or not.

The woman then found some mending to do and took her work outside in the better light. She also worked on a special gift she was making for her daughter who would soon no longer be a child, but would be considered a woman. When that occurred the mother had a special gift to honor her daughter's new role in life.

The Young One watched the activities from a vantage point that allowed him to see the wigiwa and women working and much of the rest of the village, too. Most of the women were outside working on their own projects; small children were getting in one last game of chase before dark, and he could see several groups of men talking, and hear their laughter. A few were mending their arrows or restringing their bows.

As the sun started going down, the Young One saw the mother quickly collect her eating paraphernalia and put it away. The small fire inside the lodge was added to, so it began to give off more light and warmth, because as darkness came so did the humidity and coolness. By this time the woman's family was beginning to reappear and the young boy was ready to go to bed, as was his father, who had hunted a long distance that day. The tired father and son went to their beds and went right to sleep. The Young One realized by now that he was unseen by these people, so he lay down beside them, testing the comfort of their bed. The wife told the husband she would be back shortly but needed to check on one of the elders who had been ill earlier that day, and she would take their daughter with her.

The mother took a gourd bowl full of the leftover stew and wrapped several pieces of bread in clean corn husks that she took from a storage basket. Quietly the mother and daughter walked to a wigiwa about half way through the village. The Young One was now by their side. The mother knocked on the door and an old woman's feeble voice bade them to come inside. Entering, they could see that the elder's fire had almost burned out. Rapidly they found a few small sticks of wood to kindle the flame, and some larger pieces to ensure its lasting the night. After tending to the fire, they could see that the old woman was indeed still ill and needed their assistance. The young girl began to help the old woman eat as the mother began to tidy the old woman's house, straightening the bedding and sweeping the floor. After sweeping out the top dust and debris, the mother sprinkled water on the floor and did a quick shuffling-style stomp dance that repacked and reglazed the surface to an almost glass-like shine. So that was how the floor shining was done, the Young One thought. He tried to imitate the mother's dance but wound up stepping on his own foot and not adding to the finished product at all.

While the Mother was treating the floor of the wigiwa, the daughter finished feeding the old woman, and then took the broom and swept the yard outside around the house. Shawnee were given very serious rules about their housekeeping and their yards by Kohkumthena. In a lifetime, women would use many brooms, which were usually made by taking a piece of wood about four feet long, stripping off the bark, and then split-ting up one end, a little over a foot long. Splitting the pieces until they were about one-eighth to one-quarter inch wide, the women would tie some sinew at the base of the splits to strengthen it. Sometimes the women would just take stiff weed stems of a particular type and tie them together around a two or three-inch diameter stick. Again, the Young One won-dered why they used such short handles on their tools. He must remember to ask the Old Watcher, he thought.

The mother collected the dirty eating utensils and promised to take and wash them and return them the next day. The Shawnee have rules about washing dishes after sundown. It isn't done for fear of offending the spirits who might want the leftovers in the dishes. Then the young girl collected fresh water so her mother could help the old woman bathe. Shaw-nee bathed every day in every kind of weather, sometimes bathing twice in hot weather. Discreetly the Young One stepped outside while the women freshened up the old woman and her bed. After the bath a fresh garment was found for the old woman to put on, and the mother gently helped her brush her hair.

The old woman was most appreciative of their care and remembered the mother as having been an especially considerate person when she was young. How happy she was to find that the mother was teaching her daugh-ter to be kind and considerate also! She was feeling strengthened by the nourishing food they had brought her. She began telling one of the old oral tradition stories about how the red children were created. She di-rected her story at the young girl, whom she could see was about to enter young womanhood and would be doing some creating of red children of her own some time in the foreseeable future. Young One listened too.

"Oh, it was in the beginning that 'He Who Creates By Thinking' cre-ated the first twelve people of the world. But creating people must be very hard work, for when he had finished making them he was tired, and he said to Kohkumthena, 'I will let you make the rest of the red children to populate Turtle Island.' And so, Kohkumthena began making the red chil-dren. She made several, and then, she too became very tired and wanted to quit. But she knew that many more red children were needed to fill Turtle Island. As she complained about how tiring it was to make people, her silly grandson, Roundsided One, came up. 'Grandmother,' he said, 'let me make the red children for you.' After thinking it over for a while,

Kohkumthena finally agreed to let Roundsided One make the rest of the red children. But because he was a silly boy, always playing around and not paying very close attention to how Grandmother Kohkumthena had made them, he forgot to give them any genitals. For many years they tried to mate but could not because they did not have all their parts. Finally Roundsided One noticed their plight and tried to fix them. But, because he was just a silly boy and had not paid close attention, he put their genitals in strange places. He put one on the forehead, and another behind the knee, and another under someone's arm, and another on an elbow. It was so funny seeing the people try to mate and trying to get their parts to fit together. After several more years of experimenting, Roundsided One finally got it right, and now the red children can make themselves."

Everyone, even the Young One, laughed at the images the story produced in their minds. This delighted the old woman and encouraged her to use up her gradually returning strength, by telling just another short oral tradition to the young girl. "Do you know that Kohkumthena keeps all the babies up there with her? When people get married and want a baby, they must ask her. She thinks about it very hard. If she thinks you will be good parents she opens her door and lets one tumble out. Of course, all the babies want to be born so they crowd the door and even pinch each other trying to be the one that gets to come down. That is why babies sometimes have black and blue marks, given by their friends at Kohkumthena's door.

"It takes nine months for the babies to journey here to be born. Once the baby comes, the first four years he or she is only here on a trial basis. If the parents are not good ones, or if the baby is unhappy being away from Kohkumthena, he can go right back. Parents do not even spank their babies until after they are four years old, for fear it will make them want to go back to Kohkumthena or she will think they are bad parents and take the child back to her house. Little ones still speak Kohkumthena's language until they are four years old. And when they are infants, never let them play with their fingers; always give them something to amuse themselves with. It is said when they play with their fingers they are counting the days until they leave you and go back to Kohkumthena."

The old woman was growing tired speaking so much, but her glowing smile told the Young One she was grateful to have someone to pass on the old traditions to, and to be still useful.

The mother and her daughter tended the fire so it would last the night and the old woman would not be cold. The last thing they did was to make her a cup of herbal tea which had been prescribed by the medicine man, and with the promise of seeing her tomorrow, they bade her, "good rest," and went to their own lodge.

"This is the way that parents taught their children in those times, Young Watcher," the Button continued. "They took the children with them and had the children participate in their activities. The young girl learned many things that night, not just about housekeeping, but about how the elders are to be given respect and taken care of when they are not able to do for themselves any more. Old Woman was continuing her responsibilities in life as the keeper and transmitter of the ancient oral traditions. Her words, whether of the legends of the People or advice to the mother and girl, were respected."

The Button's voice sounded softly in his ear. "Young One, your elders have knowledge of life that you can use to help you have a better and easier life, or you can ignore and make your life hard and full of pain. It is the way of your ancestors to love, honor, and respect the elders. Be wise. Try their way and it will convince you that the old ones are of a value beyond money. They are equal to the value of children, the nation's treasures and as such, priceless."

Time was rushing by; the sky was changing color from the rich blue to a rich peach. The sun was not yet up, but he could see the mother up from her night's sleep, sweeping her front yard, and he could smell the warm food she had prepared for her family's breakfast. Just a few minutes before the sun broke over the horizon the family came out and greeted one another and then filled their bowls with the sweet-smelling breakfast foods that had warmed to perfection. It was the belief of the People at that time that the sun was a witness, and he reported every day to Creator how you were doing. The sun's first impression of you was what counted because it took it a whole day to get to Creator's home. So the people tried to be up, happy, well fed, their surroundings clean, and involved in some industrious work by the time the sun's first rays touched their shoulders.

The little family had finished breakfast now. The mother and young girl had washed the dishes, and the young girl was being given some instructions on working with skins. The young boy had skipped towards a friend's home Their father had brought home two deer yesterday, so the first thing they needed to do today was to process the meat and skins. First the mother set aside two roasts and a portion of the ribs which she would cook today. The ribs she would take to the old woman who was sick and let them cook all day until the meat fell off the bones and then leave the bones to cook until all the marrow was out of them and in the stew.

The mother was cutting the meat from the bones, creating long slabs which could be cut thin. These she hung over tall drying racks of green saplings placed close to the fire. The meat would be dried slowly near the heat and smoke from the fire until it was almost totally dry but still was ever so slightly chewy. The mother knew many ways to add to the meat's savory flavor when it would be cooked next winter. Some of it she dried, using wood from a sugar maple tree that had blown down in a storm. For other parts of the meat she changed the type of wood she used, putting large pieces of loose bark from the shag hickory tree on the fire. For one batch she used wood from the walnut tree, just for variation. Salt was available with which to cure the meat, but the mother thought it was not good to use very much salt, as she believed it ruined her stews, overpowering the seasonings she liked to add, so she chose not to use any salt to preserve the meat.

The mother showed the young girl how to separate the meat from the bones. She then showed her where to cut the meat to make it thin and chewy, and then where to cut it to make it tender when it was cooked fresh. It was not too long until all the meat was hanging for drying and the women's attention was directed towards a pile of fur that was in a heap near the stretching rack. The mother helped her daughter take some coarse pawpaw cord and sew the skin to the four corners of the rack. Then they secured the skin about every four inches until it was quite taut.

The mother then called the young girl's attention to the bones from which they had just taken the meat and showed her how to choose a good leg bone to make her flensing, or scraping, tool. For comfort and leverage the bone needed to be at least ten inches long. The rest of the bones would be cooked to make a nourishing broth to which they could add whatever kinds of vegetables and fruits they wanted. The men of the family would then create tools from the bones, such as needles and paint applicators, and even use some of the bones to carve into beautiful gifts.

The Young One watched with interest as they created the flensing tool. The mother showed her daughter how to chip it away on one side, then she chiseled it some more in such a way that it was blunt, with blunt teeth. This tool would be used to gouge and scrape the fat from the inside of the skin, for any fat left on would cause the skin to rot. Later they would have to decide if they were going to remove the hair or not, and if they were, the flensing tool would be traded for another scraper, probably of flint.

After all the fat and hair was removed and the skin had been tanned, either by soaking in an oak bark solution or a brain paste and urine solution, the skins would be stretched again and dried and then the hard work of softening the hide would begin, again using the flensing tool part of the time and rubbing the hide other times over a pointed tree stump, or twisting it with ropes. It took much work to make a skin usable for the beautiful, soft clothing they wore.

The young girl thought she would never become good at this. It called for strength in muscles she was just now developing. It also took the ability to turn off your nose, because some of the solutions began to smell wretched after the second day, and then the skins became slippery and slimy and had to be hand-washed many times before they were dried and softened. The young girl recognized the truth of her father's words; she was really going to have to try hard to overcome her sensitive nose, for no one would want to marry a young woman who could not make clothes from the deer skins he would be providing her.

The Young One got a whiff of one of the containers of the soaking skins. His stomach jolted and he recoiled from the stink. He instantly felt sorry for the young girl who would have to learn to do this. How fortunate he was that his mother could go to the fabric store and buy what she needed to make clothes by the yard from a bolt of cloth, and not have to go through this disgusting and difficult process. In his mind though, the Young One admired the old ancestor mothers for their perseverance, time, and talent in making the beautiful buckskin and sueded deerskin clothing he had seen in pictures and at museums. Secretly the Young One was also happy it would not be his lot in life to have to go hunting deer and carrying them home on his back, as he had seen the father of this family do.

It was time for the noonday meal now. The Young One realized that the mother had put something on to cook before she and her daughter had begun to work with the deer carcass. They had worked hard this morning, and in spite of the smell of the skins they were both very hungry. The father returned from visiting with his friends. He would not go hunting that day but instead would stay around the village, replenishing his arrowheads, mending his bow, doing the small chores he needed to do and socializing with his friends. Because they got up so early in the mornings, most of the work was done by noon. The noon meal was the most substantial of the day, and everyone ate heartily. The young boy did not come home for lunch. Instead, he had gone home with a friend where he was as welcome as if he lived there. He had homes of several friends and many surrogate 'aunts' which would function as his homes-away-from-home. Although he was free to go where he chose, he would still let his mother know his whereabouts so she would not worry.

The noon meal was cleared away. The mother then had the daughter go to the family storage pit where squashes were kept. She knew that by now most of them would have become soggy and moldy, but wanted her daughter to see if there were two still firm enough to bring up. The mother wanted to prepare squash seeds for planting. She would split the squash open with one of her large knives and scoop the seeds out to dry. By the time they were dried it would be the right time of the moon to plant them. While the mother showed the daughter how to do this, she was talking and teaching her about planting by the moon and star signs. Then she had her daughter prepare the other squash while she watched.

Near the entrance to the yard around the wigiwa were several pieces of bark, seeming to be just lying on the ground. The daughter had gone to the farthest one and lifted it, so the Young One could see it was actually a cover to a storage pit. He stepped close to look inside. It appeared to be only four or five feet deep, and he could see that it was lined with grasses, held in place with supple branches, probably of willow. There were squashes of at least five varieties inside, some deep yellow and orange, some green. Young One could also see there were braids of dried corn still on the cob, wound around inside the perimeter of the pit.

How perfectly it seemed to be constructed. Even today it would take much talent and practice to create its equal. He had seen drawings of these pits, but had never seen anyone try to duplicate them. He knew you had to select and place the several different vegetables and fruits carefully, because foods give off different natural gases and chemicals. If mixed incorrectly, they can cause the foods around them to spoil before they can be used, in the winter when food was precious.

72

"Daughter," said the mother. "The old woman we visited yesterday is right about you. Someday soon you will be creating red children yourself and you must know how to take care of them. It is time for you to learn about some of our medicines. We will take a walk each day in a different direction so you can learn the medicine plants. When we run out of directions we will repeat our paths. We must do this every day from the end of the Hunger Moon until the Moon of the Falling Leaves. Even then it will take three years to teach you the very least you will need to know. You will have to pay close attention and remember well what I show and teach you. All things do not grow every year. Some grow every other year. Some grow every third year. There are some plants which take longer than three years, but right now we will concentrate on just those we will see in that period of time.

"Do you remember when Sunbird, your cousin, was so ill and the medicine man needed medicine to make him well? Do you recall him asking the old woman Metsikie to bring him some medicine? Many times the medicine man must ask a woman who knows her herbs to procure a cure for him. When this happens he does not tell the woman what herbs or roots to bring. He only tells her what is wrong with the patient and she must know what to bring back. There are times when she must prepare a concoction for the medicine man and bring it to him ready to administer to the patient. Someday, Daughter, you will be expected to know what to bring. Every Shawnee woman knows at least a hundred and fifty cures, but because our family has always known more of the uses of the green people, more will be expected of you too.

Arriving at the edge of the woods, the mother turned to her daughter and asked, "What is one of the first things we dig when we return from the winter hunting camps?"

"Why, sassafras, Mother," responded the girl.

"Do you know how to tell the sassafras from the other green people?"

"Of course Mother. It has a leaf like a closed hand with a thumb sticking out."

"What if you need it before the leaves are out?"

"I don't know, Mother."

"Come with me, Daughter, and I will show you the shiny, bright green, slick stem it has when it is a young and tender plant, and its rich, deeply furrowed, dark orange bark when it is old. Then we will dig. You must be able to pick out the sassafras root from all the others, an easy thing, Daughter, because of its spicy, pungent aroma. Then you must be taught how to clean and preserve it so it doesn't mold or loose its potency but will have its medicinal qualities when you need them.

The Young One found himself accompanying the two on their walk into the woods. He was trying to locate a sassafras tree himself when the mother stopped and began pointing out several sassafras of varying ages and sizes to her daughter. He could hear the mother as she continued to instruct her daughter. "Here is the 'chief' of the sassafras: It is the largest and the first one that we have seen. This is the one we must give a tobacco offering to . We must remind it of the laws that Kohkumthena gave it, and its obligation to take pity on us and give us itself and its medicinal strength. Because none of us are sick at this time, we must explain to it that we need to take some of its roots now in the summer, because it is strongest now, and it will not be right for us to come and take its roots in the winter when there is no medicine in them. We must promise to use the roots wisely. And we must thank it for having pity on us grandchildren so we may be well and strong. Begin at the east and offer your tobacco to the cardinal points in the manner of the sun's travels. When this is done we will then go to the next batch of sassafras we see and sprinkle more tobacco and remind the sassafras why we are taking its roots and what medicine we need from it for later use. If we do not treat the tree with respect, daughter, we could dig enough to fill our wigiwa and it would not make anyone well. But when we treat it with respect, it will be obedient and have pity on us and give us its medicine powers. If we do not tell it just what sickness we will be using it to cure, it might give us a different curing power that we don't know about and cause our patient to become sicker. Now let us dig, only what we will need."

The Young One watched as the two women dug with their crude hoes and digging sticks. He knew it was hard work to get the pungent sassafras roots to relinquish their hold on Mother Earth and yield themselves to humans. Still, the mother and daughter were skillful. He was amazed at the short time it took for them to fill the sack that the mother had brought. The mother was teaching the daughter now about the many uses of the root, and also the leaves and the berries. She was still talking and teaching when he noticed they had quit digging and were headed in the direction of the river. He saw by the sun that it was almost time for their evening meal and presumed they were heading for the river for a quick refreshing swim and bath before they went home. He politely looked around the scene for something else to occupy his attention, allowing the women privacy as they tended to their need for daily bathing and refreshing themselves.

The Young Watcher caught sight of the young boy of the family playing with his friends. They were using a long, weighted arrow, throwing it at a rolling woven target. The target reminded him of a tightly woven dream catcher. The young boys were yelling and loudly predicting when one of them would hit the target through one of the openings of the weave. The young boy from the family Young One had been observing took a turn and leaped with happiness when his arrow went through the middle. His friends were congratulating him and bragging about his good aim, and teasing him about his luck. Even at this tender age the young boys were beginning to wager he could not do it again. At this the Young One remembered the tales the Stones had shared about how the ancestors had loved game-playing and wagering.

The mother called from the family cook fire, telling them their evening meal was now ready, so Young One followed the boy home, reluctant to leave his new friends, even though they seemed unaware of his presence. He had not heard from the Woman's Button for some time. Again he was handed a bowl of food as though he were simply another member of the family, yet no one spoke to him or acknowledged his true presence among them. This meal was totally different from last night's. Somehow the mother had found time to roast a grouse over the hickory smoke and from the coals she dug out sweet potatoes she had wrapped in corn husks. These sweet potatoes were not seasoned with anything, even though the mother had brought out a small pot containing maple sugar for them to drizzle on top. They were utterly delicious fresh from the fire. The stew pot contained a corn and bean combination that had been seasoned with a tangy herb he wished his own mother could taste, so she could fix this dish at his home.

Shortly, the family was finished eating and the mother and girl had cleared away the residue of dirty dishes and garbage. The remainder of stew was hanging close to the edge of the fire, to keep warm for whoever might stop by, just like last night. The father had gone to visit the man in the village who had extra flint, taking a handful of deer toes with him that the flint man might want to use for a rattle. Indian people did not charge for their work or gifts, but they would accept gifts and exchanges. It was a great joy to share what you had with your tribal family and friends. The People were always so giving, to one another and to visitors.

It was a way to show respect to Kohkumthena who made everything for all her children to use to their benefit. The people who were busy using their special talents for the tribe couldn't gather the natural resources, but still needed those things. There was *always enough to share*! Sometimes the people who had those special gifts from Creator were not talented in other ways. To make something they could use to help them fulfill Kohkumthena's purpose for all the others' benefit, was another way to show honor and respect to her.

It seemed that each person in the village had something special that Kohkumthena had given them to assure a useful and honorable place among their people. Even the smallest talent was a gift from her, and thus even the children were so gifted.

It was still early enough that there was plenty of daylight left. The mother instructed the young girl to go get her basket supplies out, because they were going to have to repair the big basket the mother used for storing her sassafras, and they were going to have to make several small baskets to hold the young girl's own supply of medicinal herbs and roots. The mother then showed the daughter how to strip the outer covering off the fine vines of honeysuckle, winding them into tight coils so they would fit inside a pot of water, where they would soak and stay supple until later that day or the next when they could weave with them.

As the two worked, the mother continued talking to her daughter, stopping every now and then to show her some specific detail of the process. "Daughter, tomorrow when you finish taking the hair off the last deerskin, we will begin making a large parfleche bag of it. Tonight before you go to sleep you might ask the spirits to gift you with a beautiful design. I will let you make your paint from the plants and some of my vermilion powder, and you can decorate it yourself. If you are pleased with how it turns out I will then show you how to prepare a protective glaze for it so the design doesn't fade. There are plenty of fish at this time and we can boil their parts into a thin glue which works beautifully, or we can gather some of the yucca that was planted a few miles from here by our village trader, and boil its sap. The fish glue will have a bit of yellow tinge to it, but the yucca will be a little cloudy and will soften the colors. You will choose.

"It is time you knew how to make these things for your own wigiwa. I know you are yet young, but you will need to practice so you can be proud to show your husband your handwork and he will know you will be a good wife, one worthy of his efforts to provide for you. I will tell you a small secret that we women know. The men will often be undecided between two young women, as to which to marry, for as you know our young girls are almost always very pretty and well behaved. The young men will walk through the village trying to be inconspicuous, and they will be observing not only how you behave, but what your hands are busy doing.

"It is embarrassing for a man to have a lazy wife, so he looks for the young woman who is skillful with her hands and takes pride in making beautiful things from these necessary and useful items. Your father tells me how some men try to brag about their wives' beadwork, and if a strand of beads breaks and loose beads fall, the men tease them about their 'lazy squaw,' referring to the stitches the wife has used and to her lack of care for not taking the extra time and trouble to do the extra stitching required to make a quality piece and lock each bead in place.

"Always, Daughter, whatever you do, make it your best work and make it as perfect and beautiful as you can. You know Creator always makes things different yet very beautiful, and Creator always does the very best. By our doing our very best we are telling Creator how much we realize the effort to make our world beautiful, the Creator puts forth for us, the grandchildren. It is not just your future husband who will notice, but the adults of the village as well as Kohkumthena. We look for things to be proud of in you. Good work reflects a right-thinking mind and heart. You will be very respected for that."

As the Young One watched the two working, he was fascinated at the speed with which the mother was creating a beautiful double walled basket from the slender tendrils of honeysuckle. The young girl struggled with them for a while until suddenly she seemed to understand their nature and they stopped acting in an unruly way. She was building her little basket round by round and smiling more broadly at every round, as it finally took a recognizable shape.

The Young One then felt the rush that usually preceded the voice of one of his stone teachers. He heard the quick, smooth voice of the Button ask him, "Are you ready to return to the Great House now? Others are waiting for our return. There is so much more that the women did and so many more ways that they were important to the community, but the great Mask is becoming impatient because I have kept you so long.

"Can you understand why, if a man was murdered, his murderer might be allowed to pay the grieving family a hundred and sixty lengths of wampum, but if a woman was murdered they had to pay more than eight hundred and thirty lengths? The grieving family would have to purchase or make exchange for all the goods a woman would make, and all the things she would do for the family. A man would have provided meat and protection, both of which are essential, but the woman provided everything else. If the family wanted to, they could adopt the murderer to replace the dead family member, and he would then do all the work and provide all the things the dead person had contributed to the family. Strange as it may seem, if the family did adopt the murderer, they truly treated him as well as they had their blood family member. They never mistreated him. Work compensation was the most commonly used consequence of a murder, because wampum paid out would eventually be all spent. Rarely did the family choose to kill the murderer, because they needed manpower most of all. Only the truly worst of people were considered totally detrimental or totally useless to the People.

"I feel the Mask urging us to hurry. Remember, this is just your first night of being taught. We will try to come to you again as you grow, so your knowledge and memories will be complete. We must return now."

No sooner had Young One heard those words than he was again in the Great House. The Old Watcher now was slumped almost horizontal to the ground and emitting such a snore that in spite of himself, the Young One laughed. To himself he said, "Perhaps we aren't very good 'watchers' but we certainly let people know we are still here." His mind could not make the decision as to whether to race, whir, or shut down and nap. Entirely too many things were being implanted and impressed into his consciousness; there was no way he could remember it all, he thought.

In reality he had sat at the same spot for several hours now and his backside was becoming numb. He was so tired he wondered if this tingling numbness was only on his one end or if it had started with his head and gone clear through. He got up and stretched, doing simple movements to help his circulation restart, but trying to not wake the Old Watcher, who seemed to have a great need for much sleep. His eyes had become accustomed to the soft, flickering light of the fire, and now he could walk around inside the Great House without fear of stepping on anything important. Slowly he retraced the path of the ceremony celebrants, pausing at each station trying to remember what each person said. At the altar he saw several pipes resting on the top stone, collecting strength and blessings for their owners.

Each pipe was totally different from the others. The bowls were all made of different stones and were of all different colors, with unique carved designs. There was even one made of clay. The pipes' owners also had different ways of decorating the stems. The Young One presumed that the spirits had given each owner a vision concerning the use and decoration of his sacred instrument.

The bowl of one of the pipes was of a shiny, blackish stone. The Young One thought he could detect a faint green to its color. He had never seen this pipe before. The stem was not more than two feet long and had red felt held on with yellow yarn. There were six small eagle feathers hanging down the length of the stem. In between there were strips of braided cloth ribbon in the colors of the sacred four directions, each ending at a small carved clan totem, each in a different beautiful stone, with a pointer feather of the same color as the ribbon attached. There was one clear quartz circle hanging from the last totem representative, which was the eagle. The Young One could see even in this dimness that the circle had been worked in some way to cause it to separate the light beams into prisms of color. Attached by a small silver ring to the inside of the circle was an inch-long, perfect eagle feather, carved of bone or horn. Scrimshaw highlighted the feather's details. Young One guessed someone had used black walnut dye to accent the scrimshaw.

Loosely held onto the stem with a plain twist of handmade basswood twine were several stems of sage. The bowl, while of this hard blackish stone, seemed to be highly polished and was inlaid with delicate silver resembling filigree. One of the tribe's carvers had told him this stone was the most difficult of all to carve and polish. Whoever made this exceptional pipe must have had help from the spirits to create it so perfectly.

The pipe was not especially large, but its beauty stood out as it lay there, on top of its white elkskin bag decorated with old transparent beads, true wampum and shells. Young One could not resist stroking it gently with the fingers of his hand. It was truly a sacred object and he would never dare to pick it up, but he simply had to touch it.

Young One strained his mind for who among his People would own such a sacred treasure. He did not recognize it. He had seen most of the People's pipes at some time or another, but he had never seen this one before. He tried to remember if there were any important visitors in the camp. As it lay there it seemed to shimmer, probably from the strange light that mornings sometimes give in the early hours. He thought, this truly is a medicine pipe, I can feel its power almost throbbing.

The Young One tried to walk away, but was held transfixed to the spot, and he found himself wondering about the history of this awe-inspiring pipe. What ceremonies had it seen, what people had it known, what events had it experienced in its lifetime before arriving here in this Great House? In the midst of his wonderings, he began to recognize the rich, resonant sound of a voice speaking to him in answer to his silent questions.

The Diorite Pipe spoke with pleasant authority to the Young One. "I have come to teach you things you need to understand. I am no longer in

the form that you are seeing me, because many ages ago I was stolen by the Aliens, taken from this land and hidden. I had lived among your people for centuries. I was one of the travelers when your people came from the far south. Because of the history I had experienced and my beauty, the Aliens coveted me with such a passion they could not resist their temptations. They induced my rightful owner, a person who knew all the ancient ceremonies, laws and blessings from Creator to allow them to see me up close, even touch and hold me. Shortly afterwards they enticed him into a secret meeting with them. They took advantage of that opportunity to kill my owner, and they stole me."

The sacred Pipe explained, "I was quickly taken across the Big Waters to the east. A wealthy and influential man was told of my existence and arranged to view me. He became obsessed with a burning desire to have me for his own. But he realized for him to possess me in safety he would have to acquire me in secret and remove the witnesses to the transaction. So he arranged to have my thief murdered and I was stolen again. I was too precious to be put on display, because he feared someone would kill him and steal me for himself, as he had done.

"He had a special container made in which to hide his exceptional Diorite Pipe, and a false panel installed in the wall beside his bed. He told the wall builders that niche was to hold his sacred black book of a special type with handwritten text and intricate drawings in color and accented in true gold. Oh, he had a book that fit those descriptions, but it never was placed in that secure spot; it stayed in a hand-carved wooden box lined in velvet, and was kept in his library in plain view where he thought it would be under constant observation. It was I who was placed in that dark and dreary hole behind the false panel.

"After a while the wealthy man needed money, as he was experiencing the difficult times then besetting his whole country. Finally he spoke of me to other wealthy men, trying to entice them to buy me. I had become a great burden to him. He was in constant fear I would be stolen or that he would drop me and break me when he got me out to admire me. Less and less frequently he took me out so he could enjoy the beauty of my design and ornaments. More and more he worried. Finally, a potential buyer came to see me, a friend of the wealthy man. I was put on display after being polished and placed just so on a silver stand.

"The friend was most respectful of my powers, but was afraid to own me himself. Instead he suggested that my owner should give me to his ruler as a good will gesture, and perhaps the king would forgive the owner's debts as a favor in return. The friend suggested that would ease the owner's situation more than a temporary fix of any money he would receive by my sale.

"Indeed, he contacted his ruler and asked for an audience. To his delight he was invited to dinner at the palace. I was taken from the vault, polished and the tarnish removed from my silver. The other ornaments were refreshed and I was once again a splendid sacred pipe, ready to help grandchildren in their communications with Creator. This ruler, though, while he admired my beauty and understood my value in terms of his coin of the realm, was not a spiritual man. But even he could tell I have great mysterious powers, and he too became obsessed with the great need to possess me for his own selfish needs. He was also afraid some ruthless person would covet me to the degree they would risk killing him for possession of me. Still, he could not bear to see me be in the possession of another, so he 'graciously' accepted me as a gift from the wealthy man, and forgave the man's debts to the crown.

"Because the ruler was so full of fear that someone would find out about my being in his possession, he had his court chamberlain escort the wealthy man out of his castle through an ancient secret way that has no end. The wealthy man perished there and I was concealed in a secret place in the palace, in a false wall. My hiding place was known only to the ruler, who from time to time would get me out, secretly gaze at my beauty, wonder at my past, and replace me before anyone discovered my existence.

"So I spent long years locked away where no light touched my sacred circle of crystal. Most of my original ornaments rotted and fell away, the feathers dissolved from age. The wrapping on my stem became brittle and eventually turned to dust. Of my beautiful adornments, only my stone clan symbols and my sacred crystal circle survived. Even my bowl had become dull with lack of care.

"The land they took me to, Young One, was racked with wars. Governments changed, kings and rulers changed, even the boundaries and name of the country changed. Yet I was not discovered, for when the ruler died, his court chamberlain had preceded him in death and the ruler had never told anyone of my existence nor of the existence of my hiding place, so I waited. We Stones have a lifetime that is exceeded only by Creator's existence. Yet I longed to be back with the People and to be useful again, to be the one who received the sacred tobacco and helped convert it to the smoke that carried the grandchildren's words to Creator.

"Eventually, there came another type of revolution. There was less killing, but much looting. Buildings and palaces were torn down by their people, stone by stone. The people became impatient with the slowness of their methods and called for huge guns to fire into the walls and finish tearing them down quickly. When the first round hit the palace, it cracked the inner walls where I had been sealed away all those years. But because the outer walls had not crumbled enough, they fired again. This one shattered my hiding place and the falling stones crushed me underneath them. I was destroyed with only small pebbles of my beautiful diorite left, the silver having tarnished black like common wire. My delicate crystal circle was mashed to a fine powder, and the clan symbols were so broken not a one resembled anything but a handful of coarse multicolored pebbles.

"It was a short time later that one of your clan mothers came to visit this place. While touring the ruins of the destroyed palace she picked up one of my larger pieces and placed it in her stone bag. Last night she gave me to one of the carvers of the tribe, as a gift. He placed me here on the altar with several other stones to receive blessings. It is wonderful to be with the People again and smell the cedar and sage smoke, to hear the old songs and feel the drum. I have heard my new owner say he will try to carve something sacred of me and then embed me into the bowl of a pipe he is now making. He can feel my strength and power. He knows I am no ordinary pebble. I shall try to teach him of Creator's ways in exchange for the honor he is showing me. But, Young One, I have a few things to share with you first.

"I once traveled with the great shaman who came with your people from Mexico. It was I who was called upon to hold the tobacco when the people were having such a terrible time trying to find their way, before they found their relatives. I helped them thank Creator for their blessings when they rejoined their separated families and again when they were happily living in the south where the giant reptile lived. It was an Alien trader who had seen me in the south who stole me. He had followed your people as they traveled until he saw his chance to acquire me.

"Before I was stolen from your people I participated in the part of your history that became the beginning of the end of your people's life as free people. I was at the first 'agreeing' with the pale Alien invaders. You should remember, Young One," said the Sacred Pipe, "treaties are just agreements between nations; they need not be from the outcome of a war. These pale Aliens professed to have come as friends, wanting nothing but your friendship, oh yes, and just enough land on which to place a chair, so they had a place to sit and talk with you. They had said they would ask for only the amount of land that would be covered by a hide they had. This was felt to be a reasonable request and so it was granted. To their disgust and amazement your ancestors watched as the Aliens then began to cut the skin into the thinnest strips, like microscopic thread and then they stretched it out from the water's edge to a place west, and then to the south, and then to the water's edge again, taking many acres if not miles of land. Your ancestors were alarmed, but they were bound by their word, and so the pale Aliens then possessed a piece of Turtle Island, and they never let it go. When they set sail again on a brief voyage, your shaman spoke with your chief and said, 'These are not right-thinking men. Beware of them. They are strange and dishonest creatures.' The shaman could not conceive of calling them humans, or even animals, as they seemed to have no knowledge of the Great Laws of Kohkumthena. From that moment on, Young One, they cheated and lied and stole your home, and moved you always out, to places with less of what you needed to survive.

"These are the same people who came and out of friendship left a metal ax as a gift for the chief when they sailed away for a few months. It was a new ax which had not been used. The chief took the ax head, put it on a stout chain and wore it around his neck. The Peoples's stone axes had worked just fine for thousands of years, and they considered this just a symbolic gesture. It was not long before the pale Aliens came back. They were astounded to see that the chief was wearing the ax head as an ornament, but not using it to make his chopping and cutting easier. They tried to explain to him its use. Finally they went to their ship, got another one and promptly went to the first tree they saw and with a few swift swings of the blade, cut it through and it fell to the ground. The people were flabbergasted. The Aliens smiled and left feeling good that they had now shown your ancestors how to use such a fine tool. The shaman said to your chief, 'These Aliens are disrespectful. See how they have no regard for offending the spirit of the tree people. They did not have a use for this tree, and they did not offer it any tobacco before taking its life. They are very dangerous.'

"The pale ones were not gone long when they returned again, this time bringing a gun to give to your chief. Remembering how your people had not known how to use the metal ax, their leader gave a demonstration. He held up his gun and he shot and killed the first animal he saw. Your people accepted the gun as graciously as they could and the Aliens left on their ship again. As they rode the wind out of sight, your shaman spoke to your chief and said, 'These people are crazy. They will kill us all.'

"These are the things I witnessed, Young One. It was not very long until these pale ones returned and as usual they were looking for things of value to take back across the Big Waters. One of the men who controlled their trading had come to the village and seen me. His heart burned with lust until he had found a way to steal me and take me away. That is how I got to the land of the rich man and the king, as I said.

"Today I see the pipes are much plainer. The decorations are still sacred, but you are more cautious in letting strangers come to the ceremonies, where they might succumb to stealing. This is a good thing. While some of the Aliens' descendants are good at heart, their values system is strange and they have a difficulty in understanding the true meaning of sacred. Often to them, 'sacredness' means objects of value that cost more money to acquire than ordinary items, but which can still be bought. Your responsibility as a Watcher is an important one. From this night on, you will be asked to guard the tribal sacred possessions. Protect them even from your people's friends, even from the temptations some of your own people will experience, for they have been exposed too long to the Aliens' abhorrent, greedy, sacrilegious ways.

"After I was stolen, because I was not available to the old shaman who made me, he could not pray in the right way until he had made another pipe. For a while the prayers he offered became lost in the wind because there was no sacred tobacco smoke to carry them to Creator. This caused great suffering for your people and the chief. They had no power to protect themselves and the Aliens gained great advantage over them. The People's vision was clouded and they were unable to see the invaders in true light. The voice of the spirits was muffled, and it was too late that the People understood their peril.

"I represent honesty and sincerity when I am smoked at momentous occasions. I was brought from Mexico to the southern area here, and then some distance up the East coast. I was smoked at that first agreement when the Aliens took advantage with their trick of the hide.

"There were several kinds of Aliens here who had agreeings with the People before the Pilgrims landed in 1620. Your people even had agreeings they'd made on paper with the Swedes, dating from 1610, as the Kispokos of the Shawnee were always the keepers of these important things. This is perhaps because they were the warriors and could defend and protect them best.

"I was smoked at several other agreeings during those very early years of the Alien invasions. But, when I was stolen, the Dutch and English began coming, and difficulties accelerated for your people.

"Although I am only a small portion of my old self, I still have strength and wisdom to offer your people. In my position as an adornment on a new pipe, I will still be respected and listened to when I feel I need to advise your people and my new owner. I can read people's hearts and their minds, and can help protect you from new injuries. It is wonderful that Creator has found a way to bring me back to you.

"As a Sacred Pipe, I sometimes am also given preknowledge of the future. I know this is an exciting time to be Shawnee. Your people are facing many new, exciting, and sometimes perilous things. Your chief will have to be strong and right-thinking. Your council will have to be clearheaded and right-minded. Your spiritual leaders will have to keep themselves busy praying for guidance and protection for you all, in doing what is best for your grandchildren's grandchildren. Ah, Young One! What a privilege to be back with my great Shawandasse grandchildren! Your people did well to go back to their old true name, Shawandasse. It shows great respect for the ancient ancestors, as well as your ancestors, the Shawanos in the east who became extinct during the early 1700s, whose name your people used as a form of honor for so long.

"Remember, when you are watching, what happened to me so long ago, and guard your people's treasures well. I will now let you see me in my present state, so you will recognize me when you see me decorate the new pipe." The Sacred Pipe then became quiet, and its shimmering seemed to dance in the eyes of the Young One, waxing and waning.

Suddenly the light from around the Sacred Pipe changed and the beautiful vision the Young One had been gazing at became a strange little stone of a greenish metallic black. It was about the size of the end of his thumb. He was struck by the history of that plain little chunk of stone, yet it was difficult for him to imagine how anyone could make anything decorative out of it. He knew some of the men in the tribe were exquisite carvers, so he did not doubt that someday he would indeed see this pebble decorating a pipe. He also knew his hands would never have the ability to create such a delicate thing. But he would be watching for it. He hoped it would be soon, for he realized it had great powers, and he wanted his people to have the benefit of them as quickly as possible. He thought it had been too long since this sacred object had been able to fulfill its purpose in helping his Shawandasse people.

The Young One sat down near the altar, wondering what wonderful things his people were about to experience that the Sacred Pipe had alluded to. It seemed to his youthful mind that they were already doing as much as the people could keep up with and certainly as much as they could afford, in the way of improvements on the land. But if that ancient Sacred Pipe was excited about the future, that future must be something truly wonderful. The Young One thought of words the Old Watcher had once said to him, that if you are right-thinking, you are never finished counting your blessings and gifts from Creator. He was beginning to understand those words.

From in front of where he sat came a voice that sounded uneven and gruff saying to the Young One, "I was the replacement for the diorite pipe. The people were living in an area in the east, where I am found in abundance. I am a form of easy-to-carve soapstone. The people found it easy to make beautiful designs on me. I hold heat for a very long time and do not easily crack from it. Pipes made of me are generally very large and fancy. I abound with authority when I am involved in ceremonies and treaties. I became one of the most sought after items, one that your people traded to other Indians. Each of the Indian men needed his own pipe, for prayers, not just the chiefs, shamans and medicine men. When no red stone was available, I was the next choice. Some used a beautiful black stone but it was rare and hard to find. The black stone was harder to carve, so was never as ornate as I. No one holds up to heat as I do.

"Let me explain some of the treaties in which I have been involved. They didn't have short titles or names, so I will just mention where they were negotiated. Not all of them were ratified, with negotiations taking months. Sometimes years later the Aliens would enforce these incomplete, nonbinding documents: Treaty of 1722, Conestogo; 1728, Conestogo; 1729, Conestogo-Philadelphia; 1632, Shawnee-Philadelphia; Philadelphia, 1742; Lancaster, 1744; Carlisle, 1753; Easton, 1753; and at least a dozen more.

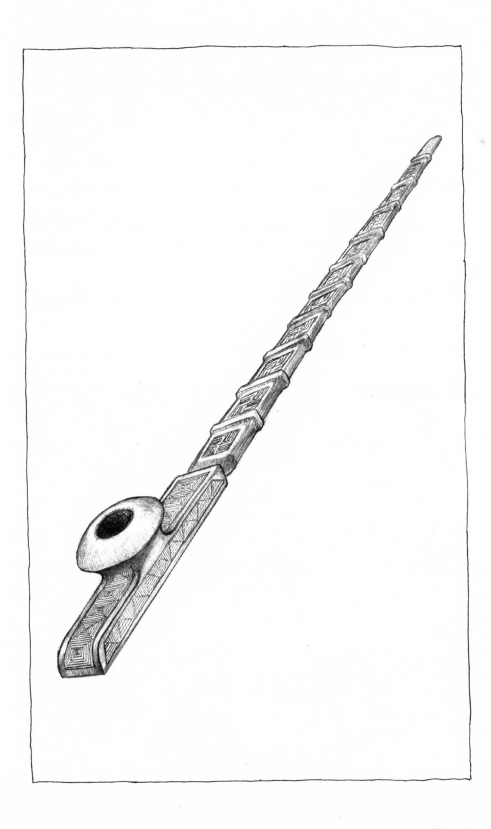

"You know, Young One, that your people were with their grandfathers the Delaware when they were in the east. They had moved out of the area on the Atlantic and gone inland to New Jersey and then to Pennsylvania. Always the Aliens were moving in and ruining the hunting, fishing, and gathering. Their domestic animals ruined the ground for the natural animals which your people depended on for subsistence. Their style of farming ruined the ground and caused many indigenous foods, like gooseberries, to become scarce. They overkilled the fowls until the succulent swans were no longer seen in huge flocks but in a few scatterings here and there. Even the wild turkey became hard to find as did the deer. So now, being pushed by necessity and the Aliens, your people were migrating to the west.

"Since the first recorded outbreak of Alien diseases in 1633 in epidemic proportions, typhus, scarlet fever, influenza, measles and small pox had thinned out the various people until many tribes had been reduced to mere weak percentages of their former strength. These remainders of people formed loosely-joined associations and began traveling together and living in contiguous communities; eventually they would wind up in the Ohio Valley. In the 1700s they were between the Allegheny River in western Pennsylvania and the Delaware River in eastern Pennsylvania. The area most populated by your people and the Delaware was the Wyoming Valley, which was bordered by the Susquehanna River and its branches and the Delaware River. Your direct Shawnee ancestors were slightly west with villages near the Juniata River as well as the ones on the Susquehanna and its western branch. There were so many treaties during their time there that even I get them confused, so I will only mention to you a few that were unique in some way.

"In 1733 I was used during the preparations of something they referred to as the *walking sale*," the Soapstone Pipe continued. "Now you talk about cheating, Young One, this one was a dandy! Years before the People had treated — talked — with William Penn about a proposed land sale. The document the Aliens finally presented as having been agreed to by the Shawnee had a 'starting point at a particular spruce tree on the Delaware River and then west-northwest to Neshameny Creek, then back into the woods as far as a man could walk in a day and a half, bounded on the west by the most westerly branch of Neshameny, from there by a line (now here there was a blank space in the treaty), then to the utmost extent of the day and a half's walk, and from there (and another blank space was in the document), to the aforesaid Delaware River and so down the course of the river to the first mentioned spruce tree.' I must point out that by that time the ancestors were quite experienced in treaties. They were not stupid nor were they any longer naive. It is incomprehensible that they would have signed a treaty that contained blank spaces. This was supposedly signed in 1733. No mention is made in this white man's document of the treaties of 1718 and 1728 which had securely fixed the boundaries so no possible advantage could be taken of the People. There were living Aliens who said they remembered a treaty being held then, but they were not brought forth to prove there had been agreement to the terms, nor that a deed or release of the lands had ever been executed. Sassoonan, the Delaware leader at the time of the treaty and a signer, was alive and well, yet he was not sought to testify to the validity of this particular document either. So this so-called treaty document was really a questionable, even dishonest one to start with. But there was more deceit in this so-called walking treaty.

"Let me tell you how things were done. Those sneaky Aliens had relay teams of men to run, not walk, without stopping at dusk as was expected, so they could cover as much ground as was humanly possible. The escorts and observers from the ancestors protested this, but the Aliens kept running. They ran so far that they passed the territory the Delaware had any rights to and into the territory of other nations. They encompassed all the good farm and hunting lands of at least five neighboring tribes, and wound up with about one million acres instead of the anticipated 330,000 acres intended. This was done to your grandfathers the Delaware, but some of your land was affected. But all of the land of the Minisinks was taken.

"September, 1718, there had been another treaty between the Delaware and the man William Penn, and it was a good one. This treaty had its terms, limits, descriptions, boundaries fully explained so there would never be any misunderstandings as to what land the Aliens could settle on and where they could not. There was a specific area that was defined, and it was stated it could never be sold and would always be the possession of the People. It was a perfect agreement. The excess property grabbed by the Aliens was part of that description of land that could never be settled by the Aliens. But those Aliens! When they wanted to settle in territory belonging to the ancestors, they simply 'lost' that original treaty agreement and brought in some piece of paper they said was a 'copy'. It was not certified or recorded. As has been said, there were still several old chiefs alive who had signed the original treaty who could have been brought to testify to its validity. Instead, the Aliens did this transaction quickly, quietly on the sly, without making any effort to validate the document. This became another of the People's dissatisfactions caused by the frauds committed by the British."

The huge Soapstone Pipe continued confidently as it said, "Other, unscrupulous tribes added to the problem. I remember back in 1685, the Iroquois sold some land that belonged to the Delaware. At that time they had been claiming they had conquered the Delaware, although no battle was ever mentioned or proof given of an actual conflict. The Iroquois said they had put 'petticoats' on the Delaware, making them 'women.' That was a way to insult the Delaware and degrade them worse than calling them sissies. For once the proprietary, the man in charge of the land deals, felt uneasy about the transaction, so he didn't act on the paperwork for a few years until he talked with the Delaware himself and got them to sign a release on that land in question.

"The Iroquois continued to sell land that they didn't own. They negotiated with the English, dispensing land that belonged to the Delaware, Shawnee, Minisinks, Munseys, Mohiccons, Susquehannocks and about eight other tribes, in deal after deal. They were what you'd call not only sneaks and dishonest, but they were cheeky and brazen about it. By 1756, the folks, especially the Delaware, were tired of these Iroquois-inspired surprises, as the Aliens kept settling on their land. Each of these tribes was too small to chastise the Iroquois, so they banded together and created the Five Nations to speak in a strong, unified voice. The Delaware leader, known as King Teedyuscung, declared the Delaware real men again and they symbolically threw off their 'petticoats' and from that moment on spoke for themselves.

"Some historians have said the Iroquois were only having fun with the Aliens, because they didn't really believe you could sell land which belongs to Creator. The affected tribes, though, didn't consider it one bit funny. As they had taken gifts in exchange for their rights to land, it was considered legal and enforceable by the Aliens, and all these other tribes had been dispossessed. But let me tell you about this Teedyuscung the Delaware, friend of the eighteenth-century Shawnee. He was quite a leader.

"Teedyuscung was intelligent and shrewd. He knew what the Aliens were up to and he knew when they weren't telling the truth, which was most of the time. The English were trying hard to keep the people under Teedyuscung, up to ten nations then, from going into business with the French, with whom the English were about to go to war. The English made beautiful promises they had no intentions of keeping in the 1740s and 1750s. They made lovely apologies and protestations of innocence for injuries the People suffered from these bad dealings. They spread false rumors, pitted tribe against tribe and cheated the People every single chance they got, and they saw to it that they had many chances.

"At meetings and councils Teedyuscung saw that for the British there were secretaries who wrote down what was said and agreed to, for future reference and to create the land transfer documents. This was deemed better than relying on one's memory. Sometimes old Teedyuscung was not at his best, as he had a drinking problem. When he would arrive at the meetings and be too drunk, they would postpone the council until the next day. Sometimes the council would already be in full swing by the time they realized that he was too inebriated to continue. I must say, Young One," said the ornate green Soapstone Pipe, "even when he was drunk he made more sense than the English and still knew what he was saying, he just couldn't remember it all the next morning. So, Old Teedyuscung demanded his own secretary to take down the words. It was a concession he had to really fight for, but the governor finally agreed he could have one. He picked the man himself. Charles Thomson had taken minutes of the last Easton Treaty. He had honestly reported an incident involving the governor's official secretary, a man named Peters. Secretary Peters had thrown down his pen and refused to record any complaints the People put forth about irregularities in the dealings with the proprietaries during the official inquiry by the governor.

"Teedyuscung had noticed during meetings the negotiations would be resolved one way. The next morning when papers were presented for them to sign, if he asked that they be read aloud first to refresh his memory before he signed, the British would get peevish and refuse to read them. When he insisted and persevered over their reluctance, the words would be wrong and say things that the People had *not* agreed to. With his own set of recorded words, it would make it more difficult for the British to cheat them so blatantly. Teedyuscung was a hard bargainer, insisting on fairness.

"In August 1757 Teedyuscung met with the governor at Easton. He had agreed to live by the actual sales that had been arranged by the Iroquois, who had received payment in exchange for the lands. In all the treaties he had studied and been involved with personally, certain boundaries would be agreed to but when the deeds and transfer documents were drafted, or when it was surveyed, the Aliens wound up with at least twice and sometimes ten times the amount of territory the People had intended to give them. Now this was not ignorance on the part of the People and not innocence on the part of the Aliens. The Aliens were fiendishly devious and dishonest. It was as if their minds were possessed by evil spirits that constantly goaded them into ever new and disgusting ways to harm and cheat your People. (We Stones think these are not right-thinking creatures — very dangerous.)

"Teedyuscung demanded to see the original documents, treaties, deeds, transfers, recordings, and minutes of meetings held in the past, so he could determine just what his people had to abide by, what territories they could live in, and what territories had been taken from them by fraud and therefore subject to compensation payments. He had asked before, but there had been years of stalling around on the production of these documents. All the while the English were trying to discredit Teedyuscung with his followers. Their plans did not work, and in the end they had to come up with documents. When they finally did so, several very important treaties and deeds were simply missing, and the English refused to produce them. Finally they produced one lacking document written on ancient paper, dated the twenty-eighth day of the sixth month of 1686, entitled, 'Copy of the last Indian Purchase,' supposedly in the handwriting of William Penn himself. It was finally confessed to be a forgery and the original never surfaced.

"Another critical deed and treaty never surfaced, the Treaty of 1718 between the People and William Penn, and on it hinged two other treaties. The terms of this treaty were so specific that it would have simplified the sorting out of all the fraudulent transactions, and the English kept hoping that by delay, some miracle would happen to keep Teedyuscung from discovering the depth of the injustices needing compensation. Finally Teedyuscung gave up on the conference. He counseled with Mr. Norris, the Speaker of the Assembly, asking him to get the proper documents together setting forth a true statement of the case and present them to the King and his Council to resolve. Although he lived long, Teedyuscung never saw a resolution of these Pennsylvania treaty issues in his lifetime."

The huge green Pipe puffed a great sigh and said, "Young One, I know something about this alcohol problem that besets the People, and I think you should know it also. 'Spirituous liquors' were a tool used against your people to get them to do whatever the Aliens wanted of them. Liquor was given to the People because they were easily talked into anything when they had been drinking. Treaties have been signed by chiefs who were gotten drunk prior to the signing so they would not complain about irregularities they might notice. Then, too, negotiations between traders and the hunters were to the advantage of the sober traders. The traders from the French, British, Dutch and even Irish traders all kept bringing in more rum and alcohol than the chiefs wanted their folks to have access to. The tribal leaders complained to the governors continually about the alcohol's being smuggled into their towns and the surrounding woods.

"The people had no experience with these chemicals before the Aliens came. Their systems were not used to the alcohol in the liquor and they reacted in terrible ways, and still do. Worse yet was the fact that after a while the traders cheated the people by substituting strange chemicals to drink for rum or whiskey. Your people only knew that what they were given tasted bad and was hot. They had no idea they were not drinking the same stuff the Aliens were drinking. In truth they often drank kerosene, turpentine, liquid pepper like tabasco, tobacco juice, niter, all manner of dangerous chemicals. Some became deranged, went berserk, had convulsions causing permanent brain damage; some never regained their sanity or health. There were no laws of the Aliens' government to protect the People from this, so the tribes created laws against allowing alcohol on tribal territory. These laws were impossible to enforce and the Alien perpetrators of these crimes were never punished. Today the manufacture of liquor is so controlled that this can't happen again, unless someone drinks what is called 'moonshine' which is homemade and illegal, and you never know what is in it. That manufacturing control could be considered a health safeguard, but, Young One, the People just should not drink. They still can't handle alcohol. At least when you realize what the People were drinking, it is easier to understand the bizarre behavior often attributed to them back then.

"At almost every occasion of Council or treaty negotiations, the Indian leaders always requested the Aliens' assistance in stopping the river of alcohol flowing into their communities. (Ironically enough, the Aliens at these negotiations always had kegs and casks full of alcohol to keep the People's leaders in a drunken stupor, so they would not be effective in protecting their lands.)

"At the beginning of the Carlisle Treaty the People begged for the Aliens' government to intervene and stop the alcohol coming into their communities. The leaders were well aware of their people's weaknesses and the devastation that was taking place, especially in families. The governor agreed that the leaders could stave, or rupture and spill all the casks of alcohol that they found on their tribal property for the next three years, and he issued a cease and desist order to the traders, warning that if they took alcohol into the Indian communities and it was spilt, they would have no recourse for monetary recovery. That one instance of the three year prohibition is the only one known which was in the least effectively administered by either side.

"It wasn't too long after that the People decided to just leave Pennsylvania and head back to the Ohio Valley. Their land base had been so diminished that they had no place to stand. They had already been involved in at least three dozen treaties with various groups of the pale Aliens. Not one of them had been lived up to. When old William Penn was in charge, he struck hard bargains with the People, but he was a man of his word. He was the only honorable man your people dealt with, keeping the terms of the treaties he made with your people until he died. But immediately after his death, the new Aliens in charge started breaking the terms as fast as they could, and so it continued for a hundred years.

"Your people had had a group of relatives living in the Ohio Valley off and on for several hundred years, at least, as you have heard. The idea to move back was a welcome one, because they knew that the Tribal People who lived there with them were decent and accepting for the most part. They knew the land was full of food and animals, and was beautiful. A good part of the People who wanted to move to the Ohio Valley had come from there about sixty years before, when they went to the East to join a different group of their relatives, the ones who had come up the East coast and from the Carolinas. But I can tell you, the Ohio Valley looked like the perfect place to them by that time.

"Some of their Delaware relatives and even a few of their brothers the Nanticokes and some Conoys came with them. About ten tribes in all came with your ancestors. It was the same time that the Wyandottes had asked your people to come protect them from those marauding Iroquois, in exchange for some land to claim for their own, so it all worked out pretty well. The Wyandottes gave them what amounted to just about the southeast portion of Ohio for coming. Your ancestors were completely tired of the Iroquois and the tall-tale-telling, land-stealing Aliens by then.

"Of course, the sad thing is that there was not to be any real peace in your people's future until the Aliens had all your land and had moved you to strange and poor circumstances. However, I am getting ahead of the story, and someone else is waiting to tell you about that. But I had better relinquish you to the others before your time is through; they really do have a lot to teach you before you leave." With this said the huge-bowled Soapstone Pipe seemed to sigh, exhaling a tiny puff of leftover ashes from his bowl. It wafted up through the leaves of sage that its owner had stuffed inside, and then the old pipe from the east became quiet.

The darkness in the Great House deepened. The Young One thought, this is almost like one of our tremendous storms in the making. A fresh wind had come up, and it was difficult to tell if it carried new moisture from an approaching storm or just the heavy dew.

Young One went back and added a bit more wood to the fire, adjusting it so it could withstand the new velocity of wind. He sat back on his haunches and stared intensely into the flames. He stared for a long time, wondering about all the ancestors who had gathered around campfires in the past. He was beginning to believe he knew what they were like. He wondered, did they ever consider if they were good enough to live up to their responsibilities? Their lives were good before the Aliens came. Their homes were comfortable and had more than just their necessities inside. He was beginning to realize how they felt when the Aliens called them savages. With all they went through and all the different people they had lived with, how were they able to keep their own identities and beliefs? What kept their spirits up when they fought decade after decade, defeat after defeat? How did they manage not to become so bitter after all the cheating and murders? He thought on that for a moment and understood that they *were* bitter, which was why they fought so determinedly, because they fully realized that the plans of the Aliens were to eliminate them from this land. Their form of worship, though, gave them strength and good moral character. He felt the ceremonies had strengthened them, as is stated in Kohkumthena's Laws. Was there something in the actual DNA of Shawnee people that made them different and strong? In his heart the Young One now believed this without any doubt.

What did it sound like to hear everyone speaking Shawnee? On his journeys with the Stones he perceived their communications but could not tell whether they were speaking Shawnee or English. He remembered what the Old Ones looked like. He remembered, when he had seen them journeying in the south, that they had been pale olive-complexioned, not dark, tall and good-looking, and with eyes not black but brown or hazel or grey. And their clothes? How did they dress after they got to this area that was so different from Mexico where it had been so warm? Was the food really as delicious as he remembered from the visit to the family on which the Women's Button had taken him? What a rich and wonderful people the Shawnee were!

The flames seemed to grow higher and more intense, and changed their shapes until the Young One was certain he could detect forms of the people he had seen tonight inside. He looked over at the Old Watcher who had now succumbed to gravity and was lying flat on the floor of the Great House, securely wrapped in his blanket that shielded his face from the light but did nothing to muffle his raucous snore. As he stared at the old man he wondered even about him. What had it been like for the Old Watcher as a young man, when he was being taught? How much did the Old Watcher's grandfather remember? The Young One finally sat on the ground in front of the fire and continued his musing.

This land that the village is on, the okima says, is between a camp of Tecumseh's and Old Man's Village, the Young One thought. It seems reasonable that they both had walked through here. Some of these trees and stones were here then and saw these great men. What did it look like before the farmers came and cut the trees and plowed the ground? The springs that have been found here, before they were plowed under — did the old people know about them and come here and use them? And the berries here, there are so many raspberries and blackberries, did the children come here and pick them? How about the wild gooseberries and blueberries? They are so rare now, were they scarce then? Did Tecumseh hunt on this land? Where did the old green squash plant come from that Okima found in the woods. It is not anything like the ones of today. Did the ancestors of old hunt the "big foot," the huge buck who has the harem of eleven does that lives here on the land? His mind churned with unanswered questions.

It seemed that all the new knowledge the Great House Stones had given the Young One only inspired more questions. His head almost hurt with his great desire for more understanding. As he sat there wondering, a crackling voice that seemed to come directly from the fire itself began to direct itself to him.

"Perhaps I can explain some things to you that none of the other stones can. You see, I am a stone that handles heat well and my kind have been used around sweat lodges, campfires and council fires by your people almost from the beginning, which is so long ago that even we stones don't remember the first time. My kind are Fire Ring Stones. We line the fire pits so no accidental fires leak out. Some of the things I can teach you about are the old Shawnee medicine customs and about some of the great Shawnee leaders in historical times.

"Let me first tell you about the sweat lodges. You must understand that in serving you and Creator, we give up our lives for your benefit. Those of us who line the fire pits live for many years if the fires are tended to in a proper manner. But those of my family who serve as sweat stones have a short life. By the very nature of how we are used, our lives are brief. Once we are heated in the coals, brought in to the pit, and have the water poured on us, the magnitude of the temperature changes can cause us to crack and disintegrate, sometimes very spectacularly. It is a stout one of my kind that can last more than three sweats of four rounds each and still be intact.

"You know your people are different from most of the others who lived here when the Shawnee arrived. Some of the customs were similar and some were very different. There are tribes that use the sweat lodge as a place of relaxation and thus these lodges are used very frequently. Some tribes allow both men and women to be inside at the same time. Some use sweat lodges for purification before ceremonies, and some use them for

ceremonies and as a place for prayers. You Shawnee have ways which are none of these.

"Your stories about your Grandmother Kohkumthena tell that at her home she has a wigiwa, a feisty little dog, a cooking pot a ways from the house, a basket or rug that she works on daily, and a sweat lodge to be used for healing her Shawnee children if they ever become sick. But they had always been so healthy that she had never had to use it. Kohkumthena herself remains so healthy that she has never used the sweat lodge for herself.

"Just when the grandchildren became so ill no one remembers, but eventually they had to use the sweat lodge for healing, and it was under the guidance of the spirits that a medicine man healed someone in it. The medicine men and sweat doctors never took credit for healing — it was always the herbs. If the medicine men claimed to have the healing power themselves, the herbs would get their feelings hurt, and the next time they would just leave the doctoring people alone and let them try to heal by their own powers, which they really did not possess, and the next patient would not get well and might even die. It was to the Plant People that healing power was originally given, and to a few animals. The sweat doctor received directions on how to apply the herbs and the proper prayers to say and sing. Even the woman assistant who gathered and dug the herbs and roots took no personal credit for curing. All credit was given to the Plant People and Creator."

The Fire Ring Stone stopped for a moment and said to the Young One, "You must remember that your people are peculiar in many ways. Your traditions and customs are not the same as those of other nations that live here. Creator has given to your people those things which will make them well, not what will make others well. Never doubt Creator. She knows what she is doing and that what she gave you is beneficial to you. There is no need to imitate the ways of others.

"Your Shawnee form of purification uses fresh flowing water, so we do know sweat lodges were not used for purification with your people. Instead, they would go to a stream, creek, or river and wash themselves. They would then force themselves to drink so much water they would vomit, and when they were all cleaned out inside they would wash again, and take a small sip of water and then some medicinal tea. This is how your ancestors purified themselves. They might even bathe in herbal tea water after they were in the stream, but the flowing water was the purifier for them. Naturally they would have said prayers prior to going into the water.

"The Shawnee had about six different kinds of doctors. There were 'baby' doctors, some who still spoke their language. There were herbal doctors, stone doctors, touching doctors, doctors who could see inside you and heal you without touching you; others, including the witchdoctors that Tecumseh and the Prophet banned and sometimes had killed, and of course, the sweat doctors. When someone was so sick they needed a sweat doctor, then the sweat doctor, or medicine man who knew how to use the sweat lodge, would build what looked like a small wigiwa for the sweat lodge just big enough for himself and the patient. This would be constructed in a sacred manner, with prayers, offerings, and ceremonies before the cutting the first sapling. The medicine man would have to purify himself and spend time in prayer and preparation before he could even begin. The depth of the pit, the diameter, and a trench to drain the extra water all had to be constructed in a particular manner. The fire for heating the stones had to be done just so, and only particular woods were used. This would all be done at least a half mile from the village, usually more like three to six miles away, especially if whoever was to be treated was a wounded warrior or many warriors.

"During war or battles with enemies our warriors would sweat prior to battle only if they felt they were not in good health. After each battle the men were all required to sweat before returning to the village. If there were many warriors, an assistant would be used, and if the battle had gone poorly, then several sweat lodges would have to be built and used. The warriors would all be kept at the site of the sweat lodges until most of the injured were able to return under their own power. The minimum time they were required to stay was four days. This was done for many reasons: it gave the men time to get calmed down and under control; and if they had been exposed to any illnesses from the enemy this was usually enough incubation time to be able to detect the disease, treat it, and protect the village from unnecessary exposure. This form of isolation was the first type of quarantine. It was after the Civil War that the Aliens also began to enforce a quarantine policy in an unsupervised manner. It is probable that had the Aliens had isolation policies earlier, they would not have lost so many millions to the plagues, cholera, and smallpox. Several times the Aliens lost millions of their people on the other side of the ocean, and once they lost a full half of their population. There had never been such a thing here, until they came.

"Your medicine men were very knowledgeable, and even today, they understand healing and the natural helpers and cures given to you originally by Kohkumthena. Shawnee healing works! Do you know, Young One, less than eight percent of your people's cures have ever even been tested by the modern Aliens? The pale Aliens have so many illnesses and diseases, while your people had very few. Your people lived about eighteen percent longer lives than the Aliens did, yet they are still blinded to the possibilities of your medicines. And the few cures they do test, they try to duplicate in an unnatural way in their laboratories and test tubes. They still have much to learn, I am afraid, about healing.

"The directions on how to make and use a sweat lodge were given to your ancestors at the time of the First Creation. After the sweat doctor had purified himself he would find twelve willow saplings about one-and-a-half to two inches in diameter, and about twelve feet long. He would peel the bark from them. Then he would insert the large end of each sapling into the ground at least one to one and a half feet deep, in a small hole, so it was held rigidly in place. He would then place the next pole six feet to the north, the next midway between to the east, and then one six feet opposite that one. The remaining poles were then used to fill in the circumference of the circle, about one and a half feet apart, creating the frame work for the outer wall. Using strips of the peeled bark, he would tie the tops of these willows together in the center of the circle in such a manner that the ceiling of the sweat lodge was about six feet high, but slightly domed and flat on top, not pointed like a tipi. He would then use either hides or reed mats to cover the sides, or both if the weather was severe. The door would be low and a person would have to stoop or crawl to enter.

"A rectangular hole about ten inches deep, twenty-eight inches long, and fourteen inches wide would be dug along the west wall. Most doctors would make the patient lie or sit along the west wall. The doctor would heat four rose-colored rocks and place them in the hole or trench in the four directions. Then he would pour the herbed water, or tea made with either rattail brush or sage, over the rose rocks. After this he would diagnose his patient.

"If it was found the only treatment the patient needed was to sweat, the doctor would then have the proper herbs brought to him. He would either add herbs to the water prior to pouring it on us stones, or after we stones were heated properly and brought inside to our pit, he would sprinkle us with the herbs first and then pour the water over us, making a strong medicine for the one who was ill. As the treatment continued, four more rocks would be brought in and the medicine poured on top, to create the medicated steam. The medicine man would use a total of twelve rocks in the sweat, adding to the original four after each round of prayers and songs, and until they had cooled and were no longer producing the needed vapors. The patient would be treated for four days in the sweat lodge, not just once. He would be removed to his home each night and returned the next morning after breakfast and before actual sunrise if possible. The very sick ones were given medicine to drink as well as the sweat treatments. If a patient was extremely sick and weak, he would stay in the sweat lodge until he was well enough to be moved.

"The doctor would give the patient medicines to take, and the doctor would take the medicine himself as well. They both would take the medicine four times a day, for the four days. The first time the medicine was given to the patient, the medicine man would have the medicinal tea brewing, but before giving it to the patient, he would chew the medicines in his own mouth, and then at the appropriate time, he would spew the saliva herbal mixture onto a spot about an inch and a half below the patient's navel, and smear it around the abdomen. Then he would take a drink of the tea and administer it to the patient.

"There would not often be an assistant; however, if one was needed, it would usually be an older woman of the tribe who was an expert on the herbs. In fact, if the doctor needed herbs or an herbal cure, he would request this old woman to get and prepare for him a cure for whatever the patient was suffering. He would not even specify what he wanted her to prepare or the herbs he wanted used, respecting her knowledge and trusting her talents and wisdom to bring what he needed. This would be a woman who knew the proper way to collect the herbs and the prayers and offerings to make, one with whom the spirits worked and who knew Creator well.

"Before going to war, the men would prepare themselves by purifying in their traditional way with fresh flowing water, vomiting, dancing, washing in herbal teas, and drinking herbal teas of sage or cedar. They *did not* have sweats before battle.

"Once the battle was over and the survivors returned, they were never allowed to make a mad dash for home, but instead would be taken, each one, for a turn in the sweat lodge. Of course, since the number of those using the lodge was greater than usual, more than one person at a time would be sweating. They would sweat a minimum of four days, and if there were no serious injuries among them, they would all return home together. The medicine man would keep the injured at the lodge for treatment until they were healed enough to make it back to the village on their own strength, or until there was nothing more he could do for them, and the medicine man would leave the rest to Creator, and send them home to finish healing."

Young One listened intently. This was very interesting.

The Stone continued, "Because we Fire Ring Stones also line the sacred fires in the Great Houses and at Councils, we have heard many things that our other stone friends have not heard. Even the fire pits in people's private wigiwas are ringed with us, and we have heard many an interesting conversation in those circumstances.

"Even if it were not already well known, we are here to testify that Shawnee women were very powerful. They did not have to fuss at their men to get them to listen to reason; their husbands knew to respect them and did listen, and most often they saw the wisdom of the women's words and followed them. Of course one woman's counsel is good in a particular area while another woman's advice would be more astute in a different one.

"Most of the councils we witnessed concerned the nation's usual business, but some have been of historical proportions. Some of the councils we have witnessed have been nothing short of a brawl, though others were orderly and productive. Occasionally the council members disagreed mightily among themselves, but the Okima usually had a clear head and guided the people back to the subject, focusing on what needed to be done and how, before things got totally out of hand.

"There were always grand councils before any treaties were signed. These were often the most difficult times for us to remain silent. Each time there would be a small group which wanted to continue fighting, or would want to simply move away from the Alien invaders, while the older chiefs usually saw things in a totally different way. Wanting to preserve what lives were left, they were willing to sign the treaties. It was heartbreaking to hear each side saying things that were true. We realized only one side would win eventually, and we feared the outcome would be terrible for all. Each time we were correct, but even we wise Stones could not foresee just how awful life would turn out for the People. Let me tell you about a couple of instances.

"There was the council in 1777 with the most respected war chief, Cornstalk, who had followed the wishes of his people. Originally he did not want to go to fight in Dunmore's War, but his people demanded it of him and he gained great respect as a skilled war chief at the battle at Point Pleasant, October 10, 1774. Even though they lost that battle he did not want to quit the fight, but his head men were determined to give up, so he went and made the best terms he could. In early 1777 his people had again changed their minds and were intending to break the peace, and even though he was now more than ever resolved to peace, he would be bound to lead them again. So Cornstalk quickly went to Fort Randolph, which is near present-day Point Pleasant, to warn the Aliens of the intentions of his people. He had his wonderful, brilliant son, Ilinipsico, go with him, and another fine young chief named Red Hawk. They were known to be friendly people, so at the fort they were allowed to walk right in when they arrived.

"Cornstalk asked to speak with the officer in charge immediately. He and the other men were taken into a room to wait for him to arrive. While they waited, word spread around the fort that they were there. There had been a small conflict between the Aliens and a couple of renegade people that ended in two of the Aliens being murdered. Tempers were running very high over the incident. Several hot-headed soldiers who had already heard about the murders went and got their guns. They found the room where Cornstalk and the others were waiting and murdered them in cold blood and then butchered their bodies.

"He had come in friendship to warn them to protect themselves, and instead they repaid his kindness with death. The deaths of Cornstalk, Ilinipsico, and Red Hawk cost the Aliens the three best friends they had among the People at that time. We Stones who were around his wigiwa fire when Cornstalk decided to go to the Aliens mourned for his loss. He was a great man.

"Young One, I need to tell you something very sad that happened to your people that we Stones were witness to, and this is as sad a thing as any that resulted from the invasion of the Aliens. They had so many ways that brought death to you that we Fire Stones feel you need a thorough understanding of the worst ones. Before there were any wars between you, they had already killed hundreds of thousands and even millions of your people, with disease.

"To fully understand all this I must explain to you the circumstances that the Aliens came from. For more than eight hundred years the Aliens could not drink the water in their European countries unless they boiled it or let it ferment in a brew or wine, where the alcohol content killed enough of the bacteria that they could drink it without being harmed. The reason for this is that it was polluted. They had no sewage systems, although even centuries before many countries had had elaborate water and sewage systems, like the early Romans in what is now Italy. But, somehow they had forgotten or just were lazy and didn't keep up the systems, so they would use a chamber pot, a small container that held a gallon or so, and when it became full, they would simply take it to a window or door and pitch the contents in the yard or towards the street. Then when it rained that nasty stuff would run into the streets, down the ditches if there were any, travel to the creeks and rivers and pollute them. The people would also track that nasty stuff into their houses and get it on their clothes. People were much poorer then and seldom had more than two sets of clothes, one for every day and the other to wear when they washed the first set.

"The people themselves would bathe perhaps once a year, never more than twice a year because the pollution in the water would make them sick. It was actually healthier for them to be dirty and stink, have festering sores, lice and fleas, than it was for them to be clean by washing in the bacteria-laden water."

The Fire Ring Stone's voice had an amused tone as it said, "You might have heard about how many Aliens drowned when they came here. The rivers and creeks were no deeper nor wider then. It was simply that they did not know how to swim. They were accustomed to so much pollution in all of their water that if they would not bathe in it, they certainly would not want to swim in it. Therefore swimming was just not done, and anyone who did was considered totally inappropriate and not right-thinking.

Your ancestors, on the other hand, taught their children to swim by the time they were two or three years old.

"When the Aliens came here and saw the beautiful rivers and streams, and all the healthy fish, frogs, crawdads, eels, water flowers, and the animals drinking it, they were just amazed. They had not tasted anything so sweet in their lives as this clean and pure water. It appears they realized at first what a treasure it was and is, but they had lost the understanding of how to preserve it in that state and so today they have almost caught up with the centuries of polluted waters they left in Europe.

"The Aliens' forests had been destroyed by overcutting hundreds of years before. There was no place for the animals to live, but they too had been overkilled. The only remaining forests belonged to the royal families and noblemen, including the game animals left there. The diet of the Aliens was very boring, as they were used to only a few vegetables at that time and a few grains. The commoners seldom had any meat. Their style of dining was predominantly a gruel equal to oatmeal or watery stews. They had heavy breads and some cheeses. Their usual meat was greasy pork. They were not healthy for many reasons. Of the foods you are accustomed to seeing at the grocery today, more than sixty-five percent came from America, and before the Aliens came to stay, the rest of the world did not have them.

"When the Aliens came here and saw the abundance of game, they thought they had become the recipients of a second Garden of Eden or a second Promised Land. In fact, that became part of the major problem between the two people. The Aliens told themselves that this territory indeed was their Holy Promised Land, even though the original, known as Canaan, had already been given to the descendants of their ancient Tribal Elder, Abraham, about two thousand years before. They wanted this place so much that they said Creator had given it to them. No words in their black book could be found to justify their claims, but they persisted in this. Those who did not claim the land under religious arguments did so by stating that God (Creator) wanted them to have it since you indigenous people were wasting it by not using it all up, as they had their homelands. These Aliens have strange ways. They are a dangerous people, Young One.

"Now your people had always said that Creator gave this place to them. The Aliens said there was only one God who created everything, and your people only knew of one Creator, so while your people were wondering if Creator could lie, these Aliens moved in and started taking everything they wanted. If permission was refused when the Aliens asked for it, they would try to buy it. They thought then, and still do today, that you can buy everything. When buying didn't work, they then just started coming and taking, and your people started trying to hold on and fighting back, and the wars began. But before that critical point, your people were thinned out by devastating diseases that the Aliens brought with them, from the filthy existences they had across the Big Waters.

"They did not originally use the diseases on purpose to kill your people. The Aliens had simply become immune to many of them through the centuries, and were no longer severely affected by them, so they really did not give them any thought when it came to their possible effects on your people. Because your people's living conditions were so clean and pure, your people had never had to develop an immunity to anything. These were strange and powerful germs and your people would die sometimes in a matter of hours from the severity of their effects. Other diseases would take months to kill them and people would dwindle away and wither like flowers out of water. Some of the people would survive the diseases but be left so scarred their faces would no longer look human. Literally millions of the original People died. Killing your people on purpose with diseases came later.

"Some say only a few hundred thousand died but on the island of Hispañola alone more than six million died from diseases. On the continent of North America the number is generally believed to be closer to two or three million lives lost.

"I wish I could say that this type of atrocious, murderous activity is in the past but that is not true because the Aliens are continuing to find ways to kill the People. Among the latest of their strategies is dumping highly toxic pollutants into the water systems and rivers, and burying radioactive wastes on tribal lands. The People are giving birth to mutated children, having many still births, and suffering from many toxic waste-induced diseases and agonies as we speak.

"To say that all this isn't true is to try and deny historical facts and responsibilities. World War II cost over eleven million lives of Jews, Russians, Gypsies, Rumanians, Blacks and others. There are those today who try to say it never happened, it was all a fiction. Young One, never be so cowardly that you can't admit to what you do in life. You will be called

111

upon to make hard decisions and do hard things. There will be times you won't understand why you are to do things. When time has passed and you wish you had not participated in it, admit that is how you feel and see to it you do what you can to make the situation better. Lying to yourself is a dreadful disease that causes everyone grief. Be brave. The truth will give you strength, even ugly truths.

"Smallpox was introduced about fifteen years after the Western 'discovery' by Columbus, and within a short period of time more than 3.5 million people in Mexico died of it. Artist George Catlin estimated that of the twelve million people here at the time of discovery, half were destroyed by smallpox alone. From time to time the theories and numbers change, all trying to make the Aliens look as though they are not responsible for much of the evil your people have suffered. Even chicken pox took thousands of lives. The Aliens have always avoided their responsibilities towards the People and while sometimes small concessions are made, on a whole, things are very bad especially for the people who were removed from their lands and put on reservations."

The Fire Ring Stone became quiet and reflective for a moment and then continued, "We Stones are a very fortunate Nation, for we are not susceptible to the diseases, nor can we be cut down like the Tree Nations. They move us, explode us, and crush us, but in some form we do get to continue and do not perish like your people and the animals and Plant People. It has never been said, but perhaps we too are to be witnesses to Creator about your sufferings here, from the hands of the Aliens. It is very hard to remember all these things, because even Stones have hearts that hurt when they witness such things.

"There are many guesses as to how many died, but we Stones who were in their homes and witnessed their suffering can tell you: there were more than ten million people, and some say seventeen million, who perished from the diseases. Later, after the fighting ceased and your people were conquered and living on the reservations and prisoner of war camps, the Aliens would send blankets taken from the corpses of those who died with these horrible diseases and were full of these killer germs, and give them to those of you who were cold. Oh, it is all enough to break the heart of even the hardest Stone, when we think of all these things your people have suffered, and we remember how healthy and happy you were before," the Stone said sadly.

"Some Aliens came and, when they could find nothing else with which to make money, would go into the houses and steal the people, ship them to other countries as slaves, and thus make their 'sacred' money.

"The practice of slavery in the western hemisphere began with the Portuguese in 1503 on Santa Domingo. The first boatload of black slaves to come into the colonies was in 1619 at Jamestown. Slavery was continued by the Spanish and then the Dutch, who made Indian slaves their major export, and various other countries who came and stole the people and made money from the slave trade.

"Young One, think for a moment of the heartbreak of the ancestors when the slavers came and stole members of their families. Husbands, fathers, brothers, and sons; and they stole daughters and mothers as well. Those were truly evil and painful times. No one even kept a record of where they were taken, or their names, or the names of the tribes they came from. At least the names of the black slaves who came here were sometimes recorded. Truly the Aliens considered your lives less than nothing and your ancestors of less value than the mosquito.

"Young One, don't you think it is strange that some of the Aliens stole people here, and shipped them overseas as slaves for money, while others stole black people and shipped them over here and made money? There were some tribes in Central America who believed in slavery, but it was virtually unknown here until the Aliens made a business out of it. Even the tribes in Central America had merely used the people they had conquered in war, not bought. During the removal of the People to Oklahoma some tribes did have slaves that went with them, mostly of southern tribes like the Cherokee.

"We Stones believe there is nothing stranger than these Aliens and their ideas.

"Your people do not make good slaves, Young One. They were used to being free and happy. Their lives were easy compared to the Aliens' lives. The land of plenty was here. Across the Big Waters the land was tired and worn out, the water scarce and foul. Very few ever survived very long in slavery. Even the ones who were well-treated died quickly of broken hearts. The old ones knew how to quit living when it was too painful to go on. They did not commit suicide, they did nothing to make themselves die. They simply gave up their spirits and crossed over from flesh and spirit to pure spirit. It was and is a mystery; some still remember how, but now life is easier so there is no need."

The Fire Ring Stone sighed sadly and continued. "The first treaties which the People signed were made before they realized that the Aliens would lie. After each treaty they became more and more disgusted with the schemes, misrepresentations, and outright lies that the Aliens told them to get them to sign. It took only a few years to learn that the Aliens did not have honorable intentions towards them and the terms of the treaties reflected that. Some began to resist more strongly than ever. Then the Aliens began to infiltrate areas that had never been discussed in treaties and they were mean and cruel to the ancestors who had lived there so long. [See appendix for list of treaties.]

"It was a common thing for the Aliens to come into the area, find a village, wait until the men were out hunting and then burn the village and the crops and kill women and children. Some of the horrible things they did to the women and children you are yet too young to be told, but soon you can read about it in a history book. They did butchery on them with knives. Young One, your ancestors learned to scalp from the Aliens. Once in a great while a warrior would take a small triangular-shaped patch no bigger than an inch or inch and a half, but the Aliens — why, they wanted whole scalps from dead men. They did great evil so they could steal the land and all the things that grew there.

"The land was rich with fruits, vegetables, herbs, medicines, berries, animals, birds, and trees the likes of which the Aliens had never seen before. They cut down the huge trees, some over sixteen feet in diameter, simply to clear a field so they could plant the vegetables they had brought with them. They burned the trees they cut down, not even attempting to use the lumber. The trees were so thick and huge and lush that they made a canopy of shade all the way from the Atlantic to the Mississippi River. Because it was so shady, there was very little underbrush and what was there was burned off from time to time to keep the area safe from accidental forest fires started by lightning.

"You know, Young One, we Stones have seen it all, but there are some of other nations who have witnessed a great deal of your history too. There is an Old Person who would like to try to explain this part to you. You know him as the Council Oak. Instead of my rambling and rumbling on, my friend here can give you some insight from a personal point of view."

There was the sound of a light breeze stirring the branches of the Council Oak, which was so tall it could see over the Great House walls. It was just a few feet from the Great House, and the Council sat in its shade as they decided the nation's business. The breeze sound began to be thicker and more substantial, until the Young One could understand its meaning. "Just as your people have suffered at the hands of the Aliens, so have mine," the magnificent Oak breezed. "We were one of the things with which they became obsessed.

"It is true that in their own homeland they had never seen anything so grand and huge as we were then. We trees had grown for hundreds of years, some for well over a thousand years, and no one had ever bothered us. Every year or so your ancestors would thin out the smaller saplings and the brush so we would not be in danger from forest fires. Maybe every three years they would start a small fire on a day with no wind, and then they would have robes and blankets to beat the flames out when the fire went somewhere they didn't want it to go. They controlled the burning very effectively in this way. The Aliens were terrified of fire and did not know of this way of putting fires out until your people taught them.

"And once in a while they would need to cut one of the smaller ones of us, perhaps a young one of only one hundred and fifty years of age, or maybe up to three hundred years, for a canoe or some other specific reason. But they never wasted us. When they came to cut or girdle us, they always explained to us what they were doing and why it needed to be done, so we would understand that we were fulfilling the purposes which Creator had given to us in the beginning. They would offer us tobacco and be respectful of us. But oh, those Aliens! How cruel and greedy they were, and their grandchildren's grandchildren are no better today.

"I do not mean to be bitter, but we Old People of today hardly deserve the title. None of us around here are older than five or six hundred years, and most are considered old at only two hundred years or so. The pitiful patches of our virgin forests are so small that it is hard even for me to imagine our former size and strength.

"They tell me that my ancestors were so full and beautiful that it took your breath away to look at us for the first time. Our elms and chestnuts were some of the most beautiful trees in the whole world. The chestnut in particular was so rich in its color, and strong of heart, it was used for holding the new-style buildings and homes up. Later when the Aliens had

115

manufacturing plants here, the chestnuts and we oaks were prized for our strength. These two-leggeds make no sense, though. They loved my ancestors and used them with a frenzy, but then they would also bring over the versions of us they were used to from across the Big Waters, thus carrying diseases to us trees the same as they did to your people. Our people were not accustomed to their diseases, and we too died in great numbers, some of us even became extinct, just like many nations of your People.

"The French Aliens once took a survey of the trees here and found that here there were fifty-one varieties that were usable for carpentry, to make the furniture and other things the Frenchmen needed for their homes, compared to only nine in their own country. They surveyed the tall trees and found they had only thirty types in their homeland that grew to a height of thirty feet or more, but here there were more than one hundred and forty.

"All these larger trees meant to the Aliens was that they could ship the wood back to their homelands in such large quantities that even the common people would be able to have tables and chairs and cupboards and chests, just as the rich people did. They would be able to make them so cheaply that everyone could afford the things they needed to have a nicer life. They had no thought of what they were doing to us or this land and its inhabitants. Even though they knew the reason they had no animals left in Europe was that they had used up their forests, they never considered they were using up the forests here at an unbelievable and irreplaceable rate of speed.

"Young One, have you ever seen a beechnut from a beech tree? We people of the Tree Nations mature slowly. The beech must be at least two hundred and fifty years old before it can produce the nuts which are its seeds, the method which Creator gave it to continue itself. The Aliens' philosophy is that once a tree reaches its maturity you can cut it down, no matter that it hasn't had a chance to produce seeds to continue its nation. The Old Ones know so much, and they have seen and been part of so much history of which the two-legged grandchildren have no idea. Oh, how cruel the Aliens are, so blinded with greed.

"It seemed to the Aliens that there were so many animals and birds that they could never be all used up, so they wasted and squandered the lives of the Tree Nations, the Plant People, and the Bird Nations. They totally wiped out the beautiful passenger pigeons which used to fly in flocks so vast, containing many millions of birds, it would take whole days for them to pass over. Flocks of swans and wild turkeys abounded, while today you see a few tame ones and rarely the beautiful birds in the wild and natural way creator made them. Even I and my people don't know all the Nations of nature that these Aliens have totally destroyed in their thoughtless, greedy rush.

"The land of the English Aliens was also very poor in tall trees. They live on an island and they had a large population that was using up their own natural resources faster than they could be found and harvested. This was one of the reasons the English were always looking for new lands to conquer, so they could take the natural resources that they wanted. Listen to my words, Young One: then they could take what they *wanted*. They were not content to satisfy what they *needed*, they always took more than their needs to sell for their nasty, troublesome money. Nothing mattered to them except their money.

"In the area on the Atlantic coast now called New England there grew huge white pines, up to two hundred and fifty feet tall and five feet in diameter. This was unheard of in the rest of the world. The English had to buy trees just over a hundred feet tall from the Baltic nations at high prices, then splice them together to make masts high enough for their merchant ships. That splice point would break during storms. These taller and stronger American-grown masts meant they could build even bigger ships to take away the natural resources they found here. In just one year in the early 1770s they shipped over fourteen thousand tons of timber from here, having cut over thirty thousand cedars, oaks, and pines. While they were enjoying prosperity, they were devastating the Tree Nations here."

The grand old Council Oak would stop from time to time and reflect, remembering what the world had been like so long ago and what had made it change. The Oak felt it his responsibility to make the Young Watcher understand what his own nation understood. He, and all who had spoken, believed that the Young Watcher's peers would be the generation to determine the quality of life and if it would continue or all would perish. It was obviously a responsibility that the Oak felt heavily.

After pausing and catching his wind, the mighty Oak began again. "Sassafras, sweet sassafras. They cut hundreds of thousands of tons of our sweet sassafras and shipped it across the Big Waters. They used it in flavoring candy, medicine, used it for medicines themselves, and for carpentry because the bugs didn't like the tang of the resin in the beautiful rich-colored bark. But again, they did not take what they needed, they appropriated more and then tried to find ways to convince other Aliens to buy the excess supply. Our air used to be so sweet smelling that it truly was like a little paradise. Why, the sassafras had trunks five feet in diameter and bigger. Now you might find one that is one or two feet, but mostly the sad descendants are just brush and small saplings.

"These Aliens don't even know what sassafras is good for. The berries have a dozen uses, the leaves are wonderful flavoring for crayfish dishes. The oil can be added to fat or even soap and it keeps the insects away. And everyone loved the tea that had the tonic effect. In the heart of winter when the grandchildren had some root left over, it was a warm delicious treat, and in the spring when people lagged, the tonic made them feel better. Now, after they took all the beautiful Old People of the Sassafras Nation and used them the way they decided, they have declared them harmful. So any sassafras tea you get now lacks the natural spiciness it once had, and only a hint of its true flavor can be tasted.

"If the Aliens did not always misuse everything and do things to excess there would be no harm in many of the things they now take away from the grandchildren. Why, I hear they are considering making tobacco an illegal substance! The idea, restricting a sacred herb! Who do these Aliens think they are — Kohkumthena? Do they think everyone is as foolish as they are?

"Tobacco is a sacred herb. It is to be used as a witness to Creator for the grandchildren. It is to be burned so its smoke can travel to Creator's home and carry the words of the grandchildren to Creator. But the Aliens found a way to change it, make it taste different, milder, better so they say, and then they brought back the new improved version and began to sell to your ancestors their version of this sacred plant. By this time half of Europe was smoking in some way and those who didn't smoke the herb, ground it up and used it as snuff. Needless to say, the Aliens had once again found a way to make huge amounts of money from something that your ancestors considered sacred, lessening its sacredness and making it something common and cheap.

"The more Aliens who came here, the more wood they needed for their own use. What they did not use in their own houses and farms and

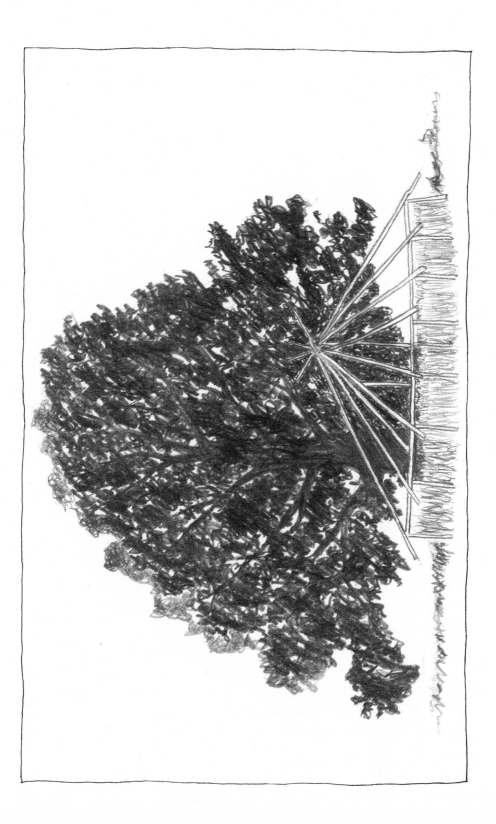

businesses they sold to others. In less than two hundred years, the New Englanders alone had burned more than two hundred and sixty million cords of wood to heat their homes with. This doesn't count what they used to build their homes and fences.

"Even today, Young One, they want to cut down the only true Old People we have left, the ancient magnificent redwoods out west. They have cut most of the hardwood trees and used them foolishly, sometimes just to make paper, which is true waste. Paper once was made of other cheaper things, without polluting, and it lasted longer. To use wood fibers, to have to pulverize and soften it in chemicals, then bleach it, dump the chemicals in the rivers and have a product that disintegrates rapidly, makes no sense to us. They say they reforest where they cut, but they plant fast-growing soft woods which cannot replace the uses of the hardwoods. It makes us frightened and angry to see this. Perhaps you can stop the devastation, and senseless waste of everything of a true value. The Aliens are driven like mad men for their wants to be fulfilled instantly. Such spoiled and thoughtless creatures, these Aliens!

"There are times that I almost wish I were a willow, so when I weep, no one would notice," the mighty Council Oak said softly. "This night of sharing and remembering your people at their finest has made me very sad. They were such a wonderful and unique people and have suffered such losses. I am sorry, I don't mean to be gloomy.

"Young One, be careful. These Aliens are very dangerous people, whom we suspect are not right-thinking.

"I have this image in my mind, Young One, of one of our most magnificent ancestors being cut off and only a raw stump remaining, and then a few years later, from somewhere deep within, this stump sends forth shoots from around its edges that grow into the shape of a beautiful full grown tree again. Of course, its middle is hollow and it only has limbs in a circle on the outer edge of the stump, but still, it is alive. It is the continuation of life for that nation, and within each shoot is all the knowledge and wisdom of the magnificent one of great age.

"My prayer for you and your people, Young One, is that you will be like those shoots sent out by the old magnificent stump. You may never have the opportunity to become exactly like your ancestors, but you will be able to grow to a person of beauty, and deep within each of you will be the knowledge and wisdom of your ancestors guiding and directing you, and helping you to be the very finest Shawnee possible at this time."

With that spoken by the great Council Oak, the breeze became strong for a moment and then just gently faded until the night was again very still.

The Young One began to feel he was turning into a philosopher, as the thought struck him that the Indians' religion and rules of life helped create a heavenly existence here on earth, while the Aliens' religion and commandments seemed to create hell on earth. Perhaps that was why there was no concept of hell in the Indians' religion until the Aliens came and brought literal hell with them. These were heavy thoughts for a youth on his first adult night watch.

Finally he directed his attention to the sleeping Old Watcher, and for a few minutes watched the lump the Old Watcher had become curled up under his blanket. He was still snoring but a little more softly now, and with an occasional snort, as though he would awaken at any moment.

The Young One smiled kindly at the Old Watcher. His affection for his mentor had grown, even though tonight the Old Watcher had been more watched than watcher, and had left the Young One to be taught by others with no interpreter. The Young One sighed softly, tiredly envying the Old Watcher his slumbers, hoping that later he could discuss all these occurrences in the Great House with him.

As he sat thinking, a strong, pleasant voice called him from the altar area. The Young One tried to identify his new teacher. There were still many objects lying on and around the altar. "Young One," the voice began. "You will now be taught about the last phases of your history in Ohio. I was one of Tecumseh's pipes. He was one of your greatest warriors. Tecumseh was born under a great sign from the heavens: a brilliant green comet streaked across the sky at the moment of his birth in 1768. I know much about his later years and the things that happened to your people during his lifetime. I am normally kept protected in a sacred bundle, hidden away for safety, but this night I was placed on the altar for the first time in many years. I believe it was so I could share with you what I remember.

"As you see, I am of the red stone they call catlinite. I lived an exciting life with Tecumseh. He received me as a gift during a time of peace, almost of calm. I stayed with him to the end, even when he no longer used me, but had begun using his peace-hawk pipe. Even though I am quite plain, I was considered a great gift, but I consider having lived the active part of my life with him my gift from Creator. While all of us red stone pipes are sacred and have rich, wonderful existences, my owner Tecumseh was the most extraordinary man the Shawnee People, or perhaps any People, ever had on this land. My bowl still feels the warmth of the embers, as this great leader would light me and begin to share me with others during a ceremony, or when he was alone and needed to pray.

"Tecumseh was the fourth child of a Shawnee war chief named Pucksinwa. When the green comet streaked across the sky at his birth, it was believed the green eyes of the Spirit Water Panther who travels over the water on occasion were showing in the sky. Tecumseh's people interpreted the sign to mean they were witnessing the birth of an extraordinary person who would do wonderful things in his lifetime for his people. He was brought up aware that he was expected to be better than his peers because Creator had something special for him to do with his life. He was taught by many, but the single most important teacher he had, after their father was killed in battle at Point Pleasant, was his older sister Tecumapease, known as Star Watcher, who taught him to be kind and humane. His older brother Chikseeka taught him about being a hunter, warrior and man, and his surrogate father, who was the village chief Black Fish, also was a fine man who taught young Tecumseh 'many wisdoms.'

"He had had another, older brother who had died when he was quite small, and a set of younger triplet brothers. Two of the triplets were normal, but the last-born was at birth misshapen and considered a runt. By practicing traditional gentle manipulation and massage, Turtle Woman, their mother, was able to ease the severity of the bean shape of his skull, but could never totally correct it.

"This little one was an ill-tempered and ill-behaved child, awkward in every way. For the first few years of his life he literally screamed and cried continuously, and so he was called Loud Noise. One can only wonder what internal problems resulting from his unusual birth he might have been suffering from. Having Tecumseh for an older brother was both a blessing and a curse for this one: he idolized Tecumseh, but it placed un-

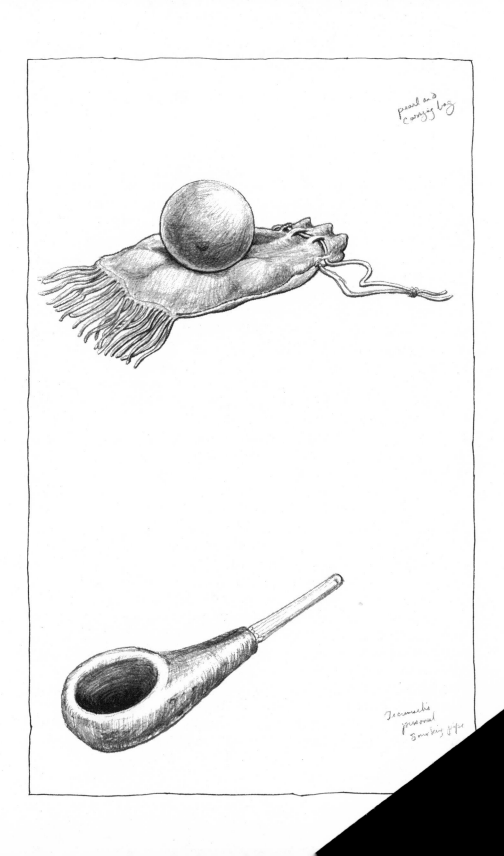

pearl and
carrying bag

Tecumseh's
personal
smoking pipe

reasonable expectations on Loud Noise which he could not physically live up to. Tecumseh seemed to possess great compassion and affection for his little brother in spite of his flaws, especially after an accident at the age of eight cost Loud Noise an eye." The Pipe paused a moment, as if relishing the kindness of the Shawnee leader.

"Loud Noise lived a life of drunken belligerence and became an embarrassment to the family. He seemed to respect nothing except his brother Tecumseh, but even that affection and respect was not enough to enable him to live a decent life. At the age of thirty-six, Loud Noise became extremely drunk and began to have seizures, finally winding up in a deep coma. It was many hours before he regained consciousness, and when he did, he had seemingly become a totally different man. He claimed to have crossed over to the land of Spirits," the Pipe said, its voice lacking conviction, "and was taken to Creator, who showed him many things. He was given the chance to come back and change his life to one of right thinking, and to help his people.

"Creator told him he had a new name, 'Open Door,' for he would be the opening for the People to change, to revert back to their own traditional ways and redeem themselves from the evil that had come to them with the Aliens' arrival. Later he would have a following of thousands from at least fourteen different tribes and help his brother Tecumseh in forming his Indian coalition. I must say," said Tecumseh's modest Pipe. "He certainly fooled me. I always thought he was merely a charlatan, but I guess thousands of people can't be wrong. But enough of *him* for the moment.

"For Tecumseh, the years from 1783 to 1813 were a time full of wars and battles with the Aliens, and times of relative peace were brief and few. Seven times in his life he saw his village destroyed by the invaders and he saw his beloved older brother Chikseeka killed by a white man's rifle ball. As a young man Tecumseh proved himself a capable warrior and in every battle he seemed to become more proficient and ferocious. Yet he was ever hon~ ~ble to his prisoners and demanded the men in his com-
n~ ~ humane manner toward them as well. All this showed
~chings," the Pipe said boastingly, as if it had been he
~ught Tecumseh instead of his sister.
~e Battle of Fallen Timbers on August 20, 1794, on the
~io, about fifteen miles from Toledo. Here the Indian

people were severely defeated by General 'Mad' Anthony Wayne and Tecumseh saw another of his brothers killed. However, Tecumseh refused to participate in the Greeneville Treaty which followed. He had given his father his word to never make his mark on an Alien treaty. Even if he had wanted to, he could not have signed for that very reason. In truth, he had studied many of the broken treaties the Aliens had made with his people, for he could read the English language. He found each had been a dishonorable deception, at best merely a ploy preceding even worse times for his people at the hands of the Aliens. He believed he had nothing whatsoever to gain by signing the Greeneville Treaty and absolutely nothing to lose by not signing. The best service he could give to his people, he believed, was to try to achieve a different and stronger form of agreeing than had been used before.

"After their Revolutionary War, the American Aliens intensified their efforts against the People to gain complete control over the land. The Shawnee were the leading power in many of the conflicts against the American Aliens and thus received the greater portion of their wrath. General Wayne had been a formidable foe on the battlefield, but after the People eventually lost the struggles he was an even more treacherous and dangerous foe at the negotiating table. The terms of the Greeneville Treaty were especially heartbreaking. Many harsh words were spoken and written before the treaty signing, and sentiments were bitter on both sides. Two-thirds of Ohio and part of Indiana would now be ceded to the American Aliens, who would have freedom to come settle in the newly-won territory and come and go unmolested as they chose. The Shawnee people would wind up in three tiny communities in northwestern Ohio. They were now the aliens in their own land.

"The councils held when the old chiefs decided to sign the Greeneville Treaty were about the most difficult we ever witnessed," the red Pipe continued. "Their hearts were near the breaking point. No one believed the Aliens would live up to all their promises, but the People hoped they would live up to at least some of them. Most of the chiefs believed that if they kept fighting, all their people would be killed and become extinct. There had been tremendous bloodshed and losses at the Battle of Fallen Timbers, and the People's resolve to continue fighting had also died. They still believed that Creator had given them this place, and although they did not want to move, they did not want to live under the Aliens' rule. In reality they had no choice. They signed the abominable treaty, wept, and prayed.

"Tecumseh knew that the beloved and respected Chief Black Hoof had been fighting for over seventy years, almost the equivalent of two normal life spans. Black Hoof had seen more of his people die than any other Shawnee chief. He had seen more Aliens crowding, encroaching, lying, stealing, cheating, and murdering than had any other chief. He had buried more of the finest of his nation than any other chief, and seen more suffering widows and children than he wanted to remember. He himself had traveled thousands of miles, having lived several places between the Crystal River in Florida, the place of his birth, to various places in Ohio. Black Hoof realized if the Shawnee were to escape annihilation, he must accept peace. All the chiefs thought that by accepting the peace terms their families and tribes would at least have a place to live in the homeland forever and have enough to eat.

"It was not widely reported, but the principal chiefs of all the different tribes were held hostage until their subordinate chiefs came to the fort and signed the treaty. This took more than two months. It took little time for the People to realize any true honor involving this treaty was not likely to come from the side of the Alien conquerors. The words of General Wayne were, "I must insist you (the chiefs) accept my hospitality and remain until all have come in and signed the treaty."

"As the various tribal chiefs arrived at Greeneville, Tecumseh would intercept them and plead with them to not sign but to join him and his men in continued resistance. None did. They continued their journey to the inside of the fort, where they set up camp and prepared to negotiate and accept terms. Their days of having any real negotiating clout were over. The concessions they won were small and insignificant. In Tecumseh's mind the negotiations were so much wasted effort, for the Aliens would still do as they pleased. He used me for many prayers during that time," the plain little Pipe reflected.

"While the old chiefs were inside the fort at Greeneville, negotiating the terms of the treaty and preparing to sign, Tecumseh and a band of followers camped outside the walls, across a small creek on a point of land, singing and praying. They burnt green wood, causing the smoke to filter into the fort to remind the old chiefs that he and his people were there to protest the signing. Across the creek and inside the fort walls a tragedy was occurring. It seemed all the battles Tecumseh had fought had been for nothing, and any respect the People had gained was being blotted out by the black ink splotches and marks. He was angry to his core; then, at accepting the reality of the treaty; he grieved for his people, for all the red children, and for his grandchildren's grandchildren — if the Aliens let them live long enough to have any.

"It grieved the old Chief Black Hoof mightily when Tecumseh refused to listen to reason and sign the Greeneville Treaty. The old chief held great affection for the young man, who reminded him of all that had been fine and beautiful about the Shawnee in better times when they were still strong. But Tecumseh steadfastly refused to even think seriously about signing any treaty, holding fast to his solemn oath and word to his father regarding that subject. He also believed the Aliens would never keep any promises, that they would continue to destroy them all. He felt the only chance for the Shawnee, and the Indian people in general, was to get these treacherous men's attention in a strong way by uniting and speaking in one voice, so the Aliens would have to deal honestly with all of them. He felt that to quit fighting and simply give in was outright cowardice, if not total madness.

"In this Greeneville Treaty, the People received twenty thousand dollars for almost twenty million acres of land, and the promise of a yearly annuity of nine thousand five hundred dollars to be divided among all the tribes who signed. The Shawnee portion was one thousand dollars. Some tribes received five hundred dollars, others received even less. This was not paid not in cash money, but in trade goods such as salt and cloth yard goods. There was special irony in this stipulation: when the People had been free, they went to the salt licks and creeks and procured salt themselves, and had hunted the deer and used their skins for clothing. But now, as prisoners on these small reservations, they had to accept such necessities from the Aliens or do without. In reality, the reservations were just short of prisoner-of-war camps.

"It took six months of negotiation to bring all the chiefs to Fort Greeneville for the treaty signing. The first two months before the chiefs arrived not a single word was sent to the chiefs about their having to give up any more land rights, only that the Aliens could freely settle unmolested north of the Ohio River. In the actual negotiations during the months of the chiefs' hostage stay, many weeks were spent arguing over another agreement called the Muskingum Treaty, in which some chiefs were accused of ceding land belonging to other chiefs who were present in Greeneville. All denied having participated in the signing of that treaty, and it was a bitter dispute and delayed the business at hand, which in itself was difficult to resolve. The Muskingum Treaty and some other un-known agreements were forced on the chiefs and caused much ill will among the various tribes. This tactic stripped the tribes of land, friend-ship, and dignity. In reality three treaties were signed and each consecu-tive one changed the agreement considerably in the favor of the Aliens, until it finally reached the form that was executed, thus relieving the People of the 'burden' of their own self-protection and their land. The three different versions were signed by different groups of the People, not always by the chiefs and certainly not always the ones with whom the negotiations had originated. This was not because the original chiefs were no longer available, but because the terms had changed without their agreement and the revisions were being slipped through on the sly. Mad Anthony Wayne proved to be as destructive to the People on paper as he was on the battle field."

The little red Pipe sounded sad as he said, "Tecumseh spent much time using me for prayers for his people and for his own state of mind and heart during these difficult times. These times were more than he could bear without help from his ancestors. Tecumseh loved his people with a fierce intensity; they were the whole reason for his existence. He felt he had failed both the People and his own sacred purpose in life. Should he have taken the war path? Tecumseh did much reassessing of his life, and continually asked for help in his prayers. If his people had to suffer the loss of their freedom, he wanted to be able to accept that honorably, even though he would never be able to tolerate that loss himself without its destroying his spirit and possibly even his mind. He was in dire need of spiritual assistance.

"After the treaty became set and was executed in all its terms, Tecum-seh and his brother Open Door, also known as the Prophet, did their best to live under the Greeneville Treaty's terms, even though they neither signed nor agreed to it. Between 1798 and 1805 they lived off and on in Indiana and Ohio; from 1798 to 1801 they lived among the White River Delaware. In 1802 the brothers moved to Greeneville, Ohio, and estab-lished their first town which they maintained about a mile from the fort.

"Remember, Young Watcher," the Pipe said to the intently listening boy, "the Prophet had had his vision by 1805 and had become a different person from the disgusting wretch he had been in his youth. He was a spiritually inspired man. He had journeyed to Creator's home and been shown many things that changed him for the good, and also shown where his own life would end if he did not change his ways. The Prophet had been shown that the red children could regain their former strength and stature by returning to the ways that had made them strong in the beginning and abandoning the things that had been designed for other creatures, including the Aliens' ways and their material goods.

"It was at this time the Prophet became a spiritual leader. He returned to Indiana to preach to the Indians there for the return of the old, strong ways. He actually traveled many thousands of miles, tens of thousands of miles by some estimates, the next few years. Many tribes west of the Mississippi River have records of his visits. The Prophet is said to have been a more compelling orator than even his brother Tecumseh, but out of the awe in which he held Tecumseh, he never spoke in councils when Tecumseh did. But the Prophet was both inspired and inspiring and was extremely effective in his new life's mission.

"The People needed internal strength, the kind that comes only from Creator and the spirits. At last the Prophet believed he had something he could contribute. His brother Tecumseh had always been especially blessed, having been born under the eye of the Spirit Water Panther, but people seemed to forget that he too was born under a great sign, as one of a set of triplets, born to a people among whom multiple births were almost unheard of. Finally he had had his own personal vision, and received his spirit helpers.

"Having returned from his spirit journey to Kohkumthena, he worked honestly and earnestly to convince the People to 'be strong by doing what is right,' in the manner taught by Kohkumthena in the first creation. They were to give up all the things of the Aliens that they had become dependent upon, to go back to traditional foods, clothing, tools, and religion. Even the pets they had acquired from the Aliens, their cats and domestic breeds of dogs, were to be given back. Buffalo were scarce by then, the elk having moved far north and west out of their range, and the deer were not as plentiful as before the Aliens' arrival, but the People were encouraged to leave the cows and pigs and be satisfied with what Kohkumthena had originally provided them. It was not an easy thing the Prophet insisted they do, but he, like his brother Tecumseh, was a powerful orator and his sincerity influenced many to join the sacred village at Greeneville that had become known as Prophet's Town.

"At the Prophet's insistence the People began returning their domesticated animals of cats, cows, dogs, and hogs. They stopped eating the Aliens' meat and reverted back to the game animals the men hunted. But when the Prophet demanded that the women give up the wheat flour, cloth, and metal needles, as well as their metal cooking pots which he demanded they replace with clay pots or old-style skin cooking pouches, the women greatly resisted. Eventually they reached a compromise: the women could continue using these items but could only acquire them through traditional barter. Positively no money was to be used.

"This compromise allowed the People to continue using the metal tools as well as guns, although they did practice more and became proficient with their traditional weapons again. Demanding that the People use barter instead of money brought back into focus the balance of life, where nothing is ever taken from life or the earth without returning something of at least equal value to it. The People had been so long under the influence of the Aliens' value system that many had forgotten this basic tenet of their life. The compromise was never graciously accepted by the Prophet. He never stopped preaching and haranguing the People to live the pure, simple life of their ancestors.

"The village of Prophet's Town at Greeneville grew from a couple of hundred revitalized converts to over three thousand. People were constantly coming and going, as if on a pilgrimage to the town. They came and stayed for a few weeks or months and then went back to their tribal homes, renewed in the old instructions of life and the way it was to be lived. As the spirituality of the town thrived it overtaxed the natural resources of the community. It was hard to feed so many people in one area. The old way of life had villages of much more modest size. To add to the stress on the natural resources, the actual town of Greeneville, a mile away, was now a growing and prospering community of Aliens. The presence of so many red children so close to Greeneville unnerved the white inhabitants. It never occurred to the Aliens to stop building so close to Prophet's Town. Their attitude continued to be that the red children had no right to exist, especially so close to them, no matter who had been there first, and most especially since the signing of the Greeneville Treaty. The Aliens continued to pressure the government to remove all traces of the red children. These Aliens are strange-thinking creatures, Young One," Tecumseh's Pipe said thoughtfully, "and I believe they are very dangerous.

"The red children thought they had given permission only for the Aliens to come share that portion of the land with them, while the Aliens thought the treaty meant the red children were to give the land to them and disappear from the face of the earth, for there was no provision for new locations for the red children to live on in exchange for the approximately seventeen million acres that were now available to the Aliens. It was an extremely confusing time, and miscommunication added to the growing hostility between the Aliens and the People.

"While the Prophet was trying to revitalize the red children, his brother Tecumseh was living peaceably under the terms of the treaty, even though it galled him. He changed his tactics and instead of being a warrior with guns and the war clubs, he began being a warrior with words. He had long been noted as an eloquent speaker, but now he was a man whose whole spirit poured into his words and so into the ears and hearts of his listeners.

"Tecumseh had studied the Aliens' government in an effort to try to discover a way to live in harmony with them. He already knew they wanted all the Indian land, but he was also familiar with the example that Benjamin Franklin had used concerning the strength of a bundle of sticks versus that of a single stick. When he spoke to the tribal people who came to visit his brother's spiritual city, he used Franklin's analogy: red children, united in their efforts, could become strong enough that the Aliens' government would have to deal with them in an honorable way and stop being deceitful and dishonest. He had given up the dream of winning anything through warfare and directed his energies toward establishing an effective diplomatic relationship. The government had pitted tribe against tribe in many ways, mainly to keep them from uniting in a common front, and it had been disastrously effective," Tecumseh's Pipe sighed.

"As Tecumseh kept trying to unite the various Indian people to stand together, and the Prophet tried to lead them back to their traditions, Black Hoof became bitter towards Tecumseh for the trouble the younger man was making, and the retribution Black Hoof believed his peaceful Shawnee were suffering because of Tecumseh's resistance. The estrangement hurt both men," the plain little Pipe commented.

"The reality of the Shawnee's being forced to resettle on small restricted communities in northwest Ohio became an increasingly bitter situation for the People there. They were forced to farm in the new Alien ways, grow the new Alien foods, breed and raise the Aliens' domestic animals, and worst of all, 'stay put.' No more hunting camps, fishing camps, or moving when the land needed to rest and replenish itself. They had no choice but to stay. The assistance from the Aliens' government in starting over in this new way was either short of the promises and a long time arriving or simply nonexistent. Had the Quakers not come to their rescue, the People would have perished early on.

"It was the beginning of the very saddest bad times. I saw them all through Tecumseh's experiences.

"Young One," Tecumseh's Pipe said, "I wish I had time to tell you about the People's lives in Black Hoof's town and how things were, but I do not. My time is so short and the story of my owner is so critical to your understanding of why and where your people are today, that it must take precedence. Later, you can be taught more. You should read a book that was written by Henry Harvey, one of the Quakers who, with his family, lived with your people for forty-two years. They helped the People on these Ohio reservations, and when the People were moved west to Kansas, the Society of Friends, the official name of the Quaker organization, sent them back to help the People again. Harvey and his family were the only Aliens who attended the funeral of Black Hoof.

"Harvey was such a good person it was difficult for your ancestors to understand how he could have been one of the Aliens. His heart was more Shawnee, even though he worshipped Creator in the Aliens' way. He and his family were part of the very few who seemed to know how to live by the words they spoke and the commandments of their black book. They worshipped Creator, not the sacred circle of money. But now I need to tell you about those last years I had with Tecumseh."

The catlinite Pipe appeared to intensify in its color, becoming bright, its simple reed stem becoming a golden yellow. Had Young One not known better he would have thought it was full of burning tobacco. The voice of Tecumseh's Pipe spoke again, with the ring of authority that made the Young One listen most attentively.

"It was prior to this time that Tecumseh was living in peace that I was given to him by one of the warriors of another tribe. While he already had several other pipes, he graciously accepted me, appreciating my fine, simple craftsmanship. He was aware that pipes of my catlinite stone have a short life span and must be replaced after several years, so he took pains to reserve me for his special occasions, usually his private prayer times. He generally used his more durable steel headed peace-hawk for all other occasions.

"I traveled with him as he made the circuits of the southern tribes almost every fall. He had relatives scattered all over, especially in the South, so he would mix business with pleasure and visit them while trying to convince the other nations to join his coalition. I do know that the leg and hip he damaged during a buffalo hunt as a young man bothered him more and more during the cold, wet winters, especially as he got older. As all Shawnee are, he was a practical man, and saw the advantage of timing his regular trips south with the bad weather here in the northern homeland.

"The constant movement of the leaders, and comings and goings of the many Indians visiting the brothers, grated on the nerves of the Aliens who had chosen Greeneville as their permanent home. Finally, faced with the growing hostility among the Aliens at Greeneville, the Prophet and Tecumseh decided they would move again. The Potawatomis in Indiana offered them a place near the junction of the Wabash and the Tippecanoe rivers, near what is now Lafayette, Indiana. So in 1808 the brothers removed themselves and their people from Ohio and began anew in Indiana. The Prophet had done well in preaching to the various tribes, and by the time they left Ohio, there were about three thousand Indians in their camp on a daily basis. The new Prophet's Town was destined to be equally successful. I was happy to be packed in Tecumseh's personal bundle which he kept close to him always," the modest Pipe said proudly.

"During those last few years Tecumseh and I traveled more than fifty thousand miles on foot, horseback, and by canoe, trying to convince other tribes to join his coalition." The Pipe's voice then grew sharp. "Young One, there is a misconception among some of the people that Tecumseh was what is termed a pan-Indian. He did not try to homogenize all Indian people into one universal tribe or culture. Tecumseh himself was totally Shawnee, refusing to think of changing himself, and he had even returned to the most traditional Shawnee culture he possibly could. He felt that was the way Kohkumthena had made him and that was what he was to remain always. He respected the varied, traditional cultures of all Indian people. He was not trying to create a new state or country or a new tribe of people, he was only trying to get everyone to band together politically to present a united front to the Government so every one would be treated equally, fairly, and honorably," the Pipe explained.

"Never forget, Young One, that it is not necessary that everyone think alike or act alike for them to be respected and be friends. Creator has made each of her children different, and each of her families of children, the tribes. The ancestors were very accepting of differences. What mattered was respect, person to person. The same is true today. Beware of those who must have everyone conform. They are a danger to free people.

"It was in the hot late July to August in 1810 when Tecumseh went to Vincennes to speak with Governor William Henry Harrison to tell him that the government's treatment of the tribes had reached a deplorable point. Tecumseh was at his most eloquent in the old French town on the Wabash. Although he could speak English well enough when he wanted to, on official parleys he always chose to speak the Shawnee which would influence his Indian brothers, leaving the interpreters to translate his words into their own ideas of proper English. Tecumseh never let the Aliens know exactly how well he understood English, which was a definite advantage for him, as he could tell when the translators misinterpreted. At the same time, he never missed the true meanings of the English-spoken words. There were rumors he could even write some English, and he did try, but beyond his own personal wigiwa he would never even hint at that capability.

"When he and his entourage of about two hundred arrived at Vincennes, Harrison had already tried to have everything staged to his own advantage. Tecumseh and his people refused to sit in the hard chairs Harrison had provided for them, though, and chose to sit on Mother Earth as they were accustomed. This simple thing seemed to irk Harrison. As the communications continued between the two leaders, each totally convinced he was within his Creator-given and legal rights, it became obvious there would be no meeting of the minds. Harrison raved on as usual, trying to make Tecumseh look like he was either stupid or dishonorable, and finally Tecumseh's temper got out of hand and he yelled at Harrison's interpreter, 'Tell him he lies!' Tecumseh went for his tomahawk, Harrison went for his sword. For a moment the two glared at each other, then drew back, and the meeting was adjourned for the day.

"Oh, what a sight my owner Tecumseh was when he was in action. He was not only handsome by even his enemies' descriptions, but his body was, strong, supple, and beautiful to watch in motion. His movements were confident without being cocky or arrogant, his perfectly erect posture regal in bearing. Tecumseh was tremendously skilled in all the activities that men were responsible for then, hunting, running, gaming, tracking, even map making for war plans. His voice was commanding without being abrasive, eloquent without being patronizing. His smile was utterly dazzling as were his perfect white even teeth. His dress was impeccable. His eyes exuded intelligence. His manner was respectful and kind, unless he was dealing with Aliens like Harrison, who were not truth-tellers, or were dishonorable in some other way. It seemed the one thing he could not do was to change the minds of the Aliens so they would let the Indian people live peacefully among them. He desperately wanted a place in the heart of the homeland for the Indian people to be able to remain living unmolested."

The red stone Pipe seemed to exude warmth as it spoke so glowingly of its former owner, causing the Young One to wish he could have known Tecumseh personally as the pipe had.

"The next day Harrison and Tecumseh met again. I have to hand it to Tecumseh," said the Pipe. "He apologized for his bad temper and manners and he and Harrison sat on a log, just the two of them, and calmly began discussing their situations. As they continued their good discussions, at the end of each point, Tecumseh would inch closer to Harrison's end of the log. After several of these movements, Harrison shifted closer to the end of the log himself, away from the encroaching Tecumseh. Several more shifts from each man occurred, when Harrison held up his hand, and told Tecumseh, 'If you shift once more I will have no place left to sit.' Then Tecumseh flashed that brilliant smile and said, 'Ah, I see you now understand. If you force my people to move any more they will have no place to stand.' Even the newspapers reported this story. The sad part is, that was precisely what Harrison wanted: for the Indians to have no place to live in his territory of Indiana, at least not as a free people.

"Harrison believed in slavery when it was dressed in pretty words. He believed farming was the American way to a good life, at least for the farm owners. Therefore the only way he thought the People could serve the American Alien interest in any useful purpose was by learning to farm the white way, or by becoming so financially dependent on the Aliens that they would more or less become indentured servants.

"By the time he returned to Prophet's Town at the Tippecanoe, fall was at hand. It was time for Tecumseh to make another trip to the South, and he coached his brother the Prophet on all that could possibly happen while he was gone, and what actions should and should not be taken. After meeting with Harrison, Tecumseh had the feeling that Harrison would wait until he was gone and then try to provoke the Prophet into some action that Harrison could use as justification to attack the tribal town. Residents of Prophet's Town included many warriors of various nations, some who had seen much battle in other circumstances. Again and again, Tecumseh warned his brother that no matter what Harrison did, the Prophet was not to allow himself to be provoked into any kind of confrontation or battle. The Prophet understood what Tecumseh was saying, but the Prophet was also totally convinced that Prophet's Town and its people were protected by Creator and could not be destroyed. Still, Tecumseh demanded that his brother promise to obey his orders. If Harrison marched on them while Tecumseh was gone, the Prophet was not to fight them. If need be, the Prophet should pack up the People and run away from Harrison's advance. Tecumseh knew towns and villages could be rebuilt; rebuilding coalitions and lives was another matter.

"Tecumseh had been gone for several weeks before trouble came." The pipe stopped speaking for a moment as if collecting its thoughts. "I was with Tecumseh on the trip south. He had planned to see the tribes who were almost persuaded to join, to see if he could convince them this time to unify their efforts in dealing with the Aliens. The leader felt things went reasonably well with the Cherokee; he had managed to extract some promises of warriors who would join him in the spring. But the Choctaw were hard to convince, as were the Chickasaw. The Creek at Tuckabatchee gathered in a crowd of about five thousand to hear him speak. But when he had finished speaking he strode into the lodge of their chief Big Warrior, and accused him of only accepting Tecumseh's words, sticks, wampum, and war hatchet, without having any intentions whatsoever of joining him in fighting the Aliens. Tecumseh accused Big Warrior of doubting that he was there because the spirits had sent him. Tecumseh said he would prove the validity of his mission with a sign. When he got back to

Detroit, he would stomp his foot and every home in Big Warrior's village would be destroyed."

The Pipe became thoughtful. "Tecumseh was not one to behave in this manner usually, and it totally unnerved not only Big Warrior, but the people of the village as well. They began to estimate when Tecumseh would arrive back at Detroit, each day dreading just a little more what might come. On the day they had determined he should arrive in Detroit, a mighty rumbling sound like thunder rolled through the land and the earth began to shake violently, until every house lay in a shambles on the ground. Some said that the very day it occurred, December 16, 1811, Tecumseh had arrived at Detroit. (In reality, he was still traveling and recruiting.) At that very moment, the word throughout the southern lands was that Tecumseh had a sign that his mission was sanctioned by the spirits. Many warriors of many nations decided that in the spring they definitely would join him in fighting the American Aliens.

"It was an awe-inspiring sign indeed that Tecumseh had given the tribes of the south. The New Madrid earthquake, which was the most devastating and powerful quake of any known to this part of the world, was commencing. Major shocks continued for almost two full months, and aftershocks for yet another two. The force of the quake caused the Mississippi River to stop flowing and to literally reverse its course, flowing backwards for many days and causing major changes in the landscape seen today along the Mississippi and the bordering states. Weeks before the quake many of the natural nations had shown peculiar behavior. Old histories of Indiana recorded squirrels migrating in swarms of tens of thousands, and birds in a constant state of unrest. Hunting for food became difficult as game seemed to disappear. The quake was felt so far east that chandeliers shook in ceilings, chimneys fell, and walls cracked as far away as New York City.

"Tecumseh, with only eight of his usual companions, returned to Tippecanoe in early January of 1812. A ferocious battle had occurred at the ground near where the Tippecanoe entered the Wabash, and he had had no prior warning of it. He was utterly stunned at the charred rubble that had been Prophet's Town. Surely his brother had not been so stupid as to have challenged Harrison, Tecumseh thought. And where had everyone gone? In a short while a few men, survivors who were hiding with the small residue of the village with the Prophet at Wildcat Creek, came to continue sifting the ashes for whatever useful items they could salvage. From them Tecumseh learned the terrible truth of the battle there. He learned that after the troops led by Harrison had overcome the warriors, the Prophet had been deserted by about five-hundred or so warriors and their families. Only two hundred survivors had followed him to the poorly constructed camp about ten miles away in the thickets of Wildcat Creek. Tecumseh's face became darker and darker as he approached the battle area. By the time he came to where his own wigiwa had stood, he had no control left. I heard him weep."

The Pipe's strong voice became hushed as it continued. "Tecumseh stared at the charred remains of his fine home and the piles of ashes everywhere. The survivors told stories of thirty-eight warriors who were killed and left on the battlefield where Harrison allowed his men to loot their bodies, and scalp and skin them. This made Tecumseh's blood boil even more. These slaughtered men had been his friends, his allies, even relatives. His rage welled up until he could no longer contain it, and he bellowed a resounding oath up to Kohkumthena's Lodge to fight the American Aliens to the death. For sixteen years he had lived peacefully under the terms of that odious Greeneville Treaty. But in his heart he had believed all along that someday the Americans would do something like this.

"Tecumseh then asked the survivors to take him to his brother the Prophet. The Potowatomis had taken him prisoner, tied his hands behind him, and tethered him by the neck to a tall post set in the ground. For a moment when Tecumseh saw his brother there was total silence as their eyes locked. The Prophet looked at Tecumseh with shame and remorse and a silent plea for mercy in his eyes. But Tecumseh's rage was still strong. The Prophet whined several sobbing excuses for what had happened, trying to shift the blame. But Tecumseh knew. He grabbed the Prophet by the throat, and we all thought for a moment he would kill the Prophet on the spot. Oh, Tecumseh's rage was terrible. Had I not been of stone, even I would have trembled. After what seemed a small eternity, Tecumseh finally gave the Prophet a violent shake, shoved him down and walked away. Most were very relieved that he did not kill his brother, even though many thought the Prophet deserved it." The Young One could almost feel the little catlinite Pipe shuddering as it remembered that terrible scene.

"By now all hope for a united front against the government had perished. But the rage inside Tecumseh now blazed more hotly than it ever had in all his life. He knew now that there would not be any hope of honorable treatment for the People. Nothing less than total annihilation of the red children would satisfy Aliens like Harrison. Over and over in his mind, the details of this battle haunted him. Harrison had traveled more than sixty miles into neutral Potowatomi territory, into true Indian territory where there had never been a problem, and had provoked the Prophet into this ultimate stupid blunder, a battle he could not win. There was *no* honor among the Aliens, especially this Harrison. But Harrison was a capable military leader, and a hard-striking foe. It would be hard for Indian warriors to fight him and win. Tecumseh had been wooed by the British lately, and their support might be necessary now if he were going to win. He would let the British know that he was now willing to fight with them to defeat the American Aliens and would come to Fort Malden near Detroit to meet with them. He would have to ask the remainder of the People if they wanted to follow him on the warpath or return to their tribal homes.

"He positively spluttered — I was the only one close enough to hear his words," confided the little Pipe, "as he kept muttering, 'I don't know who is my worst enemy, Harrison or my brother, this . . . prophet!' For months he continued second-guessing his own wisdom in letting the Prophet live instead of throttling him to death on the spot. It was a dreadful thing to hear. Tecumseh, who had always appeared tall, seemed even taller than usual now that he was filled with loathing and pure hatred of the American Aliens. Malice fairly dripped when he mentioned them, or Harrison, or his own egotistically stupid brother. These were indeed bad times, Young One," the red stone Pipe said quietly.

"It took Tecumseh many months to settle down and be able to speak to his brother again. In the meantime Tecumseh had the Prophet's captors untie the Prophet's hands and neck and allowed him to walk about near his wigiwa. It was as if the Prophet were under house arrest. Shunned by all, the Prophet fully realized his failure, and nothing he could ever do would ever change any of the past for the better. He would have to learn to live in disgrace with the results of the Battle of Tippecanoe for the rest of his life," Tecumseh's Pipe explained.

"Eventually Tecumseh calmed down enough that he could look at his brother without having to control himself to keep from beating him. And finally, he sat and talked with him, asking him about what happened. Of course Tecumseh had heard most of the details from others, but he needed to give his brother one chance to tell him something to redeem himself.

"Once again the Prophet had undergone a transformation. Gone was any vestige of arrogance. For once in his life he didn't try to lie or shift too much of the blame, although he did say that both experienced and untried warriors had influenced his decision, that he had tried to reason with them to not fight, but in the end they threatened to fight with his permission and blessings or without them. Even Tecumseh had to agree that the plan his brother had come up with had been a fine one. If the warriors had had one and a half more minutes to place all their men for effective military action, they might easily have won the battle. Some had said the Prophet had claimed to have had a dream instructing him to tell the men they could fight and not be killed, that bullets would not hurt them. Tecumseh never discussed this dream with his brother. It was a subject that was never brought up between them.

"The Prophet explained to Tecumseh how they had received word that Harrison was on the move a week before he actually arrived, but they never dreamed he would come so close. This was Potowatomi territory, and the territorial governor had no reason to come here. By the time it became apparent beyond a doubt that Harrison's destination was Prophet's Town, he was already nearby. The Prophet explained that he thought Harrison would stop and camp the usual distance of several miles away from the town, and so had been trying to think of how to handle the 'talks' he anticipated Harrison asking for, and praying for guidance. But Harrison had marched longer and farther each day than was usual and had crossed the Wabash River, and approached Prophet's Town actually before the Prophet was aware of his proximity. By then it was far too late to try to run or move the women and children out.

"Harrison had sent word he wanted to talk, but the Prophet had begged for time to prepare. And then began the worst night of the Prophet's life, as he awaited the confrontation with an Indian-hating frontiersmen's army and eventual defeat. After listening, Tecumseh only looked at his brother with a blank face, made a singular sound with his voice, and walked away. From that day forward the Prophet became a docile man who followed Tecumseh's every suggestion, with never a word of dissent. To the end he maintained a few hundred faithful followers, but never again achieved anything like his old prominence or glory. He was aware he owed his life to his brother and developed a sincerity in his dealings with others that he had never had before. Only when he spoke to the Aliens years later, telling them what he chose to think they should hear, was he dishonest, but this was allowed by Shawnee rules of life. You were permitted to treat enemies in any manner, but to your own Shawnee brothers you were always kind and honorable."

The Young One considered all this for a moment. It made sense to him.

"During the next few months I was used a great deal, especially when Tecumseh was alone. Several times he used me at councils with the British officers. The People had lost almost everything to the Aliens' torches at Tippecanoe, and the worst was that the ultimate sacred tribal bundle had been partially burned. While some of the warriors had gone back to the ruins and salvaged what they could of the food caches and items which escaped the fires, there was great need for practical utensils and essentials of living to be able to survive this hard winter. Even their iron cooking pots had been destroyed. Some men went hunting east of the Wabash, and others went to live with their Delaware relatives on the White River near today's Anderson, Indiana, while Tecumseh set off for Canada to ask the British for relief. When spring arrived the survivors moved back to Tippecanoe and planted gardens.

"Once the People were settled in back at Tippecanoe, Tecumseh started traveling again, recruiting, but this time he went as someone trying to establish a diplomatic coalition, not as a war chief looking for warriors to fight with him and the British against the American Aliens. By the middle of June he had arranged for the various groups who had pledged to join him to travel northward in small groups, so as to not alarm Harrison, until they reached Canada. The fact he was able to recruit anyone after the disaster at Tippecanoe is a testament to the persuasive oratory skills of this great man. War had been declared June 17, 1812, while he was still at Fort Wayne, but because news traveled slowly then he was safe at Fort Malden on the Detroit River in Canada before word reached him at the end of June. Meanwhile, Harrison, heady with his success at Tippecanoe, took it upon himself to destroy as many Indian towns as he could. He marched on a village on the Mississinewa River and attacked the Miami followers of Little Turtle who were trying to be peaceful and were not his enemy. Harrison had become almost frenzied in his zeal to subdue or eliminate all Indian people in his area, and, as in the case of Tippecanoe, even out of his area.

"In November of 1812 a militant posse came to the Tippecanoe camp and burned it to the ground again. Fortunately the Prophet and his people had abandoned the camp just a few weeks earlier, joining Tecumseh at Amherstburg, Ontario. The sister of Tecumseh and the Prophet, Tecumapease, and Tecumseh's son Pachetha were with the Prophet and had gone to Canada with him. The Prophet located himself several miles to the southeast of Amherstburg with his meager group of loyal followers, so as to not be a source of irritation to Tecumseh and his warriors.

"Finally it seemed Tecumseh's fortunes were changing. The British, his new allies, had a General Isaac Brock, a man who knew how to conduct war successfully. Brock and the Shawnee leader became good friends, as well as allies, and of course this built mutual respect. Tecumseh had seen many Alien military leaders, but never one who was as brilliant, courageous and honest as Brock. Their relationship quickly escalated into a deep friendship, equal to a traditional brotherhood adoption.

"Together Tecumseh and Brock executed many successful military campaigns, including the capture of Detroit. As happened all too often in Tecumseh's life, however, good fortune was short lived, for his dear friend went to another area of conflict and was killed in a battle. He was replaced by General Henry Proctor, who was such an inept and cowardly leader that Tecumseh told him he reminded him of a frightened dog who runs away with his tail tucked under his belly." The red stone Pipe made a deep-throated sound, expressing disgust. "It was Proctor's cowardice that created the scenario for the death of my owner.

"Event after event, battle after battle, this Proctor proved to be a false leader. Oh, a time or two he came up with a good idea and would have the nerve to implement it, but usually he made inept and incomplete battle plans. He seemed not to grasp the situations in their true context, or use his men or the landscape to his advantage. Worst of all in Tecumseh's mind, Proctor had no heart or stomach for fighting. Even before battle would begin, he would squirm and look furtively around for avenues of retreat. He made Tecumseh fairly nauseated with his flagrant cowardice, lack of cooperativeness and general ineptitude. Proctor for the most part treated Tecumseh's people as a diversion against the American armies, so his own soldiers could flee to safety. Soon Tecumseh realized his people were indeed being destroyed and there was to be no help from the British. His heart sank lower than it ever had in his life.

"Young One, I am still filled with grief over Tecumseh's loss, even after all these years. Never have we seen a man like him since that time. If the Ancient Mask doesn't mind, I would like to stop speaking for a while now. This is too painful for my heart to tell. Perhaps Tecumseh's war clubs will tell you this next part. They too were with him to the end, but they are made of stouter stuff than I am." And with that, and a final small sound of anguish from re-experienced grief, the catlinite Pipe became silent.

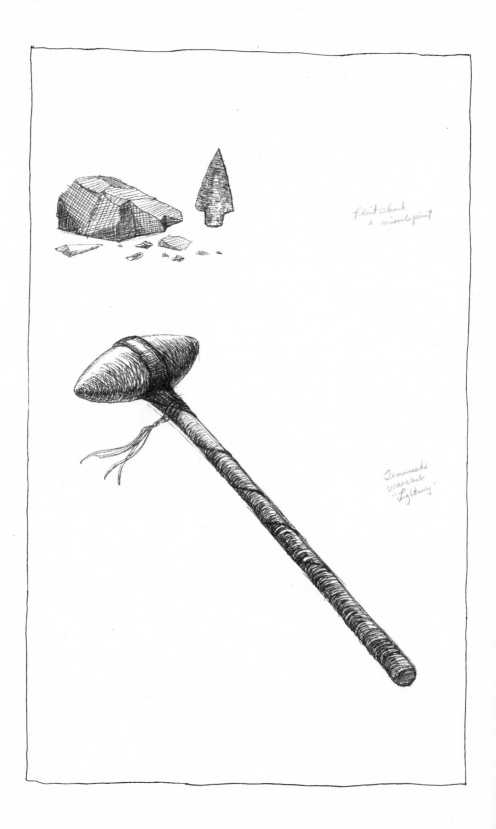

flint chank
& missile point

Tecumseh's
war club
"Lightning"

The deep rumblings that had been felt as well as heard at the beginning of the night again began to reverberate in the Young One's head. Finally he could discern the words of the Great Mask. "Ah, my friends, you Great House Stones have been doing a wonderful job of telling the old stories of Young One's people. I am proud of each of you. While it is customary for the Great House to be a sacred place, and only items used in ceremonies have been the primary speakers tonight, this occasion calls for the whole story of Tecumseh's end to be told and I agree with the warrior's sacred catlinite Pipe, that this would be best told from those who were with him at the end."

The Great Ancient Mask renewed his powerful vibrating communications, saying, "You, Tecumseh's war club with the heavy round head, I will refer to you as 'Thunder,' for truly the last thing the enemy must have been aware of was a sound like thunder as you struck him. And you, other war club of Tecumseh, I will call 'Lightning,' because of your points at each end. It is known to us that Tecumseh slept with you both at his head within arm's reach at all times. You were as intimately attached to him as anything else he possessed except his powaka bag. Which of you will begin telling this sad story of Tecumseh's end?"

Lightning spoke first: "Young One, I want you to understand about us old war clubs as weapons. Our designs are simple, ancient and effective. We are made of the hardest stones. Tecumseh himself chipped out a small groove around our middles, so when he attached the strong leather that held our handles in place, he could be certain we would never slip and fail him. His life depended on our efficiency, durability, and reliability. There could be no slippage of the handles. Thunder is a natural stone: the shape you see him in is the shape Creator gave him in the beginning, except for the small channel for his lashings. I have been worked and ground to these fine points you see. Of course, I am not a piercing point like a blade,

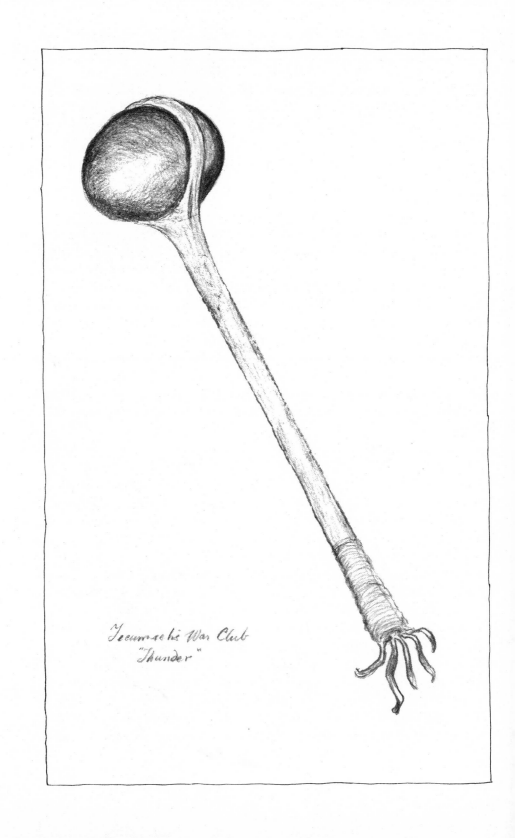

Tecumseh's War Club
"Thunder"

but very pointed for a stone. He worked with me until he had developed a fine shine on my surface and no trace of his grinding was visible. I look as if he coated me with beeswax, as some men do their pipes, but my shine is from his manual polishing so I would not snag as I worked on the battle-field. I shine from the natural polishing I acquired from contact with the enemy's heads as Tecumseh ended their earthly walk and they crossed into Spirit.

"I am proud that Tecumseh was my owner and made me as I am today. I served him and your people well. My handle is over a foot longer than Thunder's, and is still securely covered with the leather that Tecumseh himself sewed so tightly with fine sinew stitches. I still wear a few strands of tiny white seed beads, and one strand of tiny red beads with white hearts, placed there by Tecumseh, signifying war, life and truth. My longer handle made me his weapon of choice when he was on horseback, be-cause I gave his long arms an extended reach.

"Thunder is proud of the bit of fringe at the base of his short, stocky handle. Tecumseh cut that handle with his own knife. Thunder was used mostly when Tecumseh was on the ground. His weight and size gave Tecumseh reassurance that only one stroke would be needed to dispatch the enemy.

"Being an instrument of war is a great responsibility. When the blow was struck I had to gather my strength to make sure I did not shatter myself and leave Tecumseh defenseless. This was my fate, so decided when Kohkumthena created me. It was a privilege to be chosen as a weapon for a man who never used it to kill women, children, or captured prisoners," Lightning said seriously.

There was a slight pause, and then Lightning broke the silence by saying, "If I may, Young One, before I continue Tecumseh's story I have been directed to speak to you of this 'plaything' Creator gave to you hu-mans called 'war.' Creator said when your chiefs could not make sense of things the People would play with this war thing. After a time Creator would step in and calm things down and the People would live sensibly for a while. But this war changed drastically when the Aliens came here.

"They had come from a land that had just held a 'holy' war that lasted a thousand years. They called it the Crusades. The Aliens were accus-tomed to conflicts that took tens of thousands of lives in a single battle, while your People thought the loss of even a single person was not a good thing. Battles taking over a dozen lives might be stopped by the opposing chiefs, who would then renegotiate and try to resolve matters without further bloodshed and loss of life."

Lightning continued explaining: "It was said your people had 'games' of war that were very different from the types of war games that are played today with electronic weapons. Hand-to-hand combat involves looking your enemy in the eyes and making a conscious decision as to whether you will take his earthly life at that moment and send his spirit on its journey to Creator. When that kind of decision is made, you will see, smell, and hear the results of your decision, not just once, but many times before your own spirit journey.

"Life is fragile in two-leggeds, and your lives are short compared to the lives of us stones. Death is as serious as living, but much easier to cause. Destroying another's life must be avoided if it can. When it cannot be avoided, it must be done swiftly, in honorable and accepted ways, not slow and torturously, not abstractly, thoughtlessly or as a sport.

"It is far easier to learn to respect your enemies than to regret the taking of a life once it is gone.

"Today's style of warfare seems dishonorable: an electronic button can be pushed and thirty miles away ten thousand or more people will simply perish. Just when we Stones think we have seen it all, some mind that is not right-thinking comes up with another idea that surprises us," Lightning concluded.

Suddenly a clear, sweet, small voice spoke up. This was the voice of Tecumseh's Powaka Stone, wrapped inside the tribal bundle. It said, "Ancient Mask, you mentioned me, and I would like to speak to the Young One for just a little time. As you all know, I was with Tecumseh since he was about eight years old. I saw him grow from childhood to manhood. It was I to whom he would speak and tell his most intimate thoughts and fears. Small as I am, my powers gave him courage and strength uncountable times in his life. It was my power that others were trying to break by witchcraft at the end. May I speak, oh Ancient Mask?"

The Ancient Mask was astonished by the Powaka's request. It had never spoken since Tecumseh's death, and the Great House Stones had presumed its life was over and only its earthly form remained. The Mask was delighted with its offer to speak to the Young One, for the youth was not the only one who would be learning. All the Stones were eager to hear what the Powaka might say. "Of course!" the Mask said. "We will be delighted to have you contribute, sacred little Powaka. We will all be silent for as long as you wish to speak, so none of your words will be lost. The Lightning and Thunder clubs will not mind waiting for their turn. Please, begin."

The voice of the sacred Powaka was crisp and clear. " You are all aware of the story of how the Spirits placed me in Tecumseh's hand at the bottom of the cold river that icy day when he was eight. The youth had been diving into the winter river every day for over two months, and that last day they chipped the ice and made him dive four times, and on the final dive made him grab whatever he found at the bottom with one hand and then surface. I am not the typical kind of stone that is found in that river, so everyone was stunned that he had been given such a extraordinary powaka. But, after all, this was Tecumseh, the one born under the powerful sign of the Spirit Water Panther. He was always destined to be and to possess the most unusual of everything.

Scouts praying for his protection — River January 1876

"His sister Tecumapease, who raised him after his mother Turtle Woman left in 1779 and went to New Spain, taught him well. It was her influence that helped mold him into the humanitarian that he was. She taught him to value life of all kinds and nations, even though he was the ultimate warrior. It was I he asked to help him find the balance in his life and for clarity of vision. Many nights when everyone had gone to bed, he removed me from my little bag, so he could hold me and gaze into the firelight through my facets and prisms.

"I witnessed so many acts of thoughtfulness and kindness done by my friend Tecumseh that I would not know where to begin. It was hard to reconcile, when he and the Prophet were doing so much good by reawakening the Indian people to their traditions, that Tecumseh's own life was always so full of agony, turmoil, and loss. It seemed the spirits and Kohkumthena, and even He Who Creates By Thinking, had deserted the red children and left them to the murderous whims of these Aliens. But whatever terrible thing the red children had done to offend Creator, Kohkumthena and the Spirits, this punishment, Tecumseh believed, this withdrawal of spiritual help and protection, was too harsh a punishment. In his heart he admitted that the People's forsaking the old ceremonies and taking up the Aliens' ways could have been part of the reason for the extinction he saw coming. They had been warned in the Great Laws. He also realized the agony that alcohol caused, but no one seemed able to stop the flow of that poison. He agonized over what might be done to correct these problems while fighting with all his might to preserve as much of the People as he could until he could find answers.

"I used all my powers to speak to him of good purposes, and did my best to strengthen him when his own energy was spent. When he doubted and would hold me in his hand, I would strengthen myself until he could feel the warmth of my life through his fingertips, and that way he would know we Spirits were still with him.

"You see, Young One, he was the last hope your people had against the Aliens. He was the last of his kind. His brother the Prophet was out of his element, because by tradition and the laws given by Kohkumthena, he was of the wrong sept to be a medicine person, yet he was self-professed as one. Because the People were desperate, they listened to him, but his power was a false or fleeting one. But Tecumseh's power had been foreordained by the Spirits and Kohkumthena before his arrival here on Turtle

Island; that is why they arranged for the 'eye of the panther' to cross overhead and announce his arrival. He was in the hereditary position to be war chief. The outcome has made me wonder if the old ancestors' oral tradition is true, that Kohkumthena made the red children, but the maker of the Aliens is a strange and different god over whom Kohkumthena has no power. And these pale Aliens remembered the sacred words given to them as instructions for living, but they are not right-thinking.

"Let us return to Fort Malden and the British camp. As event after event transpired and General Proctor was caught lying or misrepresenting the true situations to him, Tecumseh became more and more sure that the British were even less honorable than the American Aliens. Did Proctor expect him to create battle plans that would be effective if he did not know the truth of their military situation? Tecumseh's morale was sinking fast. He prayed continuously when he was alone. He created his own network of spies and informants who kept him aware of the true happenings elsewhere. He always heard the truth from them, but it was always at the very last minute.

"Finally he convinced Proctor to stop running and to stand and fight. Even then Proctor would not accept the plans Tecumseh wanted to use and so chose a less advantageous battle site on the Thames River in lower Ontario, Canada, near Moravian Town, and current-day Bothwell. Tecumseh had been correct when he accused Proctor of wanting to run, tail tucked between his legs, all the way back to the Atlantic.

"Other rumors and information came to Tecumseh's ears. Perhaps he discovered these things with his own keen sense of hearing as he walked the camp. Certainly these walks were disheartening. It was obvious to him how much his warriors and their families were suffering. They had few provisions, and they were beginning to look ragged. If they could just hold on, winter was not far away, and the fighting would be suspended for a few months. Everyone was suffering from exhaustion and from all the retreating that had been forced on them the past few months. Tecumseh could see the eyes of the little children losing their sharpness and becoming glazed with the endless traumas they witnessed daily. There were so many orphans in camp now, with their fathers buried hastily along the way after battles and skirmishes. Their mothers without husbands broken-heartedly marched on with Tecumseh, because they had no other place to go.

"Tecumseh was no fool. He knew the only reason they were suffering was because he would not, could not quit fighting because of his sacred oath. The remaining warriors had taken oaths to follow him to the end, so they too were bound.

"His heart ached with the years of losses, of the beautiful Ohio Valley, the Tippecanoe town, his family scattered, his mother living out her life so far from him, his father and brothers lost in battles with the Aliens. He had at first had the foolish notion that if he lived in peace, the Aliens would leave him and his people alone to live out their lives as Kohkumthena had intended them to. Surely there was enough land for them all to share. He had been a good and peaceful person for over sixteen years when this unscrupulous Harrison had come out of his jurisdiction and destroyed Prophet's Town.

"His beloved sister Tecumapease had followed him. Her husband Wasegaboah served as Tecumseh's main bodyguard, and neither of them ever complained. Tecumseh loved her more than anyone in his life. She was his sister, mother, friend, confidante, mentor, advisor and support all his life, and now even more than in the past. He deeply wished to protect her and make her life right and good.

"Still, he was prepared to fight with the English against the American Aliens, come what may. There were at least twelve tribes represented in this last army of Tecumseh's besides the Shawnee, including some Kickapoo, Miami, Delaware, Wyandotte, Potawatomis, Winnebagos, Ottowa, Sauk, Fox, Creek, and Ojibway who had joined him at various times and places. There is a report that a few Sioux and several Menominee were also there. Some of his men, like his brother-in-law Wasegaboah, had been with him from the beginning. His main body of warriors of but a thousand or so were bone and spirit weary. No warrior who is in the condition he now realized his men were in fights well, yet they continued with him day after day."

The voice of the Powaka Stone became tinged with pride and defiance as it continued. "Word came to Tecumseh that a group of Shawnee elders could no longer bear the suffering of the People. They had held a secret meeting and conducted a strange succession of actions that bordered on sorcery, trying to break my powers of protection over him, so that he could be killed on the battlefield. I never felt my powers leave, though I could feel them strain and tire. Keep in mind, Young One, these elders were neither shamans nor medicine men, they were simply old men desperate to end the fighting and to try to save the remainder of the People."

The Young One's heart and mind were very troubled by this story of the Powaka Stone. He had been taught to admire and revere Tecumseh. Today he was considered the People's ultimate hero. How absolutely awful, the Young One thought, that those who were with him could even think of such a thing as bringing about his destruction.

"It was late in the afternoon of October 3, 1813, when weary-hearted Tecumseh stopped at the site of his sister's camp," the Powaka said. "He had been slightly wounded in his arm earlier in the day during a battle with his old enemy William Henry Harrison. Tecumseh looked forward to Tecumapease's presence. Her good nature always gave his spirits a lift. He had learned to do his own moccasin repairs, but his sister's cooking was always something he enjoyed, and his son would probably be there to eat as well. But on this day there was nothing cooking in his sister's pot but hot water. She went out begging from others in the camp for something to put into the pot and returned as he started to leave. Tecumseh saw she had a bag of white beans in her hands that she must have had to beg from one of the white people in the camp, for Indians never had white beans. This was Alien food. He fired dark looks and sharp words at her because she had no true Indian food to cook, and he made her weep. Later he hated himself for his harsh words, but he hated worse these desperate conditions which he felt his own personal actions and stubborn determination had caused for the people he loved the most.

"Tecumseh left his sister's camp and walked alone for a while. After calming his spirit, he returned to the camp, moved by the sights of his people's suffering he saw along the way. His personal heartache grew."

The Powaka Stone stopped speaking for a moment and seemed to take a deep breath, then it somberly continued. "It was difficult for Tecumseh to sleep that night. He tossed and turned until almost the waking hour. Finally he drifted into a fitful slumber, then he started with a violent jerk and sat bolt upright in his bed. He was drenched with sweat and deathly pale. He had had a vision of his own death. Spirits had come and shown him the battlefield with his body lying prone, small pools of his own blood surrounding him. He had felt the impact of the shot as it struck his body. In the vision the force of that shot had flung him to the ground. There on his bed the sensation forced him upward to this sitting position.

"Tecumseh had felt a moment of horror, but was then almost instantly overwhelmed with relief: Finally there would be an end to the constant running, and no longer would he have to smell the stench of death so vivid that it seemed he tasted it on the back of his tongue. He wiped away the sweat, and after a couple of minutes lay back down, considering the meanings of this vision. He had not a single doubt that it would come true. He thought that when he met Creator, he would indeed be able to look Creator in the eye as they discussed his life. No sense of shame would cause him to have to look away at his toes. Of this his heart was glad. He would be allowed to die a dignified warrior's death and not be forced to waste away on a reservation or die in any dishonorable way. He thought of what his warriors and the People would face without him, and he prayed for their future. He was suddenly tired then, and shut his eyes, instantly sleeping more restfully he had in many months. He was awakened by the voice of his sister Tecumapease, calling her beloved brother to eat some of the beans they had quarreled over the night before. It was now October 4, 1813."

The Young One was aware that the Powaka Stone announced the date as a way of preparing him for the day of the battle. A feeling of dread began to creep through his spirit, for he knew all too well what happened on October 5, 1813. Every Shawnee child knew that Tecumseh's band had fought with the British against the American forces at the Battle of the Thames, in what is known as the War of 1812. The Powaka Stone continued now in an even manner, as if it had rehearsed this story too many times. "Quickly he washed the night sweat from his lean but perfect body, dressed and joined his sister for breakfast just as the sun began to peek over the horizon. No words of apology were spoken, nor were they necessary. These two had been good at reading each other's minds and hearts for many years. She knew he was sorry for the harsh words, and that he was embarrassed at having made her weep. He would not do so again. He finished his bowl of food and ruffled her hair as he walked away, as brothers sometimes do to favorite sisters. Her eyes followed him, and admiration and deep love for him filled her heart. Tecumseh had chosen to say nothing of his vision of his death, sparing his beloved sister that pain as long as he could.

"Tecumseh found his main assistant among a small group of warriors. He told the man to get all the warriors together for a meeting, as he needed to speak to them on an urgent matter. A short time later the warriors had all gathered around him, as well as many others in the camp. He nonchalantly put his hand to his throat and held the bag in which I lay in his fingers, and I strengthened myself so he would feel my power and protection still with him. Then he let go and began to speak. He plainly told the men that they were about to engage in a battle against the American Aliens. 'The British have promised to help us,' he said. 'But they will not. They will use us to protect their rear while they flee to safety.'

"Tecumseh explained that he saw nothing but defeat for them if they advanced into this battle, a defeat that would leave even more women and children alone and defenseless. He told the warriors they were free of any and all obligations to him. Any promises they had given him to stay and fight to the end were in essence null and void. Tecumseh encouraged them to leave to return to where it was they had come from or go wherever they pleased. There would be no dishonor, no hard feelings. He would be most grateful that they chose this form of survival over the certain annihilation and defeat they would face if they chose to stay and fight.

"The warriors were stunned! This was Tecumseh, the fearless! This was the man who had taken an oath to fight to the death, and he was giving them leave to simply quit and go home. 'Why have you told us these things?' they demanded. 'I must tell you the truth,' he said. 'For I have been shown I will not leave the battlefield alive. Each of you is here because I asked you to come and join me in this fight to the death for the survival of our people. I meant the fight to my own death; it need not be yours as well. If you stay with me, there will be fewer who will live. The women and children have great need of strong and capable warriors, so the enemy does not destroy them after this battle; for the British will be of no help. They will flee for their own lives, using us to buy time for their personal escape. I beg of you to abandon this promise, and you have my blessings. Quickly gather your families and flee to safety, wherever you may find it, and when you find a home camp, preserve our People as best you can. Creator has chosen to show me my own fate.' His dream of victory was not to be. He looked into their disbelieving faces, then walked away.

"He had gone only a few paces when the voice of a young Winnebago, freshly arrived at the camp, yelled out. 'You can't quit! You made us take a vow to fight and we have come all this way to fight with you, not to tuck tail like Proctor. We will not leave! You are our leader, now lead us!' Several Chippewa, other Winnebagos and some Sioux then took up the same theme. They were for the most part young warriors, yet untried in the field. This was their chance of a lifetime to fight with the legendary Tecumseh, to make reputations for themselves in the fighting fields. They would not be denied.

"Tecumseh looked at them with his steady gaze. He understood their fiery manner and burning hearts, qualities that had appealed to him when he recruited them. He knew they would be on the battleground and would need a leader. Although he was not nearly as old as Black Hoof had been, by most standards he should have been past his prime; yet he was still in peak condition with reflexes still as keen as those of a young warrior. Experience, though, had at last brought him wisdom, and he saw no value in senseless killing. Tomorrow's battle would be just that, for there was no way they could win.

"Again he explained that the battle would be a blood bath, there would be no help from the British, that he would not be there to lead them after the battle. But the young ones would not relinquish Tecumseh from his vow of fighting to the death.

"I heard most of the warriors muttering and speaking in low tones to themselves about this unexpected turn of events," the Powaka Stone said quietly. "Many of them walked away, but first they came forward and shook Tecumseh's hand, or patted him on the back, and some gave him a brotherly hug and walked towards their camp with tears in their eyes.

"More than half of the warriors began packing to leave the camp. The young western warriors stood defiantly glaring at Tecumseh, who glared back and said, 'If you will not relinquish me from my oath, I am prepared to die a warrior's death and will lead you tomorrow.' At these words, many of his oldest comrades in arms began to return and close in about him and listen to the plans for the coming battle.

"In all, about six hundred men stayed. Before his speech he had had little more than a thousand. There had been, however, more than three thousand warriors a few days before. Tecumseh had upbraided Proctor publicly, calling him a coward and pointing out that because of Proctor's ineptitude and indecision, success was almost impossible. Nearly two thousand warriors had chosen to leave at that time, as they realized the implications of Proctor's poor leadership. So now, to those last six hundred faithful fighters, Tecumseh gave more details of his vision. He told them he had seen himself dead on the upcoming battlefield, shot in the mouth. He had seen his body with many wounds, and his life draining away in a widening pool of blood. Even so, he pledged his loyalty to them again.

"For the rest of that day Tecumseh was seen in every area of the camp, up and down the road, speaking first to this one and then that one in the camps and in the surrounding community. He sought out old friends and those who needed encouragement. Now seeming to have been relieved of a great weight, he was his usual good-humored self, and joked readily with his friends. He was serene and reflective. Those who were not at the meeting and had no knowledge of the fateful vision marveled at his composure."

The Powaka Stone slowly finished its part of Tecumseh's story. "That evening he sat and spoke with his key men, advising them on the upcoming battle. In the midst of this council, his body gave a violent jerk as he felt the precursor of the wounds to come. The men were alarmed and dismayed at the details of his vision until he finally told them that when he fell, they should tap him with a ramrod four times, and he would come back to life and be able to rejoin them in the fight. This gave them calm within themselves, thinking they would only suffer a temporary loss of his leadership and prowess. His older brother Chikseeka had given him the same instructions before the battle that took Chikseeka's life.

"While speaking with his dearest and oldest friends, Tecumseh unbuckled his sword and wrapped it neatly with its sash. He gave it to a chief who was his trusted friend, saying, 'See to it that my son Pachetha is given this when he is a warrior. Guide and help him to grow into manhood.'

"Great Mask," said the Powaka Stone. "If you will agree, I would like for the war clubs to resume telling their stories now, and I will continue with what I know when they are through. My position is a mostly spiritual one; I went through only the final segments of Tecumseh's existence here with him, and I tend to speak and relate in spiritual terms. But the clubs know more about the 'warring' than I, and can add much to the battle scenes."

The great and ancient Mask emitted a low tone that was almost a growl. His disposition was becoming very dour. "All right! All right!" the Mask fumed. "We are never going to be able to finish the Young One's education at this rate. But go ahead! Lightning? Thunder? One of you begin now! Let's not dally around. Old Man Sun is coming soon and will witness to Creator what we have done. We must be through teaching before he rises and catches us unfinished in our task. Speak quickly now."

The old Mask, who had been so somber and stately all night long was now speaking as rapidly as the Young One had when he recited Kohkumthena's Great Laws. This was the first time the Young One had been aware of more than one stone speaker at a time. While he cast his eyes around the great House trying to determine which stone object would speak next, he became aware of a rich baritone, stating, "I will begin with the details of the last day of Tecumseh's life, Ancient One." It was the war club with the thick heavy head and short handle, whom the Mask had called Thunder.

"I will continue his story. It is fairly brief at this point," Thunder said. "Before daybreak Tecumseh was up and bathed. He had decided to put aside all that was not pure Shawnee in the way of his attire, except for the medal he wore around his neck, given by the British at some time in the past. His clothes were the simple, close-fitting buckskin that he loved to wear. There was nothing colorful or showy on his person, nothing loose for the enemy to seize and hold. His face was painted for war, and for death. Even then, in his very simplicity, he was striking in appearance, and most of all, serene in his manner.

"It was October 5, 1813, by the Thames River in Ontario, Canada, about thirty miles north of Chatham, and sixty-five miles east of Detroit. The American Aliens numbered three thousand strong, a thousand of whom were fierce Kentuckians, led by the dreaded destroyer of Prophet's

Town at Tippecanoe, General William Henry Harrison. The always land-hungry Americans wanted to capture and claim all of Canada from the British. Tecumseh's army had been the deciding factor which had thwarted them. The battle to come was therefore crucial for all combatants.

"The weapons our Shawnee leader chose to take that day were his rifle, a pair of pistols his great friend, Brock, had given him, his toma-hawk, and the two of us, his war clubs. He was originally fighting from a position of ambush, from a brushy swamp area, so he had his weapons arranged around him for quick, close availability. He knew his guns would run out of ammunition and he was not sure he would have time to reload. It was well known we war clubs were his favorite traditional weapons any-way. I noticed the great leader was quite calm as he readied himself for the battle. His horse was hidden to the rear while he found himself good cover and ground with solid footing, readying himself for the hand-to-hand com-bat to come. It had been difficult for him to bid *tanakia* — farewell — to several of the oldest and most loved friends and comrades around him. But he did not dwell on long good-byes; instead seeming to banish those thoughts from his mind and concentrate on preparing himself and en-couraging others.

"Proctor had already asked him to come and review his troops and make any suggestions he might have on their deployment. Tecumseh thought it strange that now, of all times, Proctor should start behaving in a professional manner. Where had this courtesy and sense been these months? he wondered. As he reviewed Proctor's troops he shook hands with the officers, giving them appropriate salutations and good wishes. Actually he was taking his leave of them, silently extending prayerful thoughts for their fate. Proctor's army numbered about the same as Tecumseh's, about six hundred. When they had left Amherstburg ten days before, Proctor had had twenty field guns, but during the last ten days of retreats he had ordered fifteen of them to be destroyed for fear they would be overtaken by the American Aliens and the guns would be turned on the British themselves. Thus he arrived at Moravian Town with the re-maining five cannon, but with his usual stupidity and lack of foresight, left four of them in the village when his army moved downstream to actu-ally fight.

"To his own men, Tecumseh had already spoken several times con-cerning their responsibilities and positions. Just as the enemy came into view he told them *Ki la wa wishi ga tui!* —be brave and strong. These were the words they kept hearing from him as he fought by their side, until he fell.

"On the north bank of the Thames near Moravian Town, there was a slight elevation. It was there Tecumseh decided to make his last stand. The British front faced downstream while their cowering general Proctor safely positioned himself one quarter of a mile away, in the rear of his columns of men. On the right side of a small swamp were the six hundred Indian warriors under Tecumseh's command.

"Tecumseh had positioned himself where he had determined the fighting would be the thickest. In the tradition of all great Shawnee War Chiefs, he was first to be seen striking a blow if possible, and the last to quit a battlefield. The ground he chose was slightly higher than the swampy areas on each side, giving him a small advantage in sighting the Aliens as they approached."

The war club named Thunder stopped for a moment, recollecting his memories. "Lightning and I waited on the ground within his reach. Our heads were resting on the grass with our handles propped up for his easy grasp. Waiting." The heavy-headed war club again stopped speaking, trying to remember, and despising what he needed to tell next.

"Shall I continue our story, Thunder?" the thinner, double-pointed club asked sympathetically.

"Yes . . . yes, please do," said the sorrow-filled voice of Thunder.

Lightning spoke quickly. "As Tecumseh waited for the Aliens to appear he sprinkled a bit of tobacco on the ground and voiced a quiet prayer. He tucked his little catlinite Pipe back into its bag, and lay it on the ground beside us.

"The American Aliens came swiftly on horseback and all the men on both sides began to fight nobly for the causes they believed Creator had given them. The fighting was intense from the beginning and soon the visibility was clouded as the smoke from gunfire filled the air. The sounds of battle are loud, yet afterwards one usually cannot remember any noise distinctly. Tecumseh's voice was heard for well over an hour, even after his brother-in-law fell from a fatal blow. Tecumseh took many lives of the enemy that day with all of us, his weapons. Though very outnumbered, his men fought skillfully and with great courage."

There was a pause as the old war club seemed to brace itself with a deep breath, before it continued telling this most painful part of his beloved owner's end. "None who survived saw the shot that took his life. Later some could only say they saw him fall.

"All of a sudden, in the terrible din of battle, there was an empty space where his strong voice had been calling out to his men, *Ki la wa wishi ga tui!* — be brave! Instantaneously both sides became aware of his silence at the same time. The warriors stopped their struggles and retreated so silently and quickly that it was eerie. The American Aliens seemed almost stunned by the way their enemies seemed to almost melt into the woods." Lightning spoke more slowly now. "Thunder and I lay out of sight in the tall brush where he had placed us until he needed us, and we were unable to see the light in his eyes die.

"It was over. The mighty warrior was finally released from the vow that at Tippecanoe he had bellowed to Kohkumthena's Lodge, free from fighting and killing. His journeys now would be through the twelve levels of heaven to Kohkumthena's Lodge, and across the sky riding four fast horses who are pure spirit, as he is now."

As Lightning became quiet for a moment thinking on these things, the voice of Tecumseh's Powaka again spoke up. "I would like to continue now, if I may," the Powaka stated.

Lightning answered in a soft and husky tone, "Of course, tell the Young One the rest now."

The Powaka Stone's voice became crystal clear as it continued Tecumseh's story. "Many rumors and myths have sprung up concerning the details of what occurred after the great leader's death. Each witness told a slightly different version of what he saw or remembered, because in most cases, the witnesses weren't even interviewed for twenty years or more after his death. Surveying the twenty-some versions of what happened, it is impossible for anyone today to know what is the whole truth.

"I will tell you the things I, his Powaka know to be true. I speak of the facts that have been preserved by your People, though they generally refuse to speak of them to anyone.

"It is true that Tecumseh died on the battlefield at the Thames River in Ontario, Canada, near Moravian Town, now Bothwell, on October 5, 1813, in the early or mid afternoon. As soon as his warriors were aware of his death they fled the battlefield in great haste.

"Only one credible witness was interviewed immediately, a warrior called Andrew Clark who had become a naturalized Shawnee citizen and served as interpreter to Tecumseh. Clark had been an eye witness to Tecumseh's death and was himself mortally wounded. After the warriors had fled the battlefield, the American Aliens came on the field picking up their own wounded and dead. When they saw Clark they asked him about Tecumseh. He stated that Tecumseh had been killed and moved someplace by his companions. Before he could say any more, he died of his own wounds. That is the closest to the truth that anyone ever spoke, who saw what happened.

"That version that his body was retrieved from the battlefield, carried a good distance and buried is the one your okima was taught.

"Listen to me, Young One, my words will not be much different, but they will add to your understanding of the People's tradition. Indeed the warriors fled the battlefield when they realized Tecumseh was dead or critically wounded. But it has been told that the men went many miles away, and were about to partake of their evening meal when they thought about him, noticing his absence, and decided to go back and retrieve his body before the American Aliens under Harrison could do the nasty scalping and skinning ritual they had performed at Tippecanoe.

"It took more than an hour each way to travel from and to the battlefield, plus the time they spent in their camp composing themselves. Perhaps they were not in any great hurry because of Tecumseh's story to them that they could tap him four times with the ramrod and that would revive him so he could fight with them again. Perhaps. But indeed, this version of the story says that they did retrieve his body and took it with them back to their camp. Three of the men who retrieved him said he had been partially skinned, having flesh strips removed from his thigh and chest by Harrison's Kentucky 'elite.'

"The American Aliens had had more than four hours to do all the carving and peeling that they wanted by that time. It is not true as has been said that there were no people around who knew what Tecumseh looked like so they couldn't identify him. There were at least six men there who could have if they wanted to do so.

"The warriors left Tecumseh's body on a litter all night. Next morning they cleaned and prepared the body, had the medicine man perform a ceremony, did a dance, then . . . they brought out his body on the litter and struck him four times with the ramrod. When he did not respond, they took him far into the woods and buried him in a secret place."

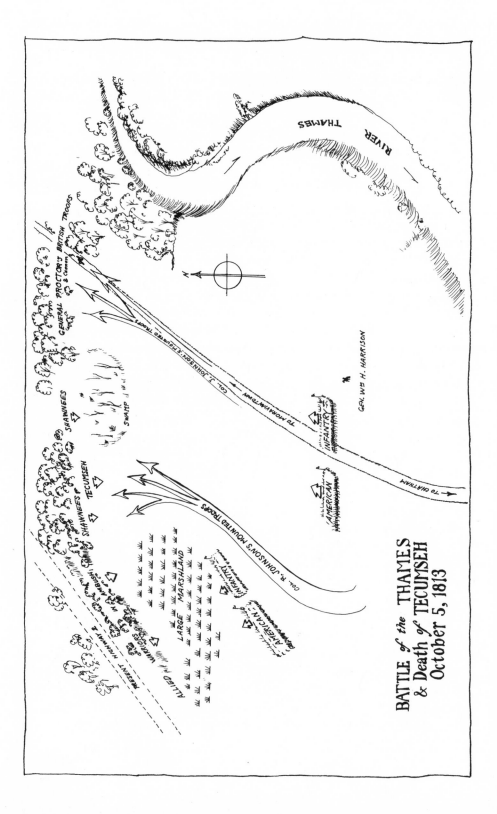

BATTLE of the THAMES
& Death of TECUMSEH
October 5, 1813

The Powaka Stone spoke with reverent tones. "Sometime during that night, a prophecy was made. 'In the seventh generation,' the wise one said, 'Tecumseh will return to his People and fight with them again. The Nation will be strong again as it was before the Aliens came.'

"The last version I have told you is an old Oklahoma oral tradition that has never been told here before, even though it has been told for decades out there. It is time now, for all to understand what happened that night. It seems each tradition contains the truth. The other controversies about where he was buried, and whether his bones were really moved later and interred in the cairn on Walpole Island, will have to be answered some other time. It is tradition that Shawnees never disturb the bones of the dead, but Tecumseh was a peculiar man who lived a peculiar and unique life. We cannot say for certain that he was or was not skinned at least partially, nor can we validate the whereabouts of his bones. It is only important that he rest in the peace he craved and so richly earned.

"Your okima here in Ohio believed that Tecumseh's body had escaped unmolested, and that is what the People have wanted to believe ever since. But perhaps not. Do you remember, Young One, the old woman who came last year, who was a descendant of one of Harrison's Kentuckians? She brought the 'family relic' for your people to bury. It was a piece of skin from the thigh of the Warrior. Her ancestor, a major in the American Alien's army, affirmed all his life that he had cut it from the man he admired most, Tecumseh. On his deathbed he said that action was his life's only regret.

"Do you remember the ceremonies for the 'return of the warrior' here at Shawandasse, close to the place of Tecumseh's birth? Do you remember the change in your okima when his hand touched the wrapped sacred bundle? Do you remember what happened during the first ceremony when the medicine person became trapped between the two worlds for a moment? And the story of how the pipe that was used became unusable when after that ceremony the hole in its stone bowl grew shut? Surely something deeply sacred occurred."

The Powaka Stone said more confidently, "Young One, you and your people have enjoyed many unthinkable blessings since his return to his homeland here. Tecumseh had walked this land before he left Ohio. He had hunted here, there is still part of a path on the upper portion of this land, from where he and his people walked from his village on Deer Creek to Old Man's Village to the southwest. "It is as though he has truly returned to his people in Ohio during this, the seventh generation. His warrior spirit now helps you fight different battles. His dream of a homeland for his People in the place of the graves of the ancestors has become a reality.

"Tecumseh's spirit must be very happy to see Shawnee children are being taught the old traditions that he was taught," the Powaka Stone said in a firmer tone of voice. "The old language is being relearned, old forms of worship and the ancient ceremonies are back stronger every year. The Shawnee are again proud of being Shawnee.

"Tecumseh gave his whole life to the People, Young One. He sacrificed all he had and all he was, so that you might have the privilege of being Shawnee instead of having to adopt the Alien's ways.

"Perhaps the sacrifice of that strip of skin from the Warrior's thigh was the way that Creator could give him back to you, so he could keep his promise to help you fight your battles today, in the form that he is today, which is pure spirit. It is a thrilling and comforting thought, Young One, that perhaps you are now protected by the ultimate warrior — just perhaps!" The Powaka Stone's voice could not keep from sounding a bit proud. Then it became silent.

The Young One was unsettled by the long, dramatic tale of Tecumseh. He looked at the sky, eager at last for the sun to appear. Would it never be morning, he wondered, so he could ask his okima about these contradictory stories? And the Old Watcher — would he never get enough sleep so he would be available to answer some of these burning questions? "Hurry, sunrise," he whispered to himself.

A most unusual-looking stone was lying on one of the lesser altar stones. The natural markings on it were unnaturally vivid in the dim light. The Young One remembered the story the woman Wakwashbosha told of how she had needed to bring a special stone to put at the base of the Spirit Pole that was placed on Tecumseh Point, where Tecumseh and his men had camped to protest the signing of the Greeneville Treaty. She did not have a special stone, and had offered tobacco and prayed about it. Bosha searched everywhere — in creeks and lakebeds, in Ohio near Shawandasse and near the Spirit Pole. Many stones were found that were significant enough to keep, but none were truly unique enough for the purpose Bosha sought to fulfil. She decided she would wait, as Shawnee are taught to do. Bosha was sure that in time the spirits would gift her, rewarding her for both patience and prayer.

It seemed that now the Bosha Stone was ready to tell the Young One its own personal history, as well as that of his people, the Shawnee.

"Young One," the Bosha Stone began. "The truth is not always pleasant, but it is a power given to you by Kohkumthena. These things were not told to confuse you or cause dismay. They were given to you for understanding of the hard and ugly reality of the world that your hero lived in and the part he had in it, good and bad. These words are to give you better perspective and a grasp of the conditions of some of your ancestors. Some of the responsibility for their conditions belongs to the Aliens, some to themselves, and yes, some to Tecumseh." The voice was very uneven and peculiar, as though each syllable were broken into small irregular pieces.

The voice continued while the Young One looked straight ahead at the horizon. He was encouraging the sun to rise quickly; his heart was tired of attempting to sort all this out and of trying to deny the ugly parts.

"When Tecumseh joined the British after Tippecanoe, a rift developed between his followers and the Shawnee who were in the Ohio Reservations. There were some on those reservations who were sympathetic to him and what he was trying to accomplish. Others thought he should accept the inevitable and live honorably as a conquered Shawnee, as they were doing. To some it was galling that he had the freedom to come and go as he chose and that he refused to bow to the Aliens' rule. Others secretly admired him and endeavored to help him in inconspicuous ways. Still, to another group he was the symbol of the Shawnee, and they wished him success in maintaining their reputation as important people.

"During this time grudges developed, and today those hostile feelings are maintained by the descendents of those Shawnee who opposed his actions. Tecumseh's actions caused the Aliens to be harder on your people on the reservations than they might have been otherwise, or at least that is what the People believed. As the clubs Thunder and Lightning described to you, that was the belief even of many who went with him. I believe Tecumseh came to think that the People would be punished because of him at the end; he certainly realized the ones with him were suffering because of him," the uneven voice of the Bosha Stone said quietly.

"Immediately after Tecumseh's death the People in Canada were unsure as to what they should do. A few went back to the reservations in Ohio. Some went to Cape Girardeau, Missouri, but most stayed in Canada for ten, fifteen, thirty-five years and even longer, before they came back after the war and hostility died down and they could return without attracting much attention. Some never came back and made Canada their permanent home. Some had quietly come back into the Ohio Valley and hidden away in the hills of Ohio, Indiana, and West Virginia. What has always been true of your People was true then: they simply were never in the same spot all at the same time. They stayed to themselves, practicing another form of invisibility and interacting with only a few of their own and with old, trusted friends. Loose, well-spaced communities covering many miles might contain twenty or more Shawnee families, but of course they claimed to be of Alien descent and that was their excuse for peculiar speech. Eventually the children were sent to local schools and intermarried with the local Aliens."

The voice was scratchy and erratic. The Young One was tired, and it took concentration to make out what was being told him. He finally looked around toward the location of the voice. The sun seemed to have no intentions of hurrying to end this night of massive information, though the sky continued to lighten. The Old Watcher was now sleeping quietly, purring like some large cat.

The Bosha Stone, of dark slate gray color with strange markings of burnished copper outlined in vivid black, was glowing so brightly it seemed to dance at its resting place. Even the Young One knew some of its unusual story. The first time he had seen it lying near the altar, he had thought that it was most peculiarly colored. Then it was shown to him that it had the design of a stick-figure man walking, holding a long stick that had a forked bottom, as if it too were walking. The woman who had pointed out the design to him had asked if he would like to hear the history of the stone, as it was very interesting. For over an hour he had sat entranced as she told him of this particular stone's travels.

The Bosha Stone said, "Young One, I would like to teach you what happened to the Shawnee after Tecumseh died. These are hard stories to listen to because all the People experienced heartbreaking pain of one kind or another. Great Mask, may I continue?"

"Hrrrrmmmmmphphphph! How nice of you to remember to ask," the ancient Mask snorted sarcastically. "Everyone seems to just jump right in with whatever he or she wants to say. No regard for how I had decided the Young One should be taught. I might as well be just a pebble around the base of the Great House, instead of the Great Mask." Sighing, the Mask grumbled, "Yes, yes! You may teach the Young One if you hurry. Now don't go filling his head with any more sad tales. You are all going to have him so discouraged that he won't be right-thinking. Hurry, Bosha Stone, begin!" the beloved old Mask snorted testily.

Somewhat intimidated by the grouchy old Mask, the Bosha Stone began to speak unevenly, its voice cracking. "I would remind you, Young One, of the time Tecumseh visited Black Hoof after he moved to that Ohio reservation. When the distinguished principal okima came out to greet Tecumseh, Black Hoof was in terrible shape. There was not enough food in the village, but apparently there was too much alcohol. The old okima had on a frayed, raggedy coat that was not clean. It was a sorrowful sight, especially when Tecumseh realized this great old okima had contracted lice. The reservation life did not even allow the people living there to maintain the cleanliness in which they had always taken such pride. While the two men had disagreed on the tribal politics, each still had regard and affection for the other. To Tecumseh's mind Black Hoof was dying by inches under the stingy, stinking hand and oppressive boot of the Aliens. Tecumseh preferred to die when his time came, quickly as a warrior but free of what he perceived to be disastrously grim and ruinously devastating control of the Aliens. While he had life, he would live it to the fullest and continue to try to be of true help to his people, even if it seemed they no longer wanted his help nor believed in him and his sacred purpose. Even in the midst of feeling deep sorrow for the People and for Black Hoof, he could not resist the baser human impulse to hurtfully say to Black Hoof, in so many words, 'I warned you. I told you so.' Black Hoof in his wisdom understood the pathetic creature he had become on the reservation. He understood too that Tecumseh's harsh words were more an expression of anger and hurt in his own heart over the conditions of the Shawnee people on the reservations than a personal indictment to Black Hoof because he had become a 'signer' and marked a treaty. This was a time of great sorrow, pain, frustration, and anger, and a time the People were powerless to change.

"Speaking metaphorically, the old traditional Shawnee way of life was already dead. Black Hoof was powerless and only going through automated motions until his body lay down to return to Mother Earth. Tecumseh was like an angry and frightened child kicking at the body of the dead Shawnee way, trying to get it to rise one more time. Now after its death, the People were physically and spiritually divided.

"I want to explain to you some of the details of your people's divisions as they left the Ohio area. Some, of course, left long before Ohio was a state. Remember that at all of these migrations there was no singular sept or division which went, nor were the groups without some from other villages joining in, even those of other nations. The causes for the migrations were many, and few of the migrations ever ended up precisely where they started for, and fewer still stayed there once they arrived. I am sorry to confuse you so soon, Young One, but your Shawnee are a complex people, as their migrations reveal. I believe they are the most interesting I have known," the Bosha Stone expounded. "Let me describe their division as simply as I can.

"The first group to leave Ohio after 1768 went to New Spain, now known as Cape Girardeau, and to Apple Creek and New Madrid areas of eastern Missouri now but at that time a part of Spanish Louisiana. This group consisted of the Thawakila, Pekowi, and Kispoko septs.

"In 1774, after the decisive battle at Point Pleasant during Dunmore's War, another group of Thawakila moved south and settled with the Creeks. This particular group returned to the shores of the Ohio River in 1790 and from that time on has never participated in any hostilities against the Alien American government, living quietly and inconspicuously in that same vicinity.

"This part is important, Young One," the Bosha Stone emphasized, "for it shows that there are even more divisions or bands of Shawnee than are usually accounted for in government records and history books. The Missouri Shawnee were joined by some Delawares, but most of them were Chalagatha and Mekoche, plus some families of other divisions who wanted to continue the hostilities against the Alien Americans. This last group remained in Ohio and after the Treaty of 1782 are referred to as the Ohio Shawnee. Remember, Young One, this does not include the Thawakila group who moved back to the Ohio River area and refused to participate in any more hostilities.

"Still other Shawnee joined the Cherokees and Creeks in the South. All of this is well-documented by the American Alien records as well as being mentioned in English and Spanish records.

"An Indian confederacy was formed in 1783 when various tribes of the Ohio Territory met on the Sandusky River. The actions they took collectively to defend the Territory were very impressive and met with much success under their war chiefs: the Miami Little Turtle, Shawnee Blue Jacket, and Delaware Buckongahelas. They celebrated the victories of Harmar's defeat and St. Clair's defeat; but then came Mad Anthony Wayne. He was an astute warrior and war chief for the Aliens, and the defeat of the Indian confederacy suffered at the Battle of Fallen Timbers crushed them, culminating in the Greeneville Treaty.

"The results of the Greeneville Treaty were that the Ohio Shawnee had to give up their territory on the Miami River and move to the headwaters of the Auglaize River near today's Defiance, Ohio. In 1798 part of this group settled on the White River in Indiana at the invitation of the Delawares. The more hostile members of the Ohio Shawnee refused to go to the headwaters of the Auglaize and instead crossed the Mississippi River and joined the Missouri Shawnee living at Cape Girardeau.

"In the early 1800s both the Ohio Shawnee and the Spanish Louisiana-Missouri Shawnee had divided again. Most of those in Ohio had stopped their hostilities and moved to the reservation at Wapakoneta, Ohio. Tecumseh and the Prophet were among this group; but instead of moving with the rest of their people to that reservation they tried to form another Indian alliance of all the tribes. Tecumseh lived in Indiana between 1798 and 1805, although it is known he also lived for a time on the Tennessee River and on part of the Cumberland in those years. During Tecumseh's life the huge villages the Shawnee had had ages before were still well-remembered. These existed near where present-day Nashville and Knoxville, Tennessee, now stand. Tecumseh was also said to have had at least a hunting camp in Kentucky, although reports list several scattered locations, and today no one is certain where the camps were. These could have simply been the different winter camps he chose rather than long-term home bases. In 1805 Tecumseh and the Prophet founded Prophet's Town in Greeneville, Ohio, and in 1808 they moved it to Indiana at the junction of the Tippecanoe and Wabash rivers. They remained there until William Henry Harrison destroyed it in 1811, and soon after they moved to Brownstown, near Detroit, then south of Amherstberg, where they stayed until after Tecumseh's death. Tecumseh had quarters in the officers' building at Fort Malden, where he spent most of his time.

"The Missouri Shawnee remained scattered in eastern Missouri until 1822 when part of them joined eleven other tribes following a Cherokee leader, Chief Bowles, and moved to eastern Texas, which was then part of Mexico.

"The rest of the Missouri Shawnee stayed near Cape Girardeau until they began to migrate west in 1825, and took possession of a new reservation provided for them on the Kansas, or Kaw, River in eastern Kansas in 1826.

"Just before President Andrew Jackson got Congress to pass the Removal Act, treaties had been agreed to with the Shawnee who were on the reservations of Wapakoneta and Hog Creek, who were moved to the Kansas reservation in late 1832, after the death of Black Hoof.

"The reservation of Shawnee and Senecas had earlier moved from Logstown, Ohio, to Lewistown, Hog Creek, and Wapakoneta, signed a treaty and moved out the same year, 1832, except they went to a reservation in northeastern Oklahoma.

"As usual, Young One, your Shawnee were somewhat stubborn and independent, and when the people from the Hog Creek band moved in 1832, there were twelve families which refused to go. They finally arrived at Kansas in 1833. One family still refused to go and instead, after the last of the others had gone, moved to Kentucky and stated they would live like the Aliens, and forever turn their backs on their Shawnee kin. This family took the names of the pale Aliens and ceased to remember they were once part of the proud and powerful Shawnee Nation."

The Bosha Stone paused reflectively for a moment and then continued. "Creator gave us Stone Nations long lives and long memories, Young One. Without that I am not sure any nation could keep up with your people's history and travels. It is most appropriate for me to tell you this part of your people's history because I am the oldest of the traveling stones. I have thought it most wise not to burden you with any more history than this last few hundred years. The wanderings of your people before arriving here are much more complex and that history is tens of thousands of years. So you see, Young One, it could be much more confusing." The Bosha Stone seemed to chuckle.

"Once I give you this outline of the last migrations and divisions, Young One, I do have some interesting and heart-tugging stories to tell to help you remember them more easily. You will remember them all yourself one day — it will not be too hard. Ready to proceed?" the Bosha Stone asked. Oh my, the Young One thought to himself, even with an elephant's memory I think it would take a lifetime to get all this straight!

The Bosha Stone resumed its story. "The Shawnee who had gone to Texas as Chief Bowles' allies were promised land there by both the Mexican government and by Sam Houston after Texas gained its freedom from Mexico. The promises, of course, were never kept. They finally felt compelled to go into battle over the matter and were defeated. They and their allies were then forced to leave Texas. The Shawnee of this group settled on the Canadian River in Oklahoma, and these people became the nucleus of the present-day Absentee. They are mostly of the Thawakila, Pekowi, and Kispoko septs.

"There was already a thriving community of Shawnee on the Canadian River at the mouth of the Little River in the early 1850s. Other Shawnee remained elsewhere in Texas, living with other tribes on the Brazos River until 1859, when they were also forced out of the state. They too joined and became part of the Absentee on the Canadian River.

"During the Alien Americans' Civil War in the 1860s the Absentee, who had returned to live with the Creeks in Alabama, near Hickory Grove, which is less than fifteen miles north of present-day Montgomery, were pressured by the Creeks to be sympathetic to the Southern cause. The Absentee suffered from Confederate guerilla raids. Their sentiments actually lay with the Northern cause, but fearing serious retribution from Confederate troops they finally sought refuge by joining their relatives of the Ohio band in their settlement near Bellemont, Kansas. There they stayed until the war ended, and returned to their homes in 1868.

"The Shawnee-Seneca group left Lewistown, Ohio, in 1832, and separated in 1867. That division of the Shawnee is now known as the Eastern Shawnee.

"The main body of the Chalagatha and Mekoche in Kansas were incorporated with the Cherokee Nation. They moved to what is now Whiteoak, Oklahoma, and are known as the Loyal Shawnee and the Cherokee Shawnee. A small division known as Black Bob's band of Chalagathas refused to move from Kansas to Oklahoma. Black Bob's group did join the others in Oklahoma in 1869.

"The Absentee Shawnee split in 1875 over the question of government allotments. Half the group accepted allotments, but the other half, under Tecumseh's grandson Big Jim, refused and their group moved in 1876 to the Kickapoo reservation north of today's Harrah, Oklahoma, where they stayed until the government moved them out ten years later in 1886.

"In 1898 Alien land speculators developed a scheme that convinced Big Jim to leave the area and go to Old Mexico, which he and his followers did in 1900, arriving at a Kickapoo reservation west of Nacimiento, Coahuila, Mexico. An epidemic of smallpox was raging when they arrived. The Kickapoo offered to take care of the Shawnee, but the group preferred to start back to Oklahoma. The Mexican authorities quarantined them all when they reached Sabinas and isolated them in a camp on the bank of the river. Only two of those Shawnee survived. Big Jim died there in Mexico on September 29, 1900.

"Young One, this is just the story of the Shawnee now living in Oklahoma. The other Shawnee have just as complex a history as this. We will discuss those of Canada, Indiana, Illinois, Ohio, and West Virginia a little later. I will tell you a secret, Young One. I hate remembering dates. They are so confusing. Calendars change, and every group has its own markers and systems. We Stones prefer just to remember events and the stories that make them worth remembering. In a moment I will tell you a good story which is timeless, about a wonderful Quaker family and their forty-two-year history with your Shawnee. Indeed, the Quakers in general were good friends to the People. But first I must tell you the sad story of the departure years."

"The Ohio Reservation Shawnee were cheated again and again by the Aliens. It wasn't just the government which cheated them: it seemed there was a real scarcity of honest men throughout Ohio at that time. The only ones who treated the ancestors fairly were the Quaker Friends. Truly, the People would have perished from exposure and hunger had the Quakers not befriended them. The People were at times literally naked because there were no clothes for them. The tools that were promised seldom came, so the People could not build what they needed nor could they farm properly and raise enough food to survive on.

"The traders cheated the People in their dealings, made huge false claims against the People and took them to the Aliens' courts and got judgments against them. The People had to sell their land back to the Aliens' government because they needed the money to pay the inflated debts to the dishonest traders. The government promised them the land west of the Mississippi, where the government wanted them to go, and which they said was just as fertile as that on the Auglaize River. Of course this was not true. Many terms were agreed to on the sale, but the government did not live up to any of it, except to see to it that the People moved out.

"It was all such a disgrace, but that seems to be the only way the Aliens knew to treat the People. Sad to say they treated all the Nations this way. And once the People arrived at the new land in the west, it just finished breaking their hearts," the Bosha Stone sighed. "Here the ground was truly rich and fertile, but out there was hardly any soil, just rock with a skiff of soil and some clay, all hard. The weather is different there: the seasons bring different rainfall amounts, and they had almost nothing but their bare hands to work with. If the Aliens' government did come through with some tools as they promised, they might deliver six plows and ten hoes for fifty families to share and farm hundreds of acres with. Remember, Young One, these were hand tools; there were few people who had a horse or a mule left to pull the plow. You might ask, how did the government expect them to survive? In truth, we Stones believe they neither expected nor wanted the People to survive, so they didn't 'waste' anything on them.

"I remember the admonishment of the Great Mask not to depress you, so I will change the subject and explain how your people divided up as they left Ohio. It has taken me this long to lead up to it, as we have spoken of the other groups of Shawnee as they divided. But let us go back to the earliest days in Ohio, so you will have a full picture. The first group to leave Ohio was a mixed group of Shawnee and Seneca who, in the late 1700s had moved to Lewistown and Logstown. After the Treaty of 1817 these villages and Wapakoneta became official reservations. The first group to leave was headed by Tenskwtawa and left in 1826. They went to Shawnee Mission, Kansas, in what is now Kansas City.

The irregular voice of the Bosha Stone said, "Let me explain that after the People were confined to the Ohio reservations they were not allowed to pursue their old ways of existence. They were to eat what they grew or cattle and hogs they raised themselves. That meant abandoning hunting the natural animals given them by Creator for food. They were supposed to farm in neat little rows, year after year, using the animal manure for fertilizer on the soil. The forests were quickly disappearing and being replaced by farm land turned by plows. The deer and other animals the People had relied on for food and clothing had almost been annihilated. There was no natural habitat for them in which to recover and repopulate. There was to be no more beautiful, soft deerskin clothing; now they bought from the traders the bright and colorful but thin fabrics that hardly lasted a whole season before they became worn and tattered. They looked pretty for a short time but certainly did not last the years that a deerskin dress or shirt would, nor were they as warm.

"From the beginning the People viewed cattle, which was the basis of the Aliens' farming, with pity. A cow or steer was obviously not a sacred animal, it had no soul and very little intelligence. The cattle were not hardy as the buffalo had been, and when butchered and dressed out held less meat and had triple the amount of waste. Their skins were hard but not durable. The type of fat gleaned from cattle was insufficient for the People's uses and even tasted different. Cattle were always breaking fences. Fences were one of the things the People found the hardest to accept; their use seemed against Creator's teachings and even their cattle seemed to understand that. In the hard parts of winter the cattle could not survive without much personal attention from the People, and they did not even have the sense to scratch the ground with their hoofs to rake off snow so they could eat the plants underneath. Cattle also got sick.

"Then there were the hogs, filthy animals, extremely mean in nature. The only good thing about using them was they did supply the fats needed in the women's cooking, as great quantities of lard would be rendered when they were butchered. Remember, Young One," the Bosha Stone said, "your people had always enjoyed a healthy diet and much exercise, so they never had weight problems and no one had heard about cholesterol at that time. But the new foods were inferior to the old, wild foods. Lard quickly became rancid and smelled terrible and tasted bad after a few short weeks, and the food prepared with it was not easy to preserve and store and quickly turned rancid and rotten.

The voice of the Bosha Stone fairly shuddered as it said, "The practice of using any type of excrement in areas where food was grown was one of the most difficult concepts for the People to grasp. Since Creator put them here on Turtle Island, they had been cautious about their human waste and always buried it out away from the village and water supply. They would burn off old gardens and use the ashes as a type of strengthener for the soil, or occasionally the women would add fish bones to the plants as they grew. But excrement of any kind was considered a contaminant, something to make you sick, not something to make your food good and you strong. But when you are conquered by an Alien People you must do as they say to survive even when they are not right-thinking.

"The People were to 'buy' everything they needed from the Alien 'traders.' These traders would sell shoddy goods, and they had a minimal selection to choose from at that. Then they would charge the People twice or three times the normal price. Of course the People just got deeper into debt with no way to pay. I will add that by this time the only thing some people had much heart to buy was whiskey, which for a moment caused them to forget their pitiful situation.

"When their debt cases came to court, the People admitted they owed money to the traders. Not knowing the system of money, nor how to keep their own records, they agreed that the specified amounts claimed by the traders (which were unjustifiably huge) must be correct. The judge demanded they pay up immediately, even if it meant selling their lands to do so. Amazingly, the very next day the government agents were there with offers to buy tribal lands cheaply and quickly.

"So now we arrive at the time we were speaking of, after the War of 1812. The government insisted that the conquered Shawnee must leave Ohio. Black Hoof, for his part, insisted that the Great Spirit had placed the Shawnee in Ohio, and if they moved He would take his protection of them away. The people of his village were divided in their opinions: Some were eager to believe the stories about the rich farm lands, the better life and no Aliens crowding them, and saw moving westward as an opportunity to go back to their old traditional way of life. Others believed they could take their new knowledge of farming the Alien way and make a better life for themselves in the new place.

"The Shawnee who were in Missouri had been reinforced by some of the Shawnee who were formerly located in Alabama and had been building their economic base. They looked forward to being joined by the newcomers. Black Hoof died early in the year of 1832 near the age of a hundred and ten. Later that year his village was moved out.

"They had been allowed to remain so long partially because they had been so docile and obedient. But the People who were reluctant to move showed some of the old traditional Shawnee traits of stubbornness. They sold off all the possessions they could not carry and converted the proceeds into whiskey. While they packed they consumed the whiskey continually and in great quantities. The federal agents responsible for escorting them to their new home were terrified at the thought of escorting six hundred drunken Indians through the white communities for almost a thousand miles, so they made arrangements for the people to travel by steamboat, down the Wabash, the Ohio, and on to the Mississippi. The People absolutely refused to even consider traveling in this manner.

"An ancient women's chief of the Wapakoneta group expressed their sentiments in terms even the Aliens could understand by saying, 'We will not go by steamboats, nor will we go in wagons; but we will go on horseback. It is the most agreeable manner for us; and if we are not allowed to go so, we can and will remain here and die and be buried with our relatives; it will be but a short time before we leave this world anyway, and let us avert our heads from as much unnecessary pain and sorrow as possible.'

"The federal agents did not press the issue and the Shawnee were left with their horses. The last community act they performed in Wapakoneta was to plant prairie grasses in their cemetery so that no traces of the graves of their fathers might be seen under the green sod.

"The People began departing in mid-September, traveling in an almost leisurely manner to Greeneville to partake of some springs that they believed held medicinal powers. They continued on down the Miami River valley on what they called Tecumseh's Trail, where they visited Old Piqua. They directed themselves eventually west and were in Indianapolis the first week of October, crossing the Mississippi at the end of that month. It was there that the People made another division, with part of them continuing to Kansas and others going to the scrub lands of Oklahoma.

"Young One, trying to sort out the migrations of your people through all their history is enough to give even us Stones a headache. What you must remember is that there were at least four different groups who left Ohio within this period from 1826 to 1832. And as we just explained, some of them divided on the trail to their newest homelands. Then too, Young One, there were pockets of people living among many other tribes such as the Creeks, Delaware, and others, as well as living quietly and separately from the other recorded villages. This does not even mention those at Cape Girardeau or the warriors who had fought with Tecumseh and stayed in Canada, nor the ones who sneaked back into the Ohio hills and hid. It does not account for the individual families who had gone off by themselves to live, never renouncing their citizenship as Shawnee, but just saying nothing of it either to outsiders or to their Alien neighbors.

"There had been Shawnee communities in Pennsylvania and West Virginia that were low-keyed and nonaggressive, as was the Ohio community of Carmel. Many of these are listed on maps once printed by the Bureau of Indiana Affairs as late as the 1970s. That bureau stopped allowing anyone to have copies of the maps for fear too many descendants would use that information to validate their tribal identities, thus raising the expenses of the government by their having to provide more entitlements due some of your people. Because these villages and settlements were not considered hostile by the Aliens' government, they were left to themselves and never forced to move. Those People were self-sufficient and ceased interaction with the world around them, including other Shawnee. Pockets of old Chalagatha sept Shawnee and a few Mekujes remain today in southern Ohio and West Virginia, still speaking the old language to a privileged and trusted few young ones. They still hold some of the oldest oral traditions of the Shawnee, but continue to have great fears of retribution, so refuse to speak to outsiders concerning these things.

"All of these complicated factors cause great sorrow and confusion among the Shawnee today. Because of treaty obligations to the People, a census was established by the Aliens, listing those who left the Ohio reservations and moved west, so the government would not be required to provide benefits for any Shawnee who were not represented at the treaty signings. That is a good business practice. The Aliens never provided all for which they were obligated, to the people who were involved in the treaties, so the census was not as useful a document as might have been expected for your people. Many times partial payments or benefits would be delivered en masse and the current chiefs would be responsible for disbursing it. Again, the census served no real function except to provide a loose head-count for the Aliens as they figured out how to short-change the People.

"Many times some People who had gone to Oklahoma would show up among the Kansas Shawnee. Some who went to Oklahoma didn't like it so they went to Arkansas, and some of that group went on to Texas and old Mexico, only to show up later with one of the other groups that had stayed put.

"Do you see what I mean, Young One, about confusion? Then add to it the fact that the young people intermarried. The group called the Absentee had people intermarry with some Loyals and Easterns. And they all intermarried with other tribes such as the Miamis, Seneca, Eyuchies, Cherokees, Kiowa, and others who became their new neighbors in these western locations.

"When all of this was going on, those loose censuses became even more important, as the People truly needed the benefits of those entitlements from the treaties to live. This was not a matter of improving the quality of their lives, but was a matter of living or dying. Again, Young One, had it not been for the kindness of the Quaker Friends and some

Methodists and Baptists, those divisions of your people would have perished of starvation.

"It is obvious that at the time they were drafted those censuses were probably correct concerning the people who arrived in Kansas and Oklahoma, but there were some Shawnee people that were not included. We Stones of the Great House will try to impart that knowledge to your mind as best we can.

The Bosha Stone's voice cracked as it spoke. "There were Aliens who loved your people and treated them as family. These Alien people actually practiced what they preached and acted out the good words that were written in their Black Book. I was privileged to be present when the People took their leave of their good Quaker friends, Henry Harvey and his family. Let me tell you this story even though it is a sad one. I feel your education will not be complete until you hear it."

At this the Ancient Mask interrupted, "You are correct, Bosha Stone. The Young One needs to understand the heartaches of his people as well as the wonderful stories of long ago. But continue quickly, please. I too, remember the Harveys well and with great fondness. It is just that the night is quickly being spent. Hurry!"

The Bosha Stone spoke quickly. "Harvey and his family had spent two years with the People at Wapakoneta before their removal west. He had visited the People several times at their new homes, never failing to petition his mission board for more assistance for them. Then the mission board had him come to minister to and teach his Shawnee friends in Kansas. He had helped construct a large school for their children, and then he was told by his board he must move on to other works. He kept news of his family's departure until the very last, when he finally had to tell his Shawnee friends they would be gone before the next week. The People were overcome with sadness at losing such a valuable friend.

"Many times the Harveys had clothed the little Shawnee children who were truly naked and cold. Mrs. Harvey always found some kind of food to share with them when the People had gone for days with nothing to eat, even when all she could do was bake loaves of bread and let them divide it among themselves, while she let her own family appreciate the Shawnees' plight by asking them to prayerfully fast and thank God for the meager rations they had to give so the People did not perish.

"Harvey wrote his own account of their departure:

One old chief came with an interpreter to say the People had held council on the matter of the Harveys' departure, including the women's council, and they had sent through him their last farewell. He lined our family up from the oldest to the youngest and went shaking hands and telling each a tearful and solemn farewell. As he held the hands of the children, weeping, he told them to never forget him and the little Shawnee children with whom they had lived in peace so long. When he had gone around the family in that manner, speaking with each one, he turned back, and after again taking each by the hand, he left us without saying another word.

For several days we were visited by each chief and others to individually say farewell.

"In a few days all the chiefs, except George Williams, a near neighbor, came together to deliver a message and say farewell for the whole nation. Many kind things were expressed and an understanding of the People that though they loved the Harveys' presence among them, they realized the Harveys must yearn for their own home, and so the People must give them up. Harvey wrote:

When evening drew near, after solemnly speaking among themselves, they divided up something among themselves that looked like fine seeds, which John Perry had wrapped in a cloth. The chiefs then loosened their hair and their clothes. Henry Clay, one of the chiefs who had served as interpreter, said they were now ready to go to their own homes.

Again the Harvey family was lined up according to their ages so the chiefs could take one last look at them as they bade them farewell.

The chiefs came one by one according to their stations. John Perry came first. As each chief reached the door he put something in his mouth, presumably the tobacco seeds, and chewed it.

As they took the Harveys by the hand tears were streaming down the cheeks of the chiefs, and the Harveys too. They cried hard when they told the children farewell; this lasted for some time. Many tears were shed by all.

When all the chiefs had come forward, they all mounted their horses with John Perry leading, and in single file they rode back to their homes across the prairie. Not one looked back, they observed the same order as if they were returning from a funeral. This was a solemn time for us. Here were the celebrated Shawnee chiefs, great men among the Indians, some of them in time past brave warriors, now here in mourning — in tears, and all this in sincerity, and for nothing more than parting with us. They surely did love us.

It was but a few days later that we took leave of the school children, having left this to the last, because we knew it would be so hard. These children had been given up to us on our arrival among the Indians, some were the children of those who had attended our schools back in Ohio. All wept, from the largest to the smallest. Some of the little girls followed us to the wagon, and begged to ride across the fields with our girls. We let several of them ride, but when we stopped for them to get out of the wagon, they refused to leave our children. We had to put them out by force. They clung fast to our little girl, and screamed as loud as they could, and so did our own poor little girl. We had to tear them apart, and put them out of the wagon, and go off and leave them in this situation, which was a very hard trial to us.

My object in penning these accounts is that those who may read them may see what the "savages," as they are so wrongfully denominated, are when treated as human beings. They are such utter strangers to such treatment as Christians should bestow on their fellows, that if they receive ever so small a favor, they can scarcely avoid magnifying it into something very great.

I am sure, that to see these great and strong-minded chiefs melted into a flood of tears — weeping in agony, holding us firmly by the hands, their eyes turned towards heaven, and in their native language invoking the Great Spirit to shower down blessings upon each member of the family, as they parted from us; this I am sure, was enough to tender any heart that could be moved; it was enough for us — more than we expected — more than we deserved. We can only regret that everyone who may read this cannot have the opportunity we had, of witnessing the gratitude of these Indians, of these "savages." If they could, the term "savage," if ever applied to the Indians, would be spared from the Shawnees.

The Bosha Stone was silent for a moment and then said, "Young One, it is so sad that today the Shawnee are divided even more than they were then, partially because of those censuses and other records that were provided by the Aliens and their government. It is a great sadness to see the great Shawnee using records of the Aliens who are notorious for falsifying records, who have never in over three hundred years produced a single accurate accounting of any of their transactions with your people; yet because these are the only written records the modern People have to use, they cling to them as if they were the Shawnee Sacred Fire. Perhaps, Young One, your place in life will allow you to help resolve these strains and help all your people to rejoice in one another again. Perhaps!"

The Young One was startled that the Stone had spoken of the possibility that he might have an important part to play in the future of his people. His elders had always taught him that each person was important, but this thought of the Stone's could be overwhelming. He decided he would have to think for a long time on that.

"Young One," the Bosha Stone continued. "When the woman who owns me told you of my past she did not have much time. I think you should know more about me and my travels with your people.

"You have been taught that your people were always in groups that usually lived separately, with a mixture of all the septs or divisions represented in each group. This is true. Each village needed administrators, medicine people, ceremony people, and warriors. Each sept had its own responsibility. The Thawegila and Chalagatha septs were the only ones who could provide you with a principal chief. The Mekujay were in charge of food, medicine, and health matters. The Pekowe maintained order and tended to the celebrations pertaining to your religion. The Kispokos took care of war and the training of the warriors. Because they were best equipped, the Kispokos guarded the Shawnee sacred fire, various sacred bundles, copies of the treaties and other sacred items.

"When it became evident that a village needed to move so the land could rest and the animals replenish themselves, a new place would have to be located before the People packed up. The People had to have a destination in mind before a move could be implemented. The council, having decided on the move, would advise the medicine man or shaman that he would have to go find a location for the new village. The medicine man would then go purify himself, offer tobacco, and pray for guidance. It was at times like this that he would seek a vision. Once the medicine man felt he had been given either a vision or what he thought was a sign of permission from Creator and the Spirits, he would then pack for several days' or even weeks' journey and set out, usually with an assistant. He would have to find a place with plenty of game, water, and good ground for the village, not too swampy or rocky nor near a flood plain. When he found a suitable location, he would hold a purification and blessing ceremony over the land. Then he could return to the People, making a trail to the new place by leaving markers of a sort, as hunters of old did. Then he returned to the People and told them where they were to go and what to look for along the way.

"As you look on my surface, Young One, you see that on my top is etched the image of a holy man holding out a stick with legs in his hand. Many ages ago when your oldest ancestors, the Fort Ancient Mound Builders, had come here from the land where the south wind begins, some of them went back to tell their families and friends about the beauty of this area. One of them found me in an Ohio creek and was so struck by my uniqueness that he picked me up and took me on his journey home. I reminded him of the times the medicine man had led them on their migration to the northeast, holding a walking, two-legged staff in his hand to show those in back the way they were to travel.

"The medicine man in the homeland thought I had a sacred purpose, so he placed me in the tribe's bundle until the second group of your ancestors decided to come here. The leader of that group, whom people refer to as the Lennape, brought me back with him and used me as a guide by following my markings in some sacred way. Again I was taken back to the homeland to stay until I was needed again. The last time I came with your immediate ancestors who eventually became known as Shawnee.

"I thought my life of wandering had finally come to an end and I would stop being a traveling stone, but when the Aliens came, your people had to constantly move, trying to put safe distance between themselves and the Aliens. After the warring stopped and your people were confined to the reservations in northern Ohio, I again had hope I could settle down and lead a respectable life for a stone, and just stay put." The Bosha Stone sighed sadly, "But the period after the War of 1812 arrived. At that time came the final push of your people to move west to what the Aliens called 'Indian Territory,' what you know as Kansas and Oklahoma. The People started packing and this time was the saddest I ever witnessed.

"The old traditional ways of the Shawnee were suffering too, as the People just didn't seem to have heart enough to perform their ceremonies. The new territory was defined by the Aliens' government in acres, miles, and markers. Again the medicine man went and searched out a reasonable place for the People to start a new village so they wouldn't

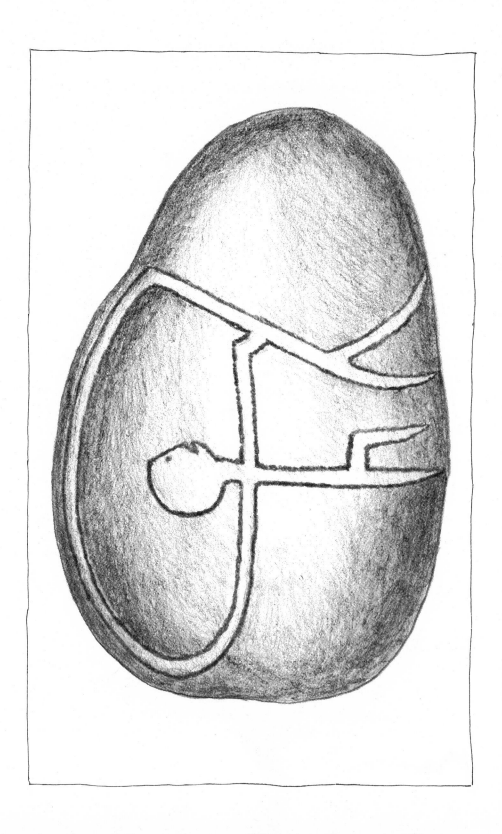

have to wander and mill about when they were tired and had traveled so far. He returned and gave the chief and council and the people all the information they needed to find the location of their new home. He had held ceremony at the new place and asked Creator to bless the place and the people when they arrived. It was still months before the people would be packed and could move out, because they had gardens to harvest, animals to sell, and much business to tend to. Their hearts were heavy.

"The old medicine man took advantage of the time and made a trip to places familiar to his own heart in the Ohio region the Shawnee people had loved for over a thousand years and that he would probably never see again. He went north to the big lake and sat for days, expressing to Creator his dismay at what he had seen in the new land for his people.

"He had seen that the land was poor and the weather different. The game they would have to depend on until the Aliens' government gave them new hogs and cattle was not plentiful. Medicine plants were rare and difficult to find, and even the trees were stunted. And discouraged as he was, it was his task to encourage the people in some way to go there and to be contented and stay put, for he realized this was the last move they could make without making the government totally angry and being themselves destroyed, man, woman, and child. The medicine man prayed constantly, Young One. Finally in exhaustion he fell asleep on the shore of the big lake.

"As his tired body and despairing mind began to rest, the Spirits gave him one last vision for the People. After he awoke he hurriedly broke camp. He needed to hurry back to his People and tell them what he had seen. He thanked Creator for sending him this piece of wisdom. It just might work. He believed he now had the words to say that would make them stay in the new land and never look back.

"After he returned to the village he asked the chief to gather the people to hear what he had been given by the Spirits in his vision to say to them. When the people had arrived at the council house and quieted themselves he began: 'I have been given a vision about our new home. It is a good place and we will be very happy there. It will be hard at first but this will not last. This is where Creator wants us to go. It is not just a place where the Aliens want us; the thoughts were put into their minds to put us there because that is the place Creator has made for us. So when we leave this place we are never to look back, we are to think as if this place has no meaning to us, we are not to remember that our ancestors' bones are part of the earth here. We will never return to this place. We are to go only in this direction. We are a new People going to a new land that Creator has made for us.' And as the medicine man finished his speech, over the sounds of gasps and sobs he said more softly, 'And we must never look back.'"

The Bosha Stone's voice became almost soft as it said, "When it came time to leave, the medicine man was up front, pointing the way with his medicine stick, and carrying me, the Bosha Stone, which had already made a thousand years or more of trips with the People, in his own sacred medicine bundle. The people drove their horses packed with the barest necessities of life. The journey was slow and almost leisurely, with the people visiting their old village sites on the way west. The government had promised decent provisions, blankets and such for the trip, and of course these had not been delivered. Many people did not survive that journey. When they finally arrived, their tired hearts had sunk to a new low. But your people's hearts and spirits are strong. They are not quitters, so the strongest of the strong survived. Still, many died those first years.

"Through the years the people tried hard to become good farmers in the style the Aliens demanded and eat just the foods they grew. Simple survival became a chore that consumed all their time and vitality. The people had no energy to spare, and displays of their natural cheer and laughter became rare occurrences. They found that they had new neighbors from other tribes, sometimes tribes who had been traditional enemies in the old days, and that too was difficult for the People. Quickly it became understood that extinction was the real enemy to fight. New friendships developed among many of the tribes as they all struggled for food, clothes, shelter, and mere survival. They survived."

The Bosha Stone gave another deep sigh and continued: "It wasn't long until the Alien government found even new ways to steal land from your People. You have already heard about the way they gave land away several times to different tribes. After the People were in the West, the Aliens' government started giving their land away to their own Aliens. This was called the Allotment Act, passed by Congress as the Dawes Act. Very simply explained, it meant the government now took away the People's land. The argument they used was that the People were not converting to using money, and the benefits and entitlements that government owed to the People cost the Alien taxpayers money. In an effort to make the People pay for their own burdens under the entitlements, Indian lands were confiscated, and 'redistributed' in smaller allotments to the People. The remainder was sold to the overpopulating Aliens. It made no difference how many acres one of the People owned, or how many there were in a household, each male head of a family of any size was given back only one hundred and twenty acres, and the rest of his land was taken with *no* financial consideration and then sold, with the Shawnee receiving not a penny of the money. The money supposedly went to the government to allow the People to make a contribution toward the government expense of keeping them. This was a 'privilege' no other people have been required to make who receive benefits and entitlements from the government. The government had so many different 'policies' that hardly anyone could keep up with them. Further complicating all of this was a lack of understanding on the part of the People."

The Bosha Stone became quiet for a moment before it continued. "I can hardly decide which of these 'policies' to tell you of next, Young One. Our time is almost over, and each one caused such suffering to your people that should I tell you of them all we would sit through another night. I will tell you of some additional policies, but I must ask you to look into the others when you can. First, you need to understand the suffering of your relatives who were removed from this beloved place in Ohio. Your people in Oklahoma fought to live in ways that were quite different from the ways of your ancestors. In Ohio they had to hide their true identities from their neighbors to keep from being murdered, for they were in the midst of the Aliens whose blood ran boiling hot with memories of wars, raids, and the People's killing of their immediate families. The Aliens always feared your people would be strong enough to reclaim what had been stolen from them. Also, your relatives who went west often struggled with starvation and disease. So the policies of the Aliens' government just added to their troubles.

"I want to tell you of the education policy that the Aliens enforced. They believed it was in the best interest of all for the People to become like the Aliens in every way. They decided the children needed to be educated in the Aliens' schools to learn the Alien ways. As adults then the People would be money-earners, no longer necessitating entitlement payments from the public treasury.

"Young One," the Bosha Stone said, "now is a good time to introduce you to a term in current usage called 'buyer's remorse' which means that a person buys something and shortly after decides he does not want to live up to the terms. He convinces himself and tries to convince others that the deal is either unfair or illegal, therefore not binding, and thus needs to be changed to suit his current desires. In reality, the transaction is legal and binding but the 'remorseful' person generally finds some way to change the execution of the terms, if in no other way than simply not performing obligations. This was true in every case with the Aliens: they invoked the doctrine of buyer's remorse. The last hundred or so years shows the constant attempt to nullify agreements and find ways for the People to pay for the entitlements the government was responsible for to pay or to change, delete, or cancel those entitlements.

"Oh my!" exclaimed the Bosha Stone. "Now I simply must tell you about the *termination policy*. But first I will finish telling you about the effects of the Education Policy. It must be stated that this policy was perhaps the only one that was truly intended to help the people as the Aliens perceived what they believed were our needs. They had no respect for and little knowledge of the intelligence, nor the forms of knowledge and teaching that your people had. Because the knowledge concerned natural life and values instead of the artificial values that had become the norm for the Aliens, they saw no value in 'Indian ways.' Because they did not truly believe there is but one Creator, they were terrified of your people's form of worship and expressing appreciation to Creator. It is a sad human failing, one we Stones are quite glad we do not have, that humans are afraid of what they don't know of or understand and so feel they must destroy it and replace it with ways with which they are personally familiar.

"Young One, throughout history knowledge has been destroyed by those who were afraid of differentness. But on with the story: It was felt urgent that your old knowledge and old teachings and especially the old teachers be replaced by the Aliens' own school teachers. And so sadly the old ways were destroyed.

"Young One, you know that it is tradition that the grandparents teach the grandchildren. With the new education policy, as soon as a child was toilet-trained and could speak well, usually around the age of four years, the government would insist that the child be sent to an Alien school. On the face of things this was unreasonable at a time when there were few schools of any type and fewer than forty percent of the Aliens themselves ever went beyond the sixth grade level of school and far fewer females went to school than males.

"Still, the government insisted on schooling for Indian children. The schools in the territory of the People were run by churches, mostly Baptists, Methodists, and the Quaker Friends. These religious denominations received contracts from the government giving them permission and some assistance to build and run schools for the People.

"Some of the schools were more than sixty or even a hundred miles from where the children's families lived, and at that time the only means of transportation available was walking. Thus, these were boarding schools. The children were taught to read and write in English and arithmetic. Actually, they were in classes only half a day, the other half being set aside for work for all the children, from age four on up. They were taught to farm, clean house and other daily 'chore' skills. This was thought to be a way to teach them how to earn a living after they graduated at age sixteen. Many did go on to become servants at the Alien homes and their farms, based on their educations received at these boarding schools.

"Young One, there is much to be said for teaching the children some of these things: they did need to know some of it in order to interact with the world outside their tribal grounds. The bad part was that some families never saw their precious children from the time they were taken at age four until they graduated eight years later. Some families were not told where their children were, and the children were basically kidnapped from their homes or while outside playing. Some children thought perhaps their families had suddenly died and they had been placed in an orphanage. They received no explanations, nor were they allowed to ask, resulting in sheer terror for the children and heart-wrenching sadness for their families. Government policy at that time literally created a cultural death many times over because persons, family structure, language, customs, and religion all died at the same time.

"If the children spoke their native tongue they were punished, usually by being beaten with a stick. Children accustomed to being barefooted were required to wear stiff, heavy shoes which caused bloody sores on their feet, yet if they took the shoes off to relieve the pain, they were beaten. So many things were done to excess that were ever so cruel, it fairly makes me weep to think on these tender dear little ones' sufferings.

193

I am certain that were this to take place today the cruelty would not be so severe because the current laws of the land protect even Indian children in more precise ways.

"Young One, do you remember your old friend the sign painter?" the Bosha Stone asked.

The Young One thought for a moment and remembered the gentle old man who always smiled so sweetly and who loved to dance. "Yes, I remember him now, he told me he once went to the Indian 'schools,' " the Young One responded.

"Well," continued the Bosha Stone. "Look at his hands the next time you see him, while he holds his dance fan and rattle. See how his fingers are all crooked, Young One. That is not from age or old people's disease arthritis, it is from being beaten with a steel-edged stick by the official *Government Child Beater*, for slipping and speaking his own language in conversation with his brother instead of using English. Oh, they gave this person an official title —'Disciplinary Officer'— but he was in fact the 'Official Government Child Beater.' I am sure the taxpayers never realized they were paying someone to beat little children who were slow in their lessons or who made mistakes."

The Young One's heart ached when he thought of how shy and kind the old painter was when he had come last time to Green Corn Celebration at Shawandasse. He remembered overhearing the last shreds of a conversation that the old painter had once had with one of the other men. It hadn't made sense to him then, but now he thought he understood what the old painter had meant when he said, "They were trying to beat the 'Indianness' out of us." The Young One's heart was very heavy indeed.

The Bosha Stone then spoke in a more forceful tone saying, "Well, Young One, it was hard on the children and it virtually destroyed the continuity of the People's culture. By the time the children did come home no one knew them. They were strangers in their own families. They could not speak the Shawnee language anymore, so they could not communicate with their elders and their grandparents. Their ideas and values had changed, reflecting those they had been taught in the Aliens' schools. And they had been exposed to the Aliens' form of religion based on 'hell' and 'punishment' which was not part of either the Shawnee religion or that of any other Native People before the Aliens came.

"It was hard to tell which was more heartbreaking," said the Bosha Stone, "when the children were stolen and taken away or when they came back total strangers.

"I must tell you though, Young One, the Aliens' policy this time began to backfire on them. As the children grew they began to relearn some of the things about their tribal ways. For every Shawnee thing they learned it seemed they lost a hundred. Some took no notice and seemed to have lost their hearts, letting their inner Shawnee fire die. But some were like Kohkumthena's feisty dog and kept their spirit. These were the ones who took the lessons they learned in the boarding schools and found ways to fight for what their People had been promised. There were only a few of these feisty ones, but they have accomplished many good things. I will tell you of them after I tell you about this *Termination* trick.

"In 1946, long before you were born, Congress began to implement a new policy they referred to as Termination. Some of the old People think this was the cruelest blow of all, with the government always trying to find ways to relieve themselves of their responsibilities to the Indian People and trying to save the money necessary for executing the entitlements. This 'termination' seemed to be the ultimate answer.

"Termination was not simply a single policy but had many segments. Congress set up an Indian Claims Commission to review, investigate, and come to conclude any yet-unresolved Indian claims against the government, and this commission was to have the final word on these matters. Strangely, a tribe that wanted to sue the government had to receive permission from Congress to do so. Amazingly, this permission was sometimes granted, although as you can imagine it was granted very seldom. Remember the chief from Oklahoma who told how it took almost forty years for this commission to conduct its investigations, and the tribe had to pay the attorneys that the government had chosen for them?

"Another segment of the ultimate solution was referred to as the Assimilation Act which took young people from the reservations and relocated them to major cities. These people were trained in factory work or the like, moved to the city by bus or train, helped to get a sleeping room or apartment, given a bus ticket and an alarm clock, and then declared to be assimilated into the mainstream of America.

"In actuality, Young One, these poor people were from rural communities where perhaps their nearest neighbor was miles away. They were used to being in constant company of their family members. The sounds their ears were used to were the sounds of nature — singing birds, trees sighing and creaking in the blowing wind, and chirping bugs. The People were accustomed to feeling the softness of Mother Earth beneath their feet, feeling the sweet winds kiss their cheeks, seeing the first rays of sun at dawn and the rich colors of sunset and the glimmer of the moon and stars at night.

"The relocation took them to areas where they felt nothing beneath their feet but the hard concrete and pavement that separated them from sacred Mother Earth. The brick buildings obscured the view and blocked the wind. The air was foul with fumes from industry and automobiles. The water held harsh chemicals and was no longer sweet. Lacking confidence, and knowing no one in these large cities, the People were like oarless canoes set adrift at sea. They were unable to worship Creator as they had been taught, and even the sacred herbs of sage, cedar, tobacco and sweetgrass were impossible to obtain in these huge cities teeming with strangers.

"Some of the young People could not bear the strain of being so far from their familiar homes and so went back to the reservations. Some tried very hard to make a success of themselves according to the Aliens' standards because the money they earned was so desperately needed back home. Loneliness was said to have been the worst part of all this. People with totally different culture, language, and religious beliefs surrounded them. With no one to talk with, no companionship, and no spiritual support, many of the young people were led to seek any type of friendship.

"Young One, I must point out that there are places in any society that are totally accepting of all types of people, even those who do not speak any English, so long as they have enough money to buy a drink, and these are taverns and bars that sell liquor. It is now known that the People's systems respond terribly to alcohol, so the young People who drank acted terribly, as was predicted in the Great Laws. They lost their heads and their ways.

"Alcohol is truly a depressant and the last thing the People needed was to be depressed, but of course, they were unaware of all of that at the time. Many became victims of suicide because they could not help themselves stop drinking and they were aware of their disgrace in the eyes of the old ones back home. Suicide was never an acceptable practice, for life is the most precious gift we all have from Creator, so for them to succumb to such an action tells you how low their spirits and hearts had sunk. More than half of those young People who were relocated committed suicide and more than eighty percent of the survivors became alcoholics. Instead of becoming assimilated the People, for the most part, became lost.

"A very few of the relocated People joined together to create urban Indian societies that blended the customs of the many nations they came from into comfortable, supportive communities. The percentages of those who succeeded in this path of mutual support versus those who either returned to their original homes or committed suicide or became resolute drunks and alcoholics were unfortunately very small.

"The final phase of this termination came as a horrible shock to many tribes. The government simply refused to acknowledge them as valid American Indian People-Tribes anymore. They refused to honor the terms of the old treaties, to send money to the tribal authorities, to assist the People in any way. Your Shawnee people were spared this horror, but many of their neighbors suffered this, some whom your People were connected to through intermarriage.

"Under termination the tribes reorganized into corporations, the members became shareholders, and the reservation became a county. The People tried very hard to make this work. Unfortunately, it was doomed to failure because of the restrictions which were placed on these Indian corporations that were never required of non-Indian corporations. They were supervised by boards of local Alien men, and the bulk of the shares were controlled by white bankers. This was true of most of the terminated tribes.

"Young One, the tribal People involved are now considered pitiful People who have no valid identification. For after termination the People are no longer recognized by any of the Aliens' governing bodies on any level, township, county, state, federal — no one. Of course they know who they are themselves and other Indian People know who they are, but the government broke them down until they were dependent on the government for their very existence and then the government refused to acknowledge their existence.

"It is sad, Young One. Your own branch of the Shawnee here in Ohio have to fight constantly to explain their identity simply because Tecumseh refused to sign any treaties. That fact did not mean you were not

Shawnee, simply that you were of a division not recorded as having accepted the so-called peace between yourselves and the American Aliens. Since you were not entitled to benefits and received no outlays of money, there are no official records of your existence, thus no official or federal recognition. You are still as authentic Shawnee as those who signed treaties, but your life's path has been a different one. Your citizenship, religion, and culture is the same, and in some ways your branch of the People has suffered less mutation of those things than the People on reservations who adopted changes from their neighboring tribes."

The Bosha Stone grew quietly reflective and finally sighed as it said, "It is difficult to understand such a dishonorable way to treat such honorable People in the name of Creator. See to it, Young One, that as you walk your own life's path that you remain honorable according to your own People's old traditional standards, not these false ones of today.

"During the 1920s and 1930s several policy changes came about, but the one that affected everyone the most was when the People officially became American citizens. This allowed them to share the same privileges as all other American citizens: they had to pay taxes and then they were 'allowed' to be drafted as soldiers in the army to protect the country in time of war."

The Bosha Stone stopped to reflect, and seemed to be almost smiling as it continued. "I promised to tell you about ways the People used the Education Act to the benefit of the People. I must tell you that what happened to your own People also happened to all the other Nations of People who were placed on the reservations. The same policies tore their lives apart and caused each of them the same hardships. Many times you hear the phrase 'you are all brothers,' and this is certainly true concerning the misery your families suffered at the hands of the conquering Alien invaders. But, as I have said, some of their people also were like Grandmother Kohkumthena's feisty dog, and they found ways to change some of the bad elements of the reservation world. By that time your people no longer had a true reservation because it had been allotted out and sold. But you were all still due many entitlements that were not being delivered correctly.

"These feisty ones became what was called 'activists.' They marched across the country protesting wrongs that were being done. They held buildings hostage, reclaiming them for the People, attracting attention to the continuing wrongs. They became politically active and helped defeat some politicians and helped to elect others, using the Aliens' own form of government to the benefit of the People. This inspired a few of the young People to go on to college and study law so they could help all the People in this way, for the Aliens' lawyers were very shrewd men who always seemed to find ways to take advantage of the People.

"Modern times enjoy an instancy in communications that was impossible in earlier times, Young One. Because of the available electronic media of television and radio, events can be reported as they are occurring. Equipment has become small enough that the cameras, microphones, and recorders can be carried in one hand. When your people were first relocated in the nineteenth century, the only form of communication to the general public was through the newspapers which sometimes published only once a week or month. Now it does not matter whether the public reads or not; they can still be aware of what is going on. It is not possible to edit a live camera on the scene to leave out the undesirable information. All the information is broadcast, so injustices can be reported firsthand. This proved to be one of the most powerful positive things to ever happen to the Native People.

"These feisty ones knew how to attract attention and they knew how to make sure there were television and radio people present to record the happenings. The general public was shocked to find the circumstances under which the People of all the native Nations lived. They began to write their congressional representatives and senators concerning what they had seen on television, demanding investigations and changes and the quality of life of the native People of all the Nations improved. It is never easy but today improvements are still being made.

"Do you remember, Young One, one of the other Stones told you that Creator gave you a power. It is called *truth*. These feisty ones believed in the truth, and they believed that the public was not evil, but simply did not know the truth. History is proving their thoughts to be true.

"There were turbulent times and even bloodshed when the feisty ones began their campaigns in the sixties. Times now are still awkward and full of troubles, but new wars are being waged on different fronts and for different problems as some of those young ones who learned the Aliens' laws now take over the old battles. These new battles are being waged for religious rights for the People. This American government was supposed to support religious freedom, which was one of the premises of the ancient documents used to guide the citizens. Yet the practice of the Peoples' ancient religion has always been thwarted in many ways. The feisty ones have undertaken the legal battles to insure that the People are allowed to use the sacred feathers of the sacred witness the Eagle as you pray and as the customs of honor allowed you in the past, and the owl and hawk feathers that you are eligible to wear and use as your birthright as a Shawnee.

"There are many things the feisty ones are doing for your benefit and yes, some of these activists are Shawnee. This is a time when many of the Native People have joined together to fight what is wrong, just as they joined Tecumseh in his battles."

The Bosha stone was exhausted. Because of the wide extent of its travels it had much to share with the Young One. But now as it paused, a very ancient-sounding voice spoke up. It was the Altar Stone.

"I have listened to all of you teaching the Young One and I wish to compliment you all on the amount of knowledge and wisdom you have shared and imparted to the Young One this short night. If no one objects, I wish to speak of the 'now' times. Our Shawnee are still vibrant and progressive people, as they have been for thousands of years. Great Mask, may I share with the Young One my perceptions of his people's present and future conditions?" the ancient Altar Stone asked.

"Oh my, yes!" responded the Mask, "We are greatly honored that you are pleased with our efforts and that you want to contribute. Please, speak."

The voice of the ancient Altar Stone was quavery, but sounded confident. "Young One, there are several things we need to have you know. First, the Shawnee who continued to interact with and be documented by the Aliens' government have fought hard to exist,. They have succeeded. Each division has much to be proud of. Their survival cost each division in many ways. Each has had to adopt the business ways of the Aliens. Eventually each ended up with some material resources needing to be managed for the benefit of all their People. They had to learn these Alien ways to protect themselves from unscrupulous dealings, and honestly Young One, the Shawnee have always been a most independent People. They did not want strangers handling their affairs forever.

"The Absentee Shawnee in Oklahoma became a governorship. They still hold meetings similar to old Councils, but the modern meetings primarily deal with the business matters of the tribe. Numbering about forty-five hundred, they are one of the two officially federally-recognized Shawnee tribes. The Absentee are considered to be the most conservative and unchanged of all the Oklahoma Shawnee. They hold more of the reli-

201

gious ceremonies in the old ways than do the other two divisions and are more knowledgeable in ancient oral traditions. But even they have lost much more of their traditions and tribal knowledge than they care to let anyone know. The Absentee Shawnee's land base is a subject they prefer not to discuss, but they believe they are in a financial position to purchase whatever amount of land they desire. This too is a good example of the Shawnee tradition of self-sufficiency.

"The Absentee were the first to go off by themselves from Ohio, and today they still enjoy their privacy and the privilege of being themselves without complaint or interference from outsiders. On a one-to-one basis, these Shawnee show the true spirit of their ancestors by being warm, pleasant, hospitable, charming, and witty. But when all is said and done they still prefer and relish being with their own. Young One, if you ever have the opportunity to meet and speak with any of this division, enjoy it, and do remember they appreciate politeness and old-fashioned respect. Most of the oral traditions you have been taught this night have been told by the Absentee for hundreds of years. It was the grandparents of those Absentee now alive who related these oral traditions to a woman named Erminie Wheeler Voegelin more than sixty years ago.

"The next group I wish to tell you about is known by two names: some call them the Loyal Shawnee, and others refer to them as the Cherokee-Shawnee. They truly are Shawnee and include the last of those of the People to leave Ohio. The Loyals have about eight thousand tribal members and are the largest group of your people, yet because of their unique legal agreement with the Cherokee they are not what is termed 'federally recognized' as Shawnee. This makes an accurate accounting of Shawnee Nation very difficult, if not impossible. It also creates complications regarding receipt of any entitlements, some of which they get through the Cherokee, others of which they must deal for directly with the Bureau of Indian Affairs.

"The Loyals signed an actual treaty with the Cherokee in 1869, a legal transaction for the use of a portion of the northern section of the Cherokee's reservation land. The northern section was chosen because it was gently rolling and reminded them of their traditional Ohio homelands, while the middle and lower sections of their reservation were quite hilly . The Delaware also had a similar transaction and live to the immediate west of the Shawnee.

"The Loyals had their last official chief in 1894. The current tribal structure of the Loyal Shawnee is similar to the Absentees but they are incorporated. Their leader is known as a chairman, and he reports to a board similar to that of a regular corporation in any business, but only on the finances and business interests of the tribe. The Loyals also have their traditional leaders who oversee and direct religion, ceremonies, and the culture. The two divisions may work hand-in-hand on a project, but only with the board managing or providing funding for whatever projects the traditional leaders have agreed upon.

"One major difference in the structure of the Loyal Shawnee from that of the ancient tradition is that the Loyals are matrilineal, tracing their lineage through the females for genealogical tracing. Other Shawnee are patrilineal, using the father's lineage. The elders of the tribe are considered the true leaders and their approval must be gained before projects are acted upon. The elders have earned this respect and it is lovingly given. Several of the grandparents of the Loyal Shawnee were also interviewed and told their oral traditions sixty years ago.

"Young One, the Loyals also deserve your respect should you be fortunate enough to meet any of them. They too are a fine, warm, and pleasant people. They have suffered greatly in the past, and in some ways still suffer, for life is hard in those western lands. They have endured the hardships and survived. They are representative of all the Shawnee, in that in time past, they were oppressed and beaten to the ground, but they have fought hard and are now standing proud. The People are together and of one mind in looking at their past for guidance in building a solid future. The People are once again proud to be Shawnee, although we Stones can say your people have always been proud of who and what they were and are. The original land the Loyals had was lost through the Allotment and Relocation Acts, so they now have individually-owned homes, but sometimes in small community clusters. The actual tribal land base is less than one hundred acres.

"The Loyal Shawnee still have some Shawnee-speaking people among their elders, and they still hold their sacred ceremonies. Through the years some of the ceremonies have changed due to influences of the neighboring tribes and for other reasons, but what they have left is considered very sacred to them, and they guard it as a most precious treasure. There was much Christian missionary work done among the Loyal Shawnee, so many today are Christians. The new universal Indian peyote religion called the Native American Church also has found many followers among the Loyals. The People fulfilled many of the old chiefs' prophecies, and they argued and were hostile toward each other and the various forms of worship that each tribe had adopted, but presently the Shawnee are reverting to their old traditional ways of tolerance, and respect each other's individual rights to worship Creator as each is guided. To have this happen is a good thing.

"Young One, there is one more group of Shawnee in Oklahoma — the Eastern Shawnee. They are the other division of Shawnee who are federally recognized. This group seems to have lost the most in the way of traditions and culture. This group no longer holds the old religious ceremonies, nor do they teach their young in the old ways. Many years ago the old people would quarrel about the oral traditions and the culture. Don't forget, Young One, that each of these Oklahoma Shawnee groups is made up of at least two septs which have different origination stories, and separate divisions whose histories and migrations have been vastly different, and have eventually coalesced to become the great Shawnee Nation that exists now.

"I remember," said the ancient Altar Stone chuckling, "one time several of the elders had come together and for once everyone got along fine. After dinner they were seen hobbling out in the meadow to admire the full moon, leaning heavily on their twin sets of canes. The next thing anyone knew the elders were fussing at one another, swearing and striking each other with one cane as they leaned on the other. They were quarreling over the month in which this full moon was shining. One old division of Shawnee held to a thirteen-month year while the other used a twelve-month year. Such was the magnitude of the subject matter of the cultural quarrels, but each person's family had different traditions and history and they were all ready to fight about the validity of what each had to say.

"The chief decided that thereafter the tribe would meet only to discuss business, and all cultural matters would be handled within the private homes. The tribe seemed to lose its focus except for the Aliens' sacred circle, the coin of the realm — money. The chief and council are now aware that to be a whole nation there must be the balance of enriching educational, cultural, and spiritual concerns, not just financial stability.

"The Eastern Shawnee still have a chief as their leader. Like the other Shawnee they too have a business committee that supervises the tribe's financial dealings. Their original land holdings have now dwindled to about three hundred acres.

"Because of the Indian Land Gaming Regulatory Act, all the Shawnee in Oklahoma now have bingo operations to supplement the people's needs no longer met by entitlements because of Congressional budget cuts. A full set of clothing for each child beginning school, scholarships for those going on to college, hot meals for the elderly, medical care assistance, eye glasses, dental work — all of these are funded from the bingo halls. Everyone thinks all the Indian people's needs are covered by the government, but government assistance is never enough. It is a good example of right thinking that the Shawnee use their proceeds from bingo to help all the People. Some funds, admittedly, are not always used in good ways. Again, the Shawnee people are proud to set the good example."

The ancient Altar Stone was silent for a moment and then continued, "You may meet some of the Eastern Shawnee some day, Young One. And when you do you will find they are very like the people here at Shawandasse. They too have a few very old ones who can remember a few of the old Shawnee words and stories, but not enough to fill the empty places in their hearts. Like your people here, they are reaching out to rediscover as much as is possible, to recover what has been lost.

"You will find their hearts sincere, their eyes steady, their hands stretched out in friendship and as long as you are right-thinking they will respect you. One ancient priceless gift from Creator at the time of the beginning they have not lost, and that is the strength of truth. They are not perfect but they do value the truth and speak it openly from their hearts. When you meet them, Young One, be most respectful, for they are a remnant of the ancestors, and even in their condition of loss, they have much to teach you."

The ancient Altar Stone breathed a heavy sigh as it finished its teaching. It was obviously remembering the full days and richly elaborate ceremonies and grand feasts it had shared with the Shawnee of times gone by.

The Mask made a gruff sound like large gravel being dumped from a truck, the equivalent to clearing one's throat, then spoke, "Thank you, ancient Altar Stone. You know of so many wonderful things you could have taught the Young One, and it was frustrating for me to listen to you speak of today's history instead of that of long ago. You did not even tell him how his Okima went to the place where you had been buried for so many years, and dug you up, and brought you to the Great House, or how for years the People did without you and only used Mother Earth, and some pebbles and sand as an altar, until they knew it was safe to retrieve you. Some night, Ancient Stone, we will all listen to your stories. I look forward to it."

The ancient Altar Stone made a sound of pleasure that seemed to magnify its already robust size. Already it was rehearsing and trying to choose the most interesting stories it knew for that fine night to come, which it hoped would be soon.

Bright streaks of melon and purple were radiating on the horizon, and the Young One could tell that the sunrise was truly not too long away. He felt a weariness unusual for one his age, but it was balanced with an effervescent excitement that kept him alert, feeling joyful inside.

Ever so faintly a sound kept repeating, as if trying to get his attention, but he couldn't quite locate or understand it. After several minutes the Mask itself groused and demanded, "Who is it? Who is trying to speak? We can't hear you — be bold!" The small, faint sound stopped.

"I am the Heart Stone!" a voice yelled at last. "I am over here, outside, in the heart of the community, on the edge of the woods. I know I am not a Great House Stone or Ceremony Stone, but I thought the Young One might remember me and would like to know that I am included as an important stone to his People."

"Yes, oh yes!" the Mask replied. "You are absolutely correct. You are indeed a valuable part of the Shawnee history which we must not forget. I agree, you are at a disadvantage being buried away from the Great House in the heart of the community as you are. At least the Altar Stone is used several times a year, but you remain buried until the village moves on, when you are unearthed and reburied at their new location. We Great House Stones consider you as vital as the heartbeat of the Nation. You are part of the continuity of their lives. Please speak, Heart Stone," the Mask encouraged.

"Young One," the distant voice inquired, "do you remember when you were a small boy of four, and the okima took you and your playmates out to the edge of the woods here at Shawandasse, where a big hole had been dug in the ground? Some of the children were frightened because they did not know what was going on, but you were trusting and brave. After several songs and a prayer your okima explained to you children that I was the Heart Stone, and was to be buried here at Shawandasse so the community would have a heart. One of the elders brought me and the children placed me gently in the hole, and then each child took a handful of dirt and gently covered me. Oh, Young One, how sweetly the children handled me and the handfuls of Mother Earth. That was truly my finest hour, for to me that was the moment you Shawnee came home and again were in fact possessors of the homeland — not when the bank loan was approved and signed for you to buy back the property of the Ancestors in Ohio.

"Someday when you are an elder, Young One, the People will move again, and you will be the one to remember where I am buried. It will be up to you to go and dig me up and carry me to your new tribal home, so the new village or community will have a heart, for so it has always been. And the smallest children will again bury me deep within the breast of Mother Earth. Remember that while I am buried I pray for you and the People and I help good things to find you, and give bad directions to evil things so they cannot approach.

"While you are remembering these things, Young One, think of the dreams of the future of Shawandasse. Your okima told the children of the permanent community to be built, a place where the old ways that were good can be recaptured and can help the People today, and a place for the protected burial grounds for the remains of those who cross over to spirit. Because I am a Heart Stone I can read hearts' innermost thoughts and secrets. I read your okima's that day. Deep in his heart he longs for what once was. He dreams of the time when all the Shawnee people will come home to the heart of the Middle Ground, to celebrate, hold ceremonies, feast, hunt, even to live. It is his idea of the ultimate gift to the Ancestors. Okima has many children and he wants for them to be able to pass on to their grandchildren's grandchildren the traditions of your ancestors, to honor Creator together, to rejuvenate the old Great Laws of respect for the earth and the other nations, and for all the Shawnee to share a common history and culture that is so good it wipes out the memories of the sad times. These are the things I read in his heart on my burial day," the Heart Stone said thoughtfully.

The Heart Stone was very happy to be included in the sacred teachings of a Young One in his fourth life, and its voice almost bubbled. Then it became very serious as it said, "Although the Bosha Stone has hesitated to tell you, I would like to give you information on its recent arrival in our midst. Perhaps it is too modest to do so.

Children Among the Heartstone

"Already you understand it is one of the most unusual Stones in the tribe. After being taken out west, the Bosha Stone stayed with the medicine man who had led the People away from Ohio. Things went from terrible to worse out there for the Shawnee. You know that each sept was responsible for some particular function in the tribal structure, and each sept had its own bundle which contained sacred items. Some of these items had special powers given from Creator or the spirits. Some of the items were emblems of authority, rather like the scepter or wand of a king.

"Well, when things became so bad in Oklahoma the People lost their senses," the Heart Stone said sadly. "In their frustration over the conditions of their lives, they began to feel jealousy and anger at their fellow tribal members of the different septs. They stole items from each other's bundles, sometimes destroying the items, sometimes replacing them with something foolish; sometimes the keepers of the bundles would get drunk and sell or give away sacred items to museums. After a few years the sacred bundles had been so depleted that nothing was left but a few stone items and a little bit of tobacco and a few feathers.

"One keeper of the bundle became so afraid the bundle might be tampered with or stolen that she buried it, and refused to tell anyone the location. When she died this bundle was lost to the People forever.

"As time passed and the medicine man grew quite old, he became increasingly worried about what would be the new history of the People. None of his apprentices seemed to have the gifts from Creator that powerful medicine men of old possessed. The People needed strong and right-thinking shamans and medicine men now more than ever but, the old one had to admit, this generation was sorely lacking in spirituality and commitment. The apprentices whined that it was too demanding to be taught and so bluffed their way, took short cuts, and resorted to cheap trickery. They no longer looked upon the position of medicine man as a sacred trust, but as an opportunity for prestige, power, and material gain. The chiefs had been made powerless by the American Aliens' government, but for a while these medicine men were still respected. The old medicine man knew he would be one of the last true medicine people of the Shawnee, that in the future there would be many pretenders.

"The presence of the Bosha Stone disturbed the old medicine man because it was difficult to find an appropriate and safe hiding place for it. He was also concerned about what part the Bosha Stone might possibly play in the People's future. The old medicine man had instructed the People to never look back to the Ohio Valley, and to never again think of it as their homeland. He didn't want his people to ever have to strike out for a new place to live. He thus decided to try to find some way to retire the Bosha Stone as a guide, and began praying for help. The medicine man spent weeks purifying, praying, offering the sacraments, and asking for Creator's help to change the Stone's purpose.

"It seemed that the medicine man was failing in his quest, for no wisdom came, no visions, and no messengers. In fact, it appeared the sacred messengers were refusing to even carry his words to Creator, because his sacred fire — *skota* — would not start, his tobacco would not burn, the eagles and hawks were nowhere to be seen, and even the wind would not blow. He became very disturbed at the implications." The Heart Stone fully understood the old medicine man's fears.

"Finally, the medicine man began all over again," the Heart Stone continued. "He purified himself with cedar, and offered tobacco and sage and sweet grass. Then he quietly picked up the Bosha Stone and went for a walk in the woods. He came to a rushing creek, and with a final prayer for his people, and all the strength in his old, feeble arms, he flung the Bosha Stone far into the water. As it sank and the ripples subsided, the medicine man felt great relief.

"The Bosha Stone was relieved too, as it returned to the waters of Mother Earth from which it had come so long ago. For over one hundred years the waters of the creek caressed the Stone's surface. Occasional spring floods and rushes would dislodge the Bosha Stone and move it downstream, closer to where the People had now expanded their activities and were building small communities.

"In 1992 a group of your people were invited by a division of the Oklahoma Shawnee to attend a ceremony to dedicate a new building. Oh, it was a red-letter day! The woman, Wakwashbosha, had come from Ohio with the others. The morning before they returned home, she was walking through the woods near their lodging place, and came upon a creek. She had already chosen several unusual stones to take home with her as remembrances of the hospitable manner in which everyone had treated the visiting Ohio Shawnee. She decided to wade a bit in the shallow creek before leaving, and it was there she found the Bosha Stone vibrantly "beaconing" to her. And you know the rest of the story about how she brought it home. The Stone now rests on her own private altar, and she placed a different stone at the base of the spirit pole at Tecumseh Point.

"Since the Bosha Stone returned to the Ohio homeland, all three Oklahoma divisions of the Shawnee have officially returned, and have been here on many different official occasions. One Oklahoma leader has worked with the local People and his division now possesses a small piece of ground, including a burial mound. Another division also holds a small amount of land in another part of Ohio. You see, Young One, the sacred messengers did not cooperate with the old medicine man because they knew that the People would in fact return one day to the Ohio Valley, and that the Bosha Stone would come first, blazing the trail for the homeward return.

"We Stones know also the part of the tradition of your first ancestors who came here and eventually sent a few people back across the Big Water to tell the others about this wonderful land. One of those going back to Mexico had scooped up the Bosha Stone from the creekside in Ohio and took it with him. And thus it went, the Bosha Stone went to Mexico and came back north a thousand years ago when the People came back to North America. It took its sad trip west to Oklahoma, and now is back in its beloved homeland of Ohio, with its beloved People, the descendants of the ancient Shawnee travelers, and it remains a symbol of hope for the future of the People."

The Heart Stone concluded its speech just as the first rays of the morning sun cleared the horizon, and a hush fell over all the community.

The Young One flinched and came fully awake as someone touched him lightly on the wrist. It was the man who had come to relieve him on the night watch. He quickly looked over at the Old Watcher who had been sleeping so soundly that his blanket had wrapped around him like a cocoon, and who now fumbled to extricate himself. Tired though he was, the Young One could not suppress a smile. Finally the tousled hair and sleep-matted eyes of the Old Watcher came into view. He sat upright and shook himself like an old hound dog after a dip, and the relief man gave the Old Watcher his arm for support and helped him to his feet.

By this time the Young One was up and clutching his own blanket to comfort himself in his great fatigue. He was so very tired, but he was so excited and there were so many things he wanted to discuss with the Old Watcher now that he too was awake. But the Old Watcher was still dazed with sleepiness; the Young One would have to wait.

The old man and the young boy left the Great House and walked towards the woods, and Old Watcher asked the Young One if he had learned anything that night. His answer came in such a jumbled rush that the Old Watcher finally raised his hand to stop the onslaught of words and smiled. He realized that the ancient, sacred Great House Stones had decided to teach the Young One themselves that night and that the boy had indeed learned many things. The Old Watcher softly told the Young One how he envied him the course of adventures he had now begun.

They neared the place in the path where they would separate when the Old Watcher stopped and pulled a small, beautifully beaded bag from his pocket. It was lumpy and obviously quite old for a skin bag. The Old Watcher reached inside and took a small piece of diorite out and handed it to the Young One, who caught the tiny piece of stone in his palm. He looked questioningly at the Old Watcher.

"Young One," the Old Watcher said, "I understand what happened to you tonight far better than you can imagine. This tiny piece of stone I have given you has been handed down from generation to generation. Its story, told to me when I received it, is vague as are most of our oral traditions: it once belonged to a powerful medicine man of ancient times when our people were in Mexico, and it has a power and a gift to return to the People when the time is right. The Spirits told me as I dreamed that it should now belong to you, for in you is the future of our people. I would not be surprised if the time is at hand for this sacred pebble to gift the People in some way. It and my prayers go with you as you journey into manhood, Young One.

"Oh, yes — I will also be speaking with your parents and the okima. I have been told by the spirits that you should have a new name. One who has received so much knowledge and wisdom must have a name that reflects it. The Spirits have chosen the name 'Night Watching Owl.' " The Old Watcher gave the Young One an affectionate pat on the shoulder. "I have a feeling last night was just the beginning of your lessons, Night Watching Owl," the Old Watcher said cheerfully.

Night Watching Owl placed the pebble of diorite into his own little medicine bag which hung on a slender thong around his neck. As he felt it slip to the bottom to nestle on the crumbles of sacred tobacco and sage there, Night Watching Owl prayed to Creator and the spirits for help on this path on which the Ancients had just placed his feet. He felt elated. What a wonderful future his people seemed to have, for the first time in hundreds of years. Night Watching Owl and the Old Watcher shook hands and parted company.

Once inside his lodge, the Old Watcher quickly spread out his blanket, lay down, and rolled up like a sausage in a roll. He felt he had only been napping in the Great House, but now with no responsibilities, in his own bed and with his own pillow, he could sleep deeply. He drifted off, remembering his own first time as a watcher in the Great House, how tired and confused he had been by all that he had experienced that night so long ago. "But this Young One," said the Old Watcher, "is already wise. He will be one to lead the People forward. He . . . will . . . bear . . . watching . . . snnnnarrkk . . . ." and the Old Watcher drifted away to sleep.

Taking care to not wake his still-sleeping family, Night Watching Owl slipped into his bed in his mother's lodge. As his weary head sank into his pillow, he wondered if he would be learning again in that special place between wakefulness and sleep. Would the Stones teach him only in the Great House? As he drifted into slumber he could feel his spirit separate from his body, and began to hear a familiar deep, resonating hum.

Appendix

Notes on Research and Verification

It should be noted that in this book, the tool of fiction has been used to tell the story of the Shawnee. It's true, though, that as we two-leggeds comprehend the world of nature today, we are unable to detect if stones do indeed communicate with us in some form other than by their visible, physical presence. That I have stones communicating with the Young One can be considered a fiction, although no one is capable of knowing this for certain.

One chapter concerns a sacred pipe made of diorite which was stolen, transported across the ocean; during its captivity most of its adornments deteriorated to dust. The pipe itself eventually was destroyed during a revolution, and a pebble of it was returned to the Shawnee People. This particular item and incident is representative of the thousands of Shawnee items and artifacts that, from the 1500s on, were taken to Europe and placed in royal vaults and private and state collections. Their former glory faded, the identifying material vanished, and the artifacts were housed unnoticed in heaps in storage areas, and today their existence and value is unknown to their possessors. It is a sad truth that only the tiniest fragment of artifacts and items in museums today can be positively identified specifically as Shawnee, as compared to items attributed to other Native Peoples. Thus oddly, such countries as Spain, France, Sweden, Germany, Austria, and even Denmark and Czechoslovakia, have more Shawnee specific artifacts in their museums than do England and the United States. I believed this matter needed to be addressed, and so I created the legendary stolen sacred diorite pipe.

One form of book writing involves using the device of placing the reader into a story at some place in time, taking the reader into the past and then bringing him full circle into the present where the story began. Because all Native Americans believe in life and time as an interconnected circle that continues, I decided to use a stone to connect all the known migrations of the People now known as Shawnee and their ancestors.

The reader will notice that oral tradition plays a great part throughout the book, especially where no written documents exist to prove authenticity. Because oral traditions of other tribes, the Cunas in particular, concerning the ancient People who left Mexico coincided with and validated what I had, I felt safe in using that information.

It is true there are and were several plain stones of some unremembered sacred significance in some of the Shawnee tribal bundles. The Bosha Stone actually does exist, but it is merely a stone found by Wakwashbosha while wading in Ohio water, after having prayed for a special stone to place at the spirit pole on Tecumseh Point. Because the markings are so unique, Bosha chose to keep it for her altar and used another stone at Tecumseh Point. The drawing in the book

219

depicts the actual markings on the stone. The stone and its peculiar markings lent itself to my need for a stone device to bring the story around from the first orally-accounted migration from Mexico to the final migration to Oklahoma. Recently all three Oklahoma divisions of Shawnee have returned to the Ohio Valley, so it's appropriate that I have the Bosha Stone do the same.

As for the rest of the material in this book, I would emphasize that I have not relied upon any of my personal knowledge but have gleaned the information from the following resources: official documents from United States, state, and county records, Colonial documents, journals, diaries, military records, and translations of foreign documents of governments and religious communities. I have pored over countless publications containing information about the Shawnee and their ancestors over the past thirty years, many when I was trying to fill in the gaps of my own knowledge base and had no intention of ever writing a book on the subject. Sadly, therefore, I kept no bibliography of any consequence, although I do have a list of a hundred or so sources that I have studied during the past three years.

I conducted interviews with various federally-recognized Shawnee, some federally-recognized Cherokee who claim they are still Shawnee, State of Ohio-recognized Shawnee, and people of Shawnee descent not affiliated with any recognized group. I have used handwritten field notes from interviews done by Erminie Wheeler Voegelin and her husband Charles "Carl" Voegelin, among many others, spanning more than forty years from 1932 through 1976, and also the audio tapes made by Mr. Voegelin. The Voegelin interviews were done in Oklahoma at the homes of the interviewees, in the presence of several credible witnesses, some of whom are still alive; these are also recorded on wax cylinders. At the time of the interviews, these elders were held in the highest regard in their Shawnee communities and were considered the most knowledgeable in traditions, culture, and religious matters. Any errors that might be found in these interviews may be that due to the great age of the interviewees, all first-generation Shawnee not born in Ohio. They possibly mis-remembered some items.

The interviewers themselves made notations that in 1932 the Oklahoma Shawnee had no knowledge or recollection of their lives in Ohio, or anything prior to coming to Kansas and Oklahoma. This is partially because they didn't have access to the same resources so readily available here in the Midwest and Ohio Valley region.

Besides the sources listed above, others include historians, linguists, anthropologists, and archeologists. I gleaned information from documents and oral traditions of the Walam Olum, oral and written traditions of the Cunas, Creek, Eyuchis, Cherokee, Delaware, Nanticokes, Seneca, and Wyandottes, among others, and from Chief Hawk Pope of Shawandasse. Every effort has been made to eliminate questionable material from the book. For example, I did not intend to use the story of the migration from Mexico until I found a treatise written in

1911 concerning the Shawnee claim that our people originated in Mexico. While the treatise gave no specific details, I considered it substantiating and thus chose to include the story.

Experts in other states that have been consulted include: Dave Costas, University of California; Jerry Malanich, University of Florida, Florida Museum of Natural History; Charles Hudson, University of Georgia; John Hann, Tallahassee, Florida; Patsy West, Florida; Lucia St. Claire Robson, Creek expert; Judith Grey, Library of Congress; Helen Tanner, Newberry Library; and dozens of others including staff at the Glenn Black Lab and Mathers Museum in Indiana. A special thank you for the wonderful information provided by author Jack Weatherford's research. Much detailed information was also found in the Indian Claims Commissions Papers. Special thanks also to Helen Tanner for permission to use the maps in her book.

Every effort has been made to distinguish fact from what is obviously fiction in this book, as there is no wish to confuse the reader nor sully in any way the fascinating history of this important People, the Shawnee. I only regret I have had to leave out so much of the history of the culture, as I believe the reader would find it as interesting as I do. Perhaps the future will bring that opportunity.

The Great Shawnee Laws

Author's Note: The Old People spoke Shawnee, which has a grammatical structure different from English. Although they had an extensive vocabulary they preferred to use descriptives instead of using nouns. They would also give an answer twice, using almost the exact same words but slightly rearranged. For the sake of clarity I have chosen to tell the Laws here in a succinct manner, with very little repetition. If time and space allowed I would have done it properly, as I am firmly convinced that changing even one word changes the context and one's comprehension. I offer these laws to you for the sake of attempting to let you see into our minds and hearts, and to help you understand why we consider all the Nations in nature sacred and important. Please remember that these Laws were spoken to someone over sixty years ago in Oklahoma by a person past the age of seventy who in turn had been taught them orally by a grandparent. We feel they have not changed nor have they become obsolete in any way since they were given to us by He Who Creates By Thinking — the Great Spirit Kiji Maneto, or the entity you refer to as Almighty God. I also ask that you try to think in a traditional manner, and if you find these thoughts and teachings peculiar, that you take no personal offense to them and respect that this is a sacred way to us; because it is our tradition that we have been taught by Creator, if it is all right with Creator, it of course is fine with you. We do not ask that you alter any of your beliefs nor practices of worship, only that you respect ours. I sincerely pray that each reader's heart and mind's eye be opened a little wider by the reading of these words.

I would have liked to have included more detail on the language and its translation from phonetic Shawnee to English. As the Sacred Stones have hinted, perhaps there will come another time when more of the language will be printed for all to share, now that more is available for the experts to work with. I look forward to that in the future.

Kohkumthena's Great Laws
as paraphrased by the Young One

The Young One began telling the Old Watcher his understanding of these Great Laws. They were similar to what he had heard of the laws that Creator gave in the Garden of Eden, except they were much more detailed. These seemed to tell everything about how to live a good life.

With a quiet firmness in his voice the Young One began. "Creator is mysterious and made us all in a mysterious way, so there is much we were not told, because we would not understand. The reason we are able to live is because of these laws that were given to us, and the way we follow them determines the way we will live. That is all we are, as we talk about Creator, that is the way we have good health and Creator will always help us. She always knows what we talk about even to one another.

"Kohkumthena handed down four great maneto, one on each side. We call each of these maneto 'Grandfather.' One in the morning who tends to the advice for us to follow, one at night to listen to our evening prayers, one grandfather in the winter who rules half of the daylight. When he makes the tree people to shed their leaves, we are then to bathe in the water with these leaves in it, to make it medicine, so we will be healthy all winter long, and it cleanses us and makes us pure. That is the reason grandfather winter has sympathy for us. The way that grandfather winter looks is his own idea.

"There are all kinds of spirits on this earth. One lives under the earth and another lives above. Now that one is one of Kohkumthena's grandfathers, and he sits in the west. He brings us the feeling of well being; when he comes we sleep and sometimes that is when this feeling comes. This is a way that Kohkumthena takes pity on us, that while we are sleeping we feel clean, safe, and well.

"There is one who sits to the south, and he rules the other half of the year. Day after day he will bring us useful things. Our grandfathers, the southerners, on the side where they sit, have all been notified by Kohkumthena. When he comes, we will remember to plant our food, the things that will benefit us in the future. We must never forget and always carry these things along with us as we live, for these are the things that will carry us along and let us survive. We must never forget that Kohkumthena gave us these ways.

"We have been given the way to carry on our relationship with what is called the supernatural. We are instructed as to the kind of respect we must have. Finally, in the end, we will be brought up to where Kohkumthena lives. We must never forget these laws or we will ruin ourselves. She has made everything on a grand scale for us so that we will survive. And Kohkumthena notified all the maneto of these things; that is how she created us. Because she favors everyone, they will talk about us too. She gave them the power to pray and to pray for us.

"She gave us a memory, so we would not forget how we should speak, when we interpret how she created us. And Kohkumthena also notified her grandfathers, the ones who sit higher up and have greater knowledge than she. She laid out everything underneath so we can find it by ourselves, and that we will have a future.

"When everyone else is speaking other languages, we are still to repeat the laws in Shawnee, because she created us with a spiritual power, so we will not make false talk. Kohkumthena gives us her notions, and when we repeat them as she created us, speaking Shawnee, we will be spiritually powerful. That spiritual power is how Kohkumthena will thank us, for repeating her notions, the way she has made for us and taught us.

"Sometimes we will not get what we pray for, but we will always get what will benefit us. We may look for benefit to any of the four sides. If we don't find what we are looking for, we will benefit from something else. The reason is, because it is all one, all the paths we follow. We will be taken up to Kohkumthena's home, by any of the paths in the way that she has devised for us.

"When we pray, our voice will reach to where Kohkumthena sits, and her voice will reach up there to the end of the world. But even Kohkumthena does not know how long the place where we live will survive. The reason Kohkumthena does not know how long we will survive is this, the world will survive as long as we correctly interpret the way we were created.

"We will guide our grandfathers and they will care for us. Everything is sacred the way that Kohkumthena created it. Kohkumthena does not hold any person higher than another, she regards us all equally.

"If we do not follow the ways she has created for us, then we will no longer receive help from that other side. We will no longer be respected from that side. And we will receive no help in keeping our right minds from the other side. We will forget everything we have been given by her. We must always remember to follow the ways that were given to us and not follow the ways of other people.

"If we lose our minds, we will not be able to think like Kohkumthena and interpret as we do now. The weather will change, we will not recognize our guides, what we eat will do us harm and not good, there will be things that harm us and we will abuse one another. But Kohkumthena did not create those things for us that will harm us or the things we will think so much about if we lose our minds. We must not lose our minds or our ways, we must repeat the laws so we don't forget, so all will go well with us, as Kohkumthena designed for us.

"Kohkumthena told us everything, so we would know how we are to live always. She knows there will be some who do things in an unnatural way, but they will realize it and go back to the sacred ways. She has left us our main guides, here where we live, and we must never forget those who guide us. We are to interpret day after day and we will be told of things one year ahead of time. We are to remember these things each and every morning so we will be healthy. Kohkumthena created fire person and the water person for us. We must always remember that Kohkumthena did all this for us.

"She gave us the corn to eat. The corn person fulfills his relationship to us and shows us pity, every time he grows following the laws she has given him. The bean and the pumpkin, they are our guides.

"We must always speak of 'pity.'

"The things that guide us look pitiful, and when we pray, we must ask them to have pity on us, and we must ask Creator to have pity on us, so we don't perish. When Kohkumthena hears us say 'pity' in our prayers she thinks our minds are right and she will make us strong because we are living like she designed us to be. These guides will always have pity on us and will follow the laws, so we won't perish. We can be certain that when we plant corn, it will have pity on us and will follow the laws and produce corn we can use for our food. When we pray and ask the water person for rain, and ask him to have 'pity' on us, he will send his water down and make sure that it is what we can use, so we don't perish. The way the law goes, that is what we will benefit by, and it was made so, because Kohkumthena loves us."

The Young One had been speaking fast, as though reciting a-well memorized, official catechism. The Old Watcher simply held up his hand to silence the onslaught of words tumbling so rapidly from the Young One's mouth. "Not so fast, Young One, you are leaving my slow, tired mind many miles behind with all that quick speech. I want to know, do you really understand those words that you have been speaking? It is obvious that your family is doing a fine job of teaching you the old laws, but I need to know how much you truly comprehend."

"Oh yes," said the Young One brightly, "my family not only makes me remember all these words, but after I remember them, they ask me questions, and we discuss these things almost every night. I am not taught anything new until they are satisfied that I know what the last words mean. They expect me to remember these words and their meanings all my life. They want me to be able to teach others some day. They say I have a keen mind for one so young," the Young One explained. "I did not mean to speak so fast but these are things I have been taught all my life and no one has ever asked me before, to tell them what I know. I will speak slower now."

"Young One, what does Kohkumthena expect us to do when one of our brothers or sisters stumbles?" asked the Old Watcher.

"Why, that is when we are to speak kind words to one another," said the Young One. "And we are never to doubt, because then the way that Creator has made for us will seem bad and we will become lost. These speeches are the way to keep remembering the laws and the guides that have been made for us, so this life will continue in the sacred manner that Kohkumthena created for us." In his enthusiasm, the Young One rattled on just as fast as he had before.

"Kohkumthena has plans for us, and she does not plan for us to forget any of these laws. She has warned us if we do not give enough thought to them, our minds will become weak and become greatly lacking. If we want to control what we do, then that is why we should watch ourselves carefully. Otherwise, we will eventually not be in our right minds. We must not be mindless of what Kohkumthena has done and fulfilled for us here on the earth. That way we will always respect the earth too. She has left some here who know everything and who will remind us should we forget, but we must remember to pay attention to them and be respectful towards them. The owl, the eagle, and the raven — they will all warn us and tell us things that are good for us and will benefit us. The grandfather who comes to remind us may even tell us to be 'small.' And all that they tell us is to benefit us in some way, because Kohkumthena has made them to know everything about us in full. They are small but they know everything and she has made it so they can pass on to one another all the knowledge they receive. They do not miss the point of what we do. Regardless of how far away we live, they will know whatever we do immediately. They will all know it, each one of their kind, so they will never misrepresent us to Creator. Kohkumthena created how each of them looks.

"There are those who will do us harm and that is the reason Kohkumthena created the Thunderers, also our grandfathers, the ones who will go after whoever would harm us. They are on guard throughout the whole world. She lets them roam the earth to protect us grandchildren. The grandfathers of all descriptions take care of us, but there is nothing that the Thunderers cannot do.

"Grandmother Kohkumthena has fixed all these guides in a certain way and given all of them to us. We must never forget to translate for our grandfathers, for

225

in doing so we will find the ones who are our guides in the way we must conduct ourselves and in what we say when we memorize these things.

"Kohkumthena created our dances and what we say when we pray. When we pray all of the grandfathers will be listening, and everything that grows will be listening to us, and Kohkumthena herself will be listening to our words. We must never forget our prayer. If we don't think enough about it, it won't be of any benefit to us and everyone will feel sad. This is everything that Kohkumthena created, in this prayer. This is where her power is. The more we pray the more powerful she can be and the more help she can give us.

"Grandfather Sun cares for us and is the daylight. Then there is Grandfather Moon who carries on the daylight but less bright. And we must keep the other Grandfathers in mind, what they look like and what they will look like in the future, so we will know the way it will look day after day. For if we know what the next day will be like, we can prepare so our children won't suffer.

"Everything that is good Kohkumthena created for us and extends it up to where she is. She told us what she thinks about everything so we will benefit from it all.

"There is an unknown sound that only certain ones can hear, they are the good ones. These are the ones that Kohkumthena has chosen to be our chiefs and our councilors, who pass these ideas around to everyone, whenever they occur. That is the way she has laid it down for the intelligent men, because they view things rightly, and they know how to repair things. This is the way she thinks about things. Sometimes their children may be slow to think, but these intelligent men will carry on, that is the way they are to conduct their tribe. They can see and hear this way because that is the way Kohkumthena created it to be. That is another reason why we must not be faulty in our speech. That is why we can translate it, the reason that our brothers can believe us when we speak of the truth, when we speak of the things that Kohkumthena has given us. This is the position we hold, and this other thing she has given us, namely 'truth', alone will always protect us and our families here on earth.

"Kohkumthena gave us intelligence so we will be able to not overlook anything in the way we manage and can then follow that way. Kohkumthena will be grateful when we repeat it correctly and that is how she will help us with our lives, by our intelligence."

The Young One felt exhausted now. He had recited all the laws he could remember concerning the way things were made for us by Kohkumthena. He could tell there was a bit of impatience in the Old Watcher's manner, but did not understand what could possibly be wrong with what he had said. His family elders had been preparing him for this examination for more than five years, ever since he earned his powaka at the age of eight. Finally, rather timidly he asked, "Grandfather, you seem displeased with what I have recited to you. Have I made an error? Have I misspoken, misremembered?"

The Old Watcher shook his head from side to side and looking the young man in the eye said, "It is only that I was taught to begin at the beginning. You have spoken correctly, but you have not mentioned how people are to treat one another. When I was taught the speech, that was the first thing I had to learn. It distresses me, and I think Kohkumthena, when things are taken out of order. Do you know the first part of the Law? Perhaps that is why our people have so many problems with one another now, they have forgotten the first part of the first law that instructs us on how we should be towards one another, man to woman, brother to sister, husband to wife."

The Young One blushed. He was just becoming painfully aware of his growing manhood, the complexities and seriousness of it, and the almost oppressive responsibility that his family reminded him of seemingly every day. He thought for a few minutes and then mustered his courage to speak to his elder and said, "I apologize, Grandfather, the fault is mine. I have been taught the words to speak, but I am yet trying to understand how to use those words in my own life and am not confident enough to speak of them. I was afraid I would not speak the words correctly since I don't fully understand them yet, and I did not want to embarrass myself in front of you by misspeaking."

The Old Watcher nodded his head in understanding, then allowed a slight smile to form on his lips. "Young One, I am glad to hear your explanation of your deletion of this important part of our instructions from Kohkumthena. It is true that it is wise not to speak of things you do not understand. But this night you may ask questions, and get clarifications and advice. Now tell me, what is it that you think you don't understand about this law?"

The Young One blushed again in the darkness and stammered, "I have been told of how things are between a man and a woman when they are husband and wife. I think I understand that. But there are rules about speaking to female relatives, whom you can ask to dance, with whom you can tell jokes, to which woman besides your mother you may speak directly. This is all so confusing to me, and I am afraid I will not know all my cousins and so speak wrongly, or embarrass us all by asking a relative to dance.

"Grandfather, there are such specific rules and laws for the women to follow, and they have not told me what they are. They have only told me that women are sometimes maneto and must be treated with great respect. That sometimes a woman is so powerful that her breath can kill a bear. There are times when women must go and be by themselves, and then they have teachings that only are given from woman to woman. These things are a mystery to me — I do not understand them."

It was all the Old Watcher could do to keep from bursting laughing out loud. "Is that all that puzzles you? Have you no other questions you need answers to, or clarifications?"

"No," said the Young One, "I do feel I understand the rest quite well."

So the Old Watcher straightened his stooped shoulders, rewrapped his blanket and began. "Your mother will tell you those with whom you may not speak, but these days hardly any Shawnee follow that old tradition. These days you must be polite to everyone, but most especially to the women. The women have different things they must do for our benefit, Young One. Let me briefly explain some of this to you.

"When young girls become young women they stop playing so much with their dolls and begin to seriously learn the ways of women, which they will need to know for the rest of their lives. They are sacred, they are the life givers. Their bodies are sacred and are to be treated with great respect. In the old days all the men were hunters. One of the tools we used in hunting was our own noses. That is what the animals use for self-defense. They would sniff the air, and if they detected a human smell they would run away and our people would go hungry. When women are on their moon there is an issue of blood which has its own peculiar scent. If that were to touch their husbands it would not wash off easily and might spoil hunting. To protect the men from this, and out of respect for their husbands and the tribe as a whole, the women would build a small wigiwa at a distance from the village, and there they would live for the few days that they were unclean. This is where much of the traditional teachings were exchanged and the young women learned the things they needed to know to be good wives and mothers.

"We have always been a people who respected the opposite sex, and took extra precautions not to be tempted into doing anything harmful or disrespectful to one another. There are special things that you will now be taught by the men in your family that the young women will not be taught, nor will they understand. And that is as it should be, and as it has always been. I am glad to know that you are a right-thinking person when it comes to the females of our people. Soon, as you grow into your manhood, you will no longer be embarrassed by these things.

"Someday you will want to marry, and we hope it will be with one of your own people. In the old times, traditions for acquiring a bride were very different from how they are now. In those times, gifts would be offered to the chosen one's family, and you would have to prove you could provide for her. It would be frowned upon if you did not wait until you were married before you had children, for they too must be provided with the things they need to live. While many of our old ways are no longer practiced, you will gain much respect of your people if, when you are ready to marry, you are capable of providing the necessities for your bride and your children without having to rely on help from others. Today the Aliens have made it seem unnecessary to meet the old requirements. The old ways, the old laws and rules were good for us, and they would be good for us again if we would simply live by them. It would be wrong-thinking for you to marry and deprive your wife and innocent children of the necessities, simply because you are selfish and impatient.

"Our marriage ceremony is beautiful and meaningful because there are no false words spoken, no vows from others' hearts, only truth between the couple marrying. Later we must discuss these things, after you have had time to grow more into your manhood.

"All of the rules and laws are based on the word 'respect.' To be a right-thinking person you must have respect for all things and all people. Especially for He Who Creates By Thinking, Kohkumthena, the maneto-Grandfathers and guides, and the Earth whom you are to consider your Mother because she carries you on her back and provides for you, and all the Nations — the plant people, the tree people, the animals, birds, fish, and the other two-leggeds, your relatives. When you understand why you were created, and how you were created, and how you survive because they all take pity on you, then you will have this respect deep inside you. When you have this respect inside you it will pour forth on all your relatives. Pray for the proper kind of respect, Young One.

"It seems you have a good understanding of how things have been made for us and how we exist. Now remember to always say the proper words and let them speak to your heart, and listen for what your guides will be telling you. These are the ones which Kohkumthena put in place to help you, even with these matters on respect and relatives. She has given you a special understanding of things, just as she thinks herself.

"Do not doubt the good sense and intelligence that she has given you. All of these make her and you strong. Pay attention when your family elders teach you these things and ask them to explain things you are not sure of. They will respect you for your truthfulness. And honestly, Young One, these things that confuse you now have always confused men when they try to sort out women. As you get older, your wisdom will come. Perhaps easily, perhaps not, but it will come as you grow older."

Relieved, the Young One again began to speak fast, blurting out some of his confusions and fears about how a man is really supposed to behave towards young women these days. He even asked the Old Watcher if he had ever been backward, or shy and awkward around young girls when he was young. Again the Old Watcher held up his hand to slow down the fast flow of words tumbling from the lips of the Young One. He smiled in the dark as he asked gently, "And what of the laws concerning the animals and the other Nations, Young One?"

"Oh, Kohkumthena thought of everything for us," the Young One answered. "She made different kinds of animals to benefit us, and we are to always respect them. She gave us laws to obey when we hunt them so we will be lucky in getting them. And She created them in a secret order and they will always be helping us as we go along on this earth. We are never to speak badly about the animals or we will not benefit from them.

"When we are hunting, we are hunting those who know the laws too, because Kohkumthena taught the animals all the laws we are to follow. We are to care for the animals and their children because that is how She created us. That is the relationship we and our grandchildren should claim with them. But this is why we must have respect for them. And we are to obey all these things as long as the world stands. If we don't understand the roads, then that is why men are to teach one another, equally, they are traveling around, so they may all have respect."

The Young One finally had to stop and take a breath. He felt exhilarated! The more he spoke, the less tired he felt and the more clearly his young mind seemed to focus. The Old Watcher was obviously impressed with the Young One's vast knowledge of the ancient directives and laws. This was indeed a young man of promising qualities. The Old Watcher had seen many such young people through the years, and most fell into one of the many traps or snares that the path of life is littered with and so lost their way before they became old enough to be elders and leaders of the People. Secretly and silently the Old Watcher prayed for this Young One, and nonchalantly sprinkled a few bits of tobacco into the fire on the Young One's behalf.

"Have you been instructed on the laws concerning the other Nations, the trees, plants, and animals? Do you know what is the right way to behave concerning them?" the Old Watcher asked, although he felt certain the Young One knew the answer.

"Grandfather, the way I have been taught, even Mother Earth herself has been given her instructions on how to care for us. She carries us on her back as the women of old carried the babies in the cradleboards. She feeds us by growing the corn and other foods that we need. Water Person helps her to do this, and they all carry us along, gently and with much sympathy. Good feelings are very important and the earth will give us good feelings so we will be happy children. The foods that she grows will have many flavors, because that is how Kohkumthena has made it to be, and that is the way it will be for as long as she allows the earth to stand. Our Earth Mother is told to never forget us or the laws that Kohkumthena has given to her, no matter how widespread we become.

"Because we are pure and clean it will be easy for the maneto Kohkumthena has placed in charge over us to have sympathy for us and help carry us along. So long as we carry along the rules she gave us, these maneto will always help us and we will respect them. Kohkumthena has deposited on the earth all the things we need to carry us along. And the maneto will always tell us what we need to understand; sometimes they will even speak to us at night, so long as we follow the Laws.

"There are those who will be medicine for us. Even the insect will pray for our good feelings, because that is how Kohkumthena has created it for them, so they will always keep us in their minds and pray for our good.

"The deer was created to look exactly as he does. Because the deer obeys the laws of Kohkumthena, it is healthy and has no diseases, so is good to eat. They live in the wilderness, but they know when we need them. When we show them the proper respect, they will come and not hide themselves from our hunters. We will speak to them about the laws and tell them why we need them and remind them of the purpose for which they were created by Kohkumthena, so when we kill them we are fulfilling the Laws. The things they eat will be medicine to us as well as to themselves. When we pray we are to speak kindly to the deer. They are to take pity on us. She has given them advice and they know about the future, which they can tell us. They are created sacred and have no harm in them toward anyone. Because they are sacred and have pity on us and send prayers to Creator, they will be taken to that place where Creator is, and they know all about this place even now. We must always show them respect for they are also our guides.

"Kohkumthena has promised the deer that they will never be hunted to extinction unless we lose our minds, and it will go hard on any who kill them all. She has promised them they will some day go up and live with her.

"The bear was given rules to live by that will be to our benefit. The bear will live in the wilderness and he will conduct himself just as we grandchildren do. He will be killed by us and he will not think ill of us for this, because this is how Grandmother created him. He too is a sacred animal and we have rules about how we are to treat him. Once we kill him we are to clean him in a special way. We will take his sacred insides and walk four times to the east, then we will place those sacred parts into the fork of a tree, where they will be eaten by a sacred bird. When cooking the bear we are to use only certain parts, none is to be given to fire person directly and we are never to use anything sharp, not even a roasting stick.

"The bear will notify Kohkumthena when we are happy as we should always be. The bear advises her on our activities. The bear also brings information and messages from Kohkumthena to us, which we relay on to others. We are to hold council from time to time to discuss these things. The bears are also to hold council from time to time and discuss the laws and how things are to be. When we hunt and kill them we will recite the laws to them so they know we are taking them in a sacred manner and for a sacred reason and are fulfilling the laws in what we do. In the end, the bear will assist us on our journey to Kohkumthena, and he too, will be brought up to where Creator is as a reward for his following the rules and advising us and telling us the truth, as he is bound by his laws. The bear is always referred to as the 'good animal,' " the Young One noted to the Old Watcher.

The Young One stopped in his recitations and looked intently at the Old Watcher. "Grandfather, I know our laws about the dog, and I also know our oral tradition of why the dog came to be. Shall I tell them both to you?"

The Old Watcher was growing tired, but knew what it was like to be young and needing to speak about these things, so he nodded his head and let the young man continue.

'The dog is to help us with his nose. He will help us in our hunting. He is to be our friend and we are to be his friend. We are never to kill the dog. We are never to eat the dog. And Creator knows that some people will eat the dog, but they are breaking the rules that were given when they do so. Sometimes the dog will have premonitions about things and will warn us. The dog is created in a sacred way and is to be respected and treated kindly, and not be abused.

"He will eat a portion of what we eat. And he will not think about his place in life but will be happy. If someone steals something from us or injures us in some way, the dog will use his nose to help us find them. But the finest dog is like Grandmother Kohkumthena's, and is feisty. These are the dogs that Creator made for us to think most highly of, yet they are quiet dogs and do not bark like ordinary dogs. We value most a dog that is like our ancestors and will withstand pain without yelping and barking and whining. They lose our respect if they are noisy.

"Our oral tradition says that the dog saw that we were without a friend and so he alone of all the animals that were created, asked to be born so we would have a friend. The dog told Creator that man needed a friend, someone to warn him of danger, help him in the hunt, to console him when he was alone, someone who would be totally loyal to him. He told Creator he would be no bother and take care of himself for the most part. He would not need much to eat and would be content with only scraps and the bones the man left, and if there were no scraps he would eat the defecation of man. So Creator saw that what the dog had said was true, that the man had no loyal friend and could use a dog to help in his hunting, so Creator allowed the dog to come and join the man, who feeds the dog his leftovers and bones, and sometimes the dog even eats the defecation.

"The eagle was also created in a sacred way, and one of its main responsibilities is to pray for us grandchildren. The eagle will know many things that we do not, and he will know things before we do. It is his duty to tell us what we need to know that will benefit us. Sometimes we will feel bad or have unhappy thoughts, but it is fixed that in the morning when we hear the eagle we will be happy. At nighttime, other birds such as the owl will warn of us things that are harmful to us and will not benefit us.

"Some of the sacred birds, for their reward, are the ones to eat the entrails of the good animal, the bear, which we have placed in the fork of the tree. The eagle is not to think bad thoughts about us, and we will not think bad thoughts about it, but we will always know it is a sacred bird and treat it with respect. It knows all the laws and will repeat them to us so we don't forget them. The eagle is a protector and screams our words up into the heavens for Creator.

"Birds will always wear their beautiful feathers and will always have the same appearance, just as we two-leggeds will always have the same appearance as we do now.

"The wolf was created to also help carry us along. Whenever he knows anything he is to tell us. He is to never do us harm but live peacefully with us, watching over us. Good feelings are what he was created with to help us feel good. He will live near where we rest, but he will live in the wilderness. The wolf was created in a sacred manner, as were we, and we are to care about one another, and care for one another, the way the rules tell us. We are to aid one another on the mutual road to where Kohkumthena lives.

"The buffalo was created in a sacred manner. He will never have bad thoughts about us. When he sees us he will be happy and will think, 'This is what we buffalo are created for.' He will be our ear to the earth. We will kill and eat him. He will be the means for us to grow and be carried along. He will be shelter, and warmth, tools and food, even medicine for us. He will not ever forget the rules and neither will we. We will bring the buffalo the things we eat, the pumpkins, dry corn and beans. When we eat him these are the things we will add to his meat in our meals. When he is killed the fourth time he will be taken up where Creator lives and will be there when we get there.

"The raccoon was asked by Creator what he wanted to look like and how he wanted to help us grandchildren along. He asked to live by the streams because he loved to play in the water and hunt for the small creatures that live there. He also asked to have his face painted with a black mask. Creator agreed that he could have the black mask on his face and that he would always live by the water's edge. Because he is always stirring things up and is so mischievous, he will never advise us on anything; but when we need to find water we need only find the raccoon who will follow the laws and lead us to it. Because he was created in a sacred manner he will never fail to find water when we need it, and he will never forget how to find it.

"The turtle was given rules to follow as he carries us along.. He will live in the water. Should any of our children be sick we are to call the turtle with special words and tobacco. We will tell him that we are going to kill him and take out his heart, and make a medicine for our sick child that it won't die and will be strengthened. The turtle will not think bad of us for doing this because we are all just following the rules that Kohkumthena gave to us. And for several days after we cut his head off the turtle will still move about, because these are the ways that have been fixed for him.

"When we need rain we will call the turtle. We will pick him up and tie his leg with bark and hang him up. We will tell the turtle how long we want it to rain. After it rains we will untie the turtle and let him run loose, and we will all be happy because we are following the rules that were given to us to carry us along.

"The turkey was told he will live in the wilderness and sleep in the trees. He is to be eaten by us, because the turkey has pity on us so we do not perish. We grandchildren have been given one rule we must not break concerning the turkey, and that is we are to never use the grease of the turkey to fry squirrel. If we do use the grease of the turkey to fry the squirrel, the turkey has been instructed to turn us into a snake, and we will be called 'monster' and have two heads. We are to lead the turkey as we travel along, and eat him but never use his grease to fry squirrel.

"Grandfather?" queried the Young One. The Old Watcher jumped with a start. He had almost dozed listening to the ancient laws for perhaps the one hundred-thousandth time in his life.

"Yes, Young One?"

"I have a question. I know the words of the next law but there is some confusion as to which bird Kohkumthena was speaking. Some of my elders say it was the raven, but others are just as adamant saying it was the crow. Which is it grandfather?"

The Old Watcher sighed a deep sigh and finally said, "We cannot be certain, Young One, so I feel it does not matter, for they and we are all related. This controversy has raged since I was small and none of my elders could resolve it either. Some felt that the confusion began when the laws were written for the first time instead of being recited as you have done tonight. I can only tell you my grandfather and I believe it means the crow, but my father and his grandfather were just as convinced it meant the raven. Remember, all these laws are about respect, so just be respectful of both birds, for each is sacredly created to be of benefit to you." The Young One nodded his head in understanding and began the twelfth and last law.

"The crow-raven is sacredly created and is a maneto. The instant he wakes up every morning he will fly and tell everyone, and especially the grandchildren, the unknown things he has been given in his dreams as he slept. If the grandchildren decide to eat him that is all right because nothing has been forbidden the grandchildren to eat. The bird will take care and eat all the snakes and other birds and will eat what the other animals leave behind, and it will eat what is left of the 'Good animal,' throwing pieces to maneto in the four directions. This shows respect.

"The grandchildren have a plaything that is called 'war.' In the future, after the fighting is over, the bird will dream in the places where the grandchildren defeated those persons. We respect the bird because he is maneto and we never go near it, nor our relatives or children. The bird must be patient with us grandchildren, and take care of us, and never forget those guides. The crow must always keep watching on this place where we live.

"Sometimes Creator might appear to it and tell it things that we do not know, and it must tell us and warn us. The crow will also talk to us about the way we raise our children. They are not to wonder about things as they wake up from morning to morning. When he wakes up and looks around he remembers all these things and all the guides.

"The maneto were all created like this so Kohkumthena would not have to wonder about us and they can help us to keep in our minds the guides that she set

down for us. This is so we will all be happy and we alone will think. When this sacred bird hears what we think then it will immediately tell all the others what we are thinking, and all the maneto and guides will help us. As the birds interpret and carry our thoughts and warn us more and more, they become more maneto until they become seated higher and higher with their understandings. Then they will guard this time that we grandchildren live because that is the way they were created.

"The Indian tobacco exists so that we can talk to our grandfather, the Fire Person, and so all the maneto can hear us plainly from where they sit high up. And they will have pity on us. Kohkumthena arranges the pity they feel towards us so that it will be beneficial to us and carry us along. We are carried along by the meaning of the guides underneath the sun, that one, who brings the light. This is so we grandchildren will never miss seeing the things that the crow has been told to tell us."

Known Location of Shawnee During Historic Times

Sixteenth Century

1566   East side of the Smoky Mountains.

1586   Sir John Hawkins expedition disbanded in Nicaragua, some went north through Mexico, east across North America to within fifty miles of Cape Breton, Nova Scotia, and met (Chouanons) several areas.

1539–44 Chalaque Chalakaatha's were northeast of the head of the Savannah River in North Carolina (Saawanua).

1584   Sir Walter Raleigh, (Chawanock) northwest of Roanoke on Chowan River in northeast North Carolina.

Seventeenth Century

1600   Warren K. Moorehead, roving bands of Shawanoes ranged north of the Ohio River.
        Captain John Smith's *History of Virginia*, Shawanoes associated with Massawomekes at head of Chesapeake Bay, Virginia.

1602-06 Barthalomew Gosnald, Shawanoes Massachusetts Bay, Cape Cod, Massachusetts.

1603-15 Samuel de Champlain, Shawanoes in the northeast.

1607   Shawanese part of the Powhattan confederacy.

1608-15 Etienne Brule, Shawanoes northeast with the Susquehannocks.

1609   Franscisco de Ecija, Santees-Sewees.

1609-10	Henry Hudson, Hudson River, Manhattans, Wappingers, and Mahicans.
1614	Dutch Carte Figurative Sauwanew on east bank of Delaware River, near the mouth in New Jersey.
1620	Pilgrims, Massachusetts and Wampanoags.
1621	South Chawonock River sixty miles from Jamestown.
1631	Peter Heyes, Delaware River, Delawares (and Shawnee).
1634	DeLaet, Sauwanoos in the vicinity of the Delaware River.
ca. 1636-38	DeLaet and Dutch Figurative, Sauwanoos and Sauuan were west of the Delaware River, between the Delaware and Susquehanna Rivers in eastern Pennsylvania.
1638	New Jersey and eastern Pennsylvania.
1640	Prior to this date the Shawnees had moved away from lower Delaware-Susquehanna.
1646	Evidence indicates they had probably all moved west or south of New Jersey by this time.
1650	Edward Blande Virginia and North Carolina, Meherrins and Nahyssans.
1651-52	Ragueneau Chaouanaquiois-Shawnee, Quebec to Acadia (four hundred leagues South West of Quebec, probably Kentucky, Tennessee or Ohio River area).
1654-69	Pierre Esprit Raddisson and Sieur de Grosseilliers, Northeast and Midwest.
1660	General force along the Cumberland and Tennessee Rivers.
1660	Shawnees engaged in lively trading with the Spanish in Florida (St. Augustine, San Mateo, and San Pedro).
1662	Father Lalemant reported Shawnees doing lively trading with Spanish from accounts of his Shawnee captives, whom he interviewed.
1669-70	John Lederer Blue Ridge Mountains and Carolina Piedmont area.
1669	Ohio
1669-70	Dollier de Casson and Rende Brehant de Galine Senecas introduced them to us in New York and Great Lakes areas.
1669-70	Claude Jean Allouez ,Great Lakes, the Mississippi, Wisconsin, and Illinois Rivers using Miamis as guides.
1669	Gallinee told by Seneca prisoner from Ohio, Toagenha, that bad, treacherous people speaking corrupt Algonkian would attack them by night unless he was guided by Senecas through Shawnee territory.
1669-70	Abbe Gallinee as by Margry at Montreal told by Senecas (Sonnontoueronons) one month south to Chiouanons.
1670-89	Nicholas Perrot, upper Mississippi River, used Miamis and others as guides.
1670	Headwaters in South Carolina, Thawakilas.

1671	Marquette refers to the Shawnee trading with the Spanish in Florida.
1671	Thomas Batts and Robert Fallam by Abraham Wood, Trader Shawnee in West Virginia.
1672	Shawanoos aided the Andaste (Susquehannocks or Conestogas of the Susquehanna River) against the Iroquois.
1672	Shawnees and Delawares supposedly conquered by Iroquois and run out of Ohio, Kentucky.
1673	Gabriel Arthur and James Needham told by trader Abraham Wood, Shawnee in Kentucky and Tennessee.
1673	Marquette Cumberland region.
1672	On the Tennessee River just before the junction of the Ohio and Mississippi Rivers, southwest of Marquette's locations for them.
1674	Henry Woodward In South Carolina met two Savannah Indians who brought Spanish beads.
1675	Shea, Catholic Missions, Garacontie, Onindaga Chief told his people to live in peace with the French, but turn their guns on the Ontwogannha.
1680	Savannah Indians in South Carolina replaced the Westos as a buffer between English settlers and the Spanish to the south.

Late Seventeenth to early Eighteenth Century

16__	Some Savannahs left to join the Shawnee bands in Pennsylvania and elsewhere, sometimes still being called Savannahs, sometimes known as Shawnee.
1682	St. Joseph's River, near portage to Kankakee, Illinois.
1682	Alabama River close to Spanish traders, Pensacola, Florida would have been the closest place.
1682	Trading with the Spanish in Florida, St. Augustine, San Mateo, and San Pedro.
1682	Some of the traders above became located at Fort St. Louis on the Illinois River.
1683	Starved Rock, Illinois.
1683	Illinois River.
1683	LaSalle invited Shawnee group to discontinue trading with Spaniards and reside on Illinois River (reported later in different journal).
1683	LaSalle mentions "Chaouanons et zoabano."
1684	Franquelin Map Assachile, probably Thawakila division, near Alabama and upper Creek country.
1684	Village on the Cumberland had a trail to St. Augustine for trading.
1687	Those at mouth of Illinois River went to Pennsylvania.

Late Seventeenth Century

| 1686 | Thawakila's and Kispoko's Tukabahchee Creek relationship first noted. |

1692	Martin Chartier traveled Ohio and Susquehanna Rivers and settled among Shawnee.
1692-94	Cornelissen Arnout Viele explored Susquehanna, Ohio, and Wabash Rivers with Shawnee guides.
1692-90	Jean Couture reported Shawnee from Mississippi River to Allegheny Mountains.
1692-97	Trader Coureur de Bois reported Shawnee among Indians of the Southeast.
1694	Approximately one thousand Shawnee migrated from the south to Delaware River.
1694	Shawnee with Minisinks, north Delaware River.

1694-1745

Many references to Delaware and Shawnee in eastern Pennsylvania along the Susquehanna River; Wyoming Valley Region of central Pennsylvania; and along the upper Ohio River in western Pennsylvania. Both Pekowi and Thawikila settled in Pennsylvania at this time (under the six nations).

1698	Thomas Welch found Shawnee from Charleston, South Carolina, to mouth of Arkansas River.

1698-1725

Pierre Le Moyne d'Iberville found Shawnee among the Southeast Indians and on the Mississippi Delta.

Eighteenth Century

1700	De l'Isle maps middle course of the Riviere des Alabamas, Chaouanons (Shawnee).
1701	Signed treaty with William Penn in eastern Pennsylvania.
1701	John Lawson reported Shawnee in North Carolina's Allegheny Mountains.
1701	On Cumberland River near Cherokees.
1701	On the Savannah River.
1709	John Lawson's *History of Carolina*, Savanoes and Shawnoes settled on the south end of the Ashley River, a second group who formerly lived on the banks of the Mississippi, removed to the head of the rivers of South Carolina. [Savannahs and Shawanoes have been proven by several anthropologists, archeologists, and linguists to be the same tribe, merely different divisions.]
1713	On the upper end of the Tennessee and Cumberland Rivers.
1714	Chickasaws and Cherokees ran Shawnee out of the Big Bend of the Cumberland at today's Nashville, Tennessee, area.
1724	Headwaters of the Ohio River.

1729	Chaussegros de Lery reported Shawnee on Allegheny River and Ohio River.
1732	Sightings at Alabama River.
1732	Reported at Detroit.
1736	DeBeauchamps's journal, some Shawnee had settled with the Alabama People.
1737	William Penn's agent (name unknown) reported Shawnee in Susquehanna River Valley from Philadelphia to Onondaga, New York.

Early Eighteenth Century

On the Chattahoochee River, Shawnee and Eyuchi among the Lower Creeks.

Chalakaatha resided among the Upper Creeks.

Thawakila division had much contact with the Upper Creeks and Alabamas.

1740	Shawnee and Delaware were pressed from Pennsylvania westward into the Ohio Valley Region. Shawnee variously settled on the Scioto River and Paint Creek, and with the Delawares who were on the Muskingum River.
1741	Mr. Sergeant, a missionary visited Shawnee living on the Susquehanna.
1742	John Peter Salley found Shawnee in the Virginia Alleghenies.
1744-48	Shawnee previously of Canada under the leadership of Chartiers, had previously also started a town in Kentucky, but now moved in three directions. Those going to Alabama traveled up the Tennessee River to Bear Creek where they went thirty miles up, placing them seventy miles above the French Alabama Garrison, between the towns of Ooe-asa and Coosa. Ooe-asa was on the Coosa River between current Talledega and Sylacauga.
1745	October, Detroit Shawnees went to Wabash, joined Ohio Shawnees, and Weas and Mascoutens.
1745-46	Thawakila came from the north to settle with kin.
1746	Shawneetown, Illinois, noted.
1747	DeBeauchamps in the spring, "Chouanons" were planning to come from the North to settle with their kinsmen there, believed to be Thawakila.
1748	Chartiers group sets out from Shawneetown, Illinois; some went to Alabama, some to mouth of Scioto.
1748-50	Thomas Walker found Shawnee at Cumberland Gap.
1749	La Jonuire, Governor of Canada Shawnee, traded with English at Sandusky.
1750	At Susquehanna, Wilkes-Barre, Pennsylvania.
1750	Village of Shawnee at mouth of Scioto on the Ohio River.

1750	A second village at the mouth of the Scioto River noted.
1750	Continuous reference to Shawano in Ohio.
1751-52	Christopher Gist found Shawnee along the Ohio River and Kentucky River and in Kentucky.
1754	James McBride found Shawnee along the Ohio River and in Kentucky.
1754	Sir William Johnson, Superintendent for Indian Affairs, Northern Dept.; Congress at Albany, New York; Shawnees then on Juniata and Susquehanna Rivers.
1755	Villages between upper Coosa and Tallapoosa Rivers at Cayomulgee. Creek, name meaning "all mulberry."
1756-65	William Johnston and George Croghan located Shawnee in Pennsylvania, New York, and Ohio Valley.
1756	Some of the southern Shawnee went north and stopped for a while at "French Lick," which is current Nashville, Tennessee.
1757	General Gage map, Osweggloes are located in Alabama Territory immediately south of the confluence of the Mobile River and another unnamed river. This is believed to be at the confluence of the Coosa and Tallapoosa, as the two rivers join to form the Alabama River (formerly the Mobile River). This Osweggloes settlement is probably the same town noted under the terms Savannah, Savanuga, and Savanogee, located near the forks of the Coosa and Tallapoosa Rivers.
1757	Ft. Massac-Chartiers Band at mouth of the Tennessee River on the north bank of the Ohio River.
1758	Christian Fredreck Post dealt with the group of Shawnee living among the Delaware in the Wyoming Valley of Pennsylvania. For detailed information, read *Enquiry into the Causes of Alienation of the Delaware and Shawanese Indians Against the Interest of the English Government* which investigates treaties from 1610 through 1758.
1760	Sixteen villages on various interior streams in Ohio.
1760	French census showed a Chalakaatha settlement on a tributary of the upper Coosa River, considered only a portion of the Chalakaathas.
1761	No record of this town appears this year. Some of its inhabitants were thought to have migrated northward toward the Ohio region and became part of the settlements on the Scioto River. Note: At approximately this same time the Shawnee traded with the Spanish in Florida and procured some etched or engraved copper plates which they gave to the Creeks as a reminder of their friendship. Some of these ancient plates still survive today. Should the Creeks ever tire of them they were to return them to the Shawnee who gave them to them. Some of the Thawakila asked for their return at one time, but as it was the Kispokos who presented them, the Creeks refused.

1760-75   Daniel Boone dealt with Shawnees in Tennessee, Kentucky, and at the Cumberland Gap.

1761   Scioto and Muskingum Rivers, had scraps of William Penn Treaty of 1701, Kispokos.

1763   People noted ninety miles up the Scioto River, and up the Muskingum River twenty miles.

1763-64   Bouquet October, down the Muskingum River met Seneca, Delaware, and Shawanoes. Shawanoes produced fragment of 1701 Treaty with William Penn.

1768   Treaty at Ft. Stanwix, William Johnson, Six Nations, Shawnees, Delawares, and Senecas of Ohio drew boundary lines near Lake Ontario at the junction of Canada and Woods Creeks, to Owegoon the Susquehanna, thence through Pennsylvania, Maryland, etc., to the mouth of Cherokee or Tennessee Rivers.

1769   Gift from Spanish to Delaware and Shawnees given at St. Louis.

1770   Purcell Map "Hickory Ground" located on eastern tributary of the Coosa fifteen miles north of the confluence of the Coosa and Tallapoosa Rivers. (Confluence is at northeastern edge of today's Montgomery, Alabama.)

1772   Scioto River settlements noted.

1772-73   Baptist missionary Reverend David Jones made two trips to Scioto region in Ohio attempting to convert Pekowi, Chalakaatha, and Kispokos. Also made trips to several smaller towns of mixed Shawnee-Delaware.

1778   Shawnee along the Wabash River and tributaries.

1778   October, Simon Kenton was stealing horses from Old Chillicothe, three miles north of Xenia,Ohio, at today's 'Old Town.' He was taken to Piqua on Mad River five miles west of present Springfield, Ohio. Then to Machack, now West Liberty, Ohio, then to Wapatomica, near Zanesville in Logan County. Then to Solomon's Town, then to Wapatomica, then the Upper Sandusky. Post-Revolutionary War, Ohio Northwest Territory Pekowi and Chalakaatha traded at Miamitown-Ft. Wayne. Hunters and warriors were at Detroit.

1780   Gen. George Rogers Clark attacked Shawnee villages on Mad River and the Little Miami River.

1781   Gen. Broadhead attacked village of Coshocton, Col. Lochry, one of Clark's men leading, eleven miles below mouth of the Great Miami River.

1784   Bellefountaine, Ohio.

1786   Miami and Scioto Rivers.

1788   Same as above.

1789   January — Spanish Territory Gov. Baron de Carondelet gave Shawnees permission to settle between the Missouri and Arkansas Rivers. They chose two locations, Cape Girardeau-New Madrid, location of the 1811 earthquake, the most powerful ever recorded on this continent, and Apple Creek. Twenty-two important battles were fought on Ohio soil prior to 1792.

1795   Located west of the Mississippi River in Missouri.

1795   The Greeneville Treaty ended resistance from Mekoce and Chalakaathas, Thawakila, Pekowi, and part of the Kispoko had already settled west of the Mississippi River.

1796   At mouth of the Saline River, Illinois.

1796-97   At Hickory Ground, Alabama. Although the Creeks and Shawnee had separated prior to this date, a Shawnee town still existed on that spot as late as 1818.

Hickory Ground and Tukpaafka Clan of Creeks. Hickory Ground belonged to the Ha'tawa Clan, or the Tukpaafka Clan, according to the Shawnee Creeks. Both Ha'tawa and Tukpaafka mean "punk" in Shawnee and Creek respectively. There were two Tukpaafka Towns, both Upper Creek communities. One had been Wakokai, ca. 1796, located on the Coosa River The second, and much older Tukpaafka from Okfuskee and the Coosa The older one was located on the Chattahoochee until 1777, when it moved to the Tallapoosa River and renamed itself "Nuyuka." The older Tukpaafka is not the same as Atciapofa, which was commonly called "Hickory Grove" by traders.

1797   Hawkins describes town mixed with Thawakila, Pekowi, with some Eyuchi and mentions the "Sha-wa-ne" had participated in the last war with the United States (doesn't specify which side they fought on).

Nineteenth Century

1804   Simon Kenton dealt with Shawnee in Allegheny Mountains and Kentucky.

1805-08   Darke County, Ohio (Greeneville), Original Prophet's Town is noted.

1806   Shawnee on Wabash River in Ohio and Indiana.

1807   Vincennes to confluence of Ohio and Mississippi Rivers on White River, Old Salt Route; Vincennes to White River to Patoka River, southwest to Wabash River near mouth of Little Wabash.

1808-11   Before May 3, 1808, Tippecanoe, Indiana, Prophet's Town II established on north side of Wabash River two miles below Tippecanoe River.

1810   Cache River, Illinois, site of Shawnee.

1810   Swan Lake, Kentucky, Shawnee settlement noted.

1811   After Harrison's destruction, Wild Cat Creek site set up within six miles of Prophet's Town II.

1812   Early in year Shawnee are on northwest White River near today's Anderson, Indiana, with Delaware.

1812   Shawnee on the war trail with Tecumseh.

1813   At Brownstown and Fort Malden, Ontario, Canada.

1817   Present near mouth of Ohio River.

1818   Shawnee reported on Ohio, Upper Mississippi Rivers and Great Lakes.

1818   Early map of Georgia shows an Ocheubofau Hickory Grove located on the east side of the Coosa River at the rapids near the confluence. This later location makes it very near the Savanogee settlement on the Lower Tallapoosa River.

1818   Hickory Ground, Alabama, Creek area a Shawnee site.

1819   John Johnston, Pequea (Piqua), Ohio, noted.

1819-36   Wapakoneta Ohio, three reservations noted.

1820   Shawnee fifteen miles north of Jackson, Missouri.

1824   Spanish Old Mexico states Shawnees helped removes twenty-four other Indian tribes to Old Mexico.

1825   White River, Missouri, Ste. Genvieve are Shawnee sites.

1826   First Wapakoneta group left, went west through Vincennes, wintered twenty miles below Kaskaskia, included the Prophet and Tecumseh's son Cat Pouncing.

1827-30   Shawnee observed at Cape Girardeau, Missouri.

1830   Painter George Catlin traveled through Kansas and painted the Prophet.

1832   Cape Girardeau and Apple Creek had been ceded and those inhabitants were living on the White River, Missouri.

1838   Last of Ohio Reservation Shawnee left Ohio for Oklahoma.

[During the first half of the eighteenth century many Shawnee and Delaware who went to Cape Girardeau later went to Mexico, both New Spain and Old Mexico.]

1840   Thawakila, Pekowi, Kispoko forced to leave Texas and had to return to Indian Country, (Oklahoma). Hickory Ground Creeks invited them to come and live among them "so long as their houses didn't leak," and they went there.

1840   Shawnee presence in West Virginia, McDowell County.

1841   Henry Rowe Schoolcraft studied Shawnees on Ohio and upper Mississippi Rivers and Great Lakes.

1860   Kansas-Kansas City area.

1862   Civil War caused the Thawakila, Pikowe, Kispoko group to leave the Creeks at Hickory Grounds. The Creeks were sympathetic to the Southern cause, and the Shawnees were sympathetic to the Northern cause, so they left and went to Kansas.

1750-1870

West Virginia, McDowell County locations include Black Wolf Town where a minor Shawnee War Chief named Black Wolf lived until 1854, Skygusky, Shawnee Mountain and the Community called War. Big Creek Owl Community of Shawnee were on the Big Creek. Johnnycake, Beartown, Puncheeancamp, Indian Ridge and along the Harmon branch of the Tug River are reported to have been Shawnee communities. Harmans who married Shawnees thereafter had to spell their names 'Harmon.' It is suspected that Sugarcamp, and White Oak are also related to earlier locations of the Shawnee. There are also many mounds suggestive of early Shawnee occupation in southern McDowell county.

1894 (January 19) West Virginia Governor William Alexander McCorkle in letter to Professor Cox relates that John Henry was hanged at Welch this date for killing two men in a nearby Shawnee camp. Many Shawnee men then worked as timberers for the Chesapeake and Ohio Rail Road under supervisor Flavious Floyd Harman, who married one of Black Wolf's granddaughters in 1901.

Mason County, West Virginia has oral traditions of several Shawnee communities now called: Mission Ridge, Gibbstown, and Broadrun. Several family archivists have found documentation their families were part of Shawnee Communities before the land was taken over by the Alien Invaders. Family names include; Harris, Russell, Proffitt, Goodnite, King, Wolfe, Redman, and others. Braxton County, West Virginia also had many Shawnee pocket communities as the area was rich in Bear, otters, and salt, where even woodland buffalo came.

Late Nineteenth Century

Contact between Tukabahchee Creek and Thawakila, Pekowi, and Kispoko Shawnee continued until after the 1920s.

1882 Shawnee, Oklahoma, an active community.

Shawnee Known Locations Not Otherwise Listed

MEXICO

• Foothills of the mountains immediately to the south of Lake Chapala, circa 995 A.D.

• Matamoros, 1839.

• Up the Rio Grande near Morelos, Coahuila with Kickapoos late 1839.

• Eagle Pass on Texas, Mexican border, 1849.

• Early 1849-50, temporarily at San Fernando de Rosas, today's Zaragoza, Coahila, at La Navaja near Presidio Monclova Viejo, and

Colonia Militar de Guerrero.

• Mid-1850, deeded by Mexican government some 70 million acres, half at the head waters of Rio San Rodrigo, and half at the headwaters of Rio San Antonio, fifty miles south of today's Ciudad Acuna, along with Kickapoos, Seminoles, Negroes and other Indians.

TEXAS

• Sabine River north of Nacogdoches, immediately after Cherokee Removal Treaty of 1817.
• Matamoros, Mexico 1839.
• Between Trinity and Red River in 1845.

OHIO

• Pike County, half moved to Darke County during the Civil War.
• Meigs County, Carmel, closed community, considered no threat to government, so left alone by them.
• Highland County, Hillsboro area, prior to 1840 were in Ross County, along Scioto River.
• Scioto County, Raven Community near Portsmouth.
• Lawrence County, Big Sandy, southern area.
• Richland County, the Marshes, as of 1880.
• Union and Champaign Counties, where they meet, Darby Creek, Buckstown.
• Monroe County, on Ohio River, Sinks.
• Adams County, Blue Creek.

INDIANA

• Hancock County, north of Shelby County on Blue River, Blue River Community.
• Rush County, Flat Rock, on Flat Rock River, Fayette County, White Water, on White Water River Miami County, Missisinewa River, Godfroy.
• Posey County, Shawnee Town, in the "toe."
• Jefferson County, Cavesville.

WEST VIRGINIA

• Mason County, Kanawa, on Kanawa River.
• Braxton County, The Owl, on the Little Kanawa River.

KENTUCKY

• Rowan County, Blue Hill, northern part of county Bell County, Red Bird, north of Tennessee line.
• Trigg County, on Kentucky River, Sandy Creek.
• Mason County, on Ohio River, Limestone.
• Breathitt County, on Buckhorn Creek, Buckhorn.

- Rockcastle County, Rockcastle River, Herrod.

ILLINOIS
- Pope County, the Bluffs, on the Ohio River.
- Vermillion County, Vermillion on Brouletts Creek.

PENNSYLVANIA
- Allegheny County, on the Allegheny River, Pitstown.

FLORIDA
- Crystal River, Black Hoof's birthplace, 1728.
- Suwannee River.

ONTARIO, CANADA, COMMUNITIES
- Walpole, on Walpole Island in the St. Clair River and Lake.
- Hannahville, northeast of Chatham on the Thames River.
- Brownstown (Michigan).
- Kingville, Ontario, southeast of Fort Malden at Amherstburg.
- Prophet's.
- Tecumseh.
- Amherstburg, Ft. Malden.

Some of these communities no longer exist. Some have appeared at various times on different maps, including BIA maps within the last fifteen years. The fact there is no longer a functioning community present does not mean there are no traces of the People or the community still there. References to them can often be found in old church records and even school records of that area.

Chronology of Shawnee Historical Migrations
based on Oral Traditions, the Walam Olum and Historical Documents

Year	Event
Pre-1000 A.D.	People lived in foothills of mountains at south of Lake Chapala, Mexico. These were the ancestors of Mekujay and Kispoko, and some oral traditions include Pikowe bands of People who eventually became known as Shawnee. These were a satellite group under Mayan rule. Aztecs invaded the Mayan empire, enslaved the people, and made human sacrifice of these people and many other satellite Mayan populations.
ca. 992 A.D.	Chief Little Fog, a Shawnee leader, led approximately twenty thousand people from the Lake Chapala area east to the coast of the Gulf of Mexico to avoid Aztecs. This group of Shawnee ancestors called themselves Lenni Lanape, meaning "True People." The other satellite

people who had mixed blood with the invaders had their own leaders, but also traveled east with the Lenni Lanape.

At the coast, each group divided in half. Those traveling north along the coast of the land mass were led by Piqua-Pikuwe leaders, all the way to Georgia. The other half, under Kispoko leadership, traveled east and then north to the tip of the Yucatan. There they built boats, and crossed the Gulf of Mexico to the panhandle area of Florida, near the Mexico Beach-Apalachicola-Tallahassee area.

Some of the Kispoko group then went north up the Apalachicola to the Chatahoochee. A few went up the Flint.

Others of the Kispokos continued east and then south to the Crystal River area and established a village where, many centuries later, Principal Chief Black Hoof claimed to have been born.

Some of those Kispokos chose not to stay at Crystal River and eventually went northward via the Suwannee River into Georgia.

ca. 996 A.D. This Kispoko group and the Piqua group reunited in Georgia and built Stone Eagle Mound to commemorate the reunion.

ca.1050 A.D. The reunited People traveled north along the coast to the Chowan River in Virginia on up to Blackwater River, established a village and stayed a long time. Some also went up the nearby Roanoke River.

Once again the People on the Blackwater divided with the Kispoko group heading north and built "Piqua" on the Susquehanna River. (It was unusual for one division to use the name of another for their village.)

ca.1100 A.D. This Kispoko group met and made an alliance with the Chalagotha People (Ainu, from across the Bering Straights) to fight against the Iroquois. Most of the Chalagathas stayed with the Kispokos. The Piqua People traveled northwest through the mountain passes to the Cumberland Falls in Tennessee and established a village there.

Piqua group traveled to Kanawa, West Virginia, and established a village there.

The Piqua group traveled to Scioto River in Ohio and established villages along the river.

Some of the Piqua group ventured into southwestern Ohio and encountered the Talegawa-Thawikila who were dying out due to their strange customs and form of religion. The two groups intermarried and became known as the Fort Ancient People. Other village sites were established and became known as present day Shawnee sites.

247

The Kispoko group and the Chalagathas traveled due west into Ohio, formed an alliance with the Wyandotte-Guyandotte to fight the Iroquois.

circa 1200 A.D.   Kispoko-Chalakathas reunited with Piqua group and the Talegawas and the "five" bands and septs of the Shawnee officially began and coexisted for the first time. They are the Kispoko, Piqua, Mekujay, Chalgotha and Thalegiwa-Hathawekila.

The Wyandotte invited the Shawnee to stay in southern Ohio. Many villages were established: Piquatown (Piqua), Old Man's Village (near present-day Urbana), Old Town (near Xenia), Chillicothe 1(Chillicothe), Lower Shawnee Town (Portsmouth).

circa 1538 A.D.   Some Chalagothas met at head of Savannah River in North Carolina.

circa 1584 A.D.   Sir Walter Raleigh met Shawnees on Chowan River in northeast North Carolina.

circa 1600 A.D.   Shawnees met traders, trappers and explorers in their own territory of Ohio for the first time.

1600-1795   Wars and treaties diminished territory and populations.

1792   Large group of Shawnee under leadership of Kishkalwa left Ohio to New Spain, Louisiana, Missouri, and became known as Absentees.

1795   Treaty of Greeneville. Tecumseh refused to participate and then refused to go to a reservation. He went to Indiana, Kentucky, Tennessee

1805-08   Tecumseh and his brother the Prophet, Tenskwatewa, started a religious revival and village at the edge of Greeneville, Ohio called Prophet's Town.

1809   Second Prophet's Town established on Wabash River, two miles from Tippecanoe River in an effort to get away from the Aliens.

1811   Prophet's Town, Indiana destroyed by William Henry Harrison.

1812   Tecumseh became allied with the British in Ontario, Canada, against the American Aliens.

1813, October 5   Tecumseh killed in Battle of the Thames River.

1813, October 6   Followers and warriors of Tecumseh decide to remain in Canada indefinitely rather than return to Ohio and become reservation residents.

1817   Treaty of St. Mary's declared all Indian People in Ohio must live on reservations, officially established Auglaize and Hogcreek reservations.

1825   Absentee Shawnee were removed from Missouri to reservation in

	Oklahoma .
1820s	Small groups of Tecumseh's followers began returning to Ohio, Indiana, Illinois, West Virginia, Kentucky, some hid out, some lived with Quakers and Amish. Prior to this only single persons or families had returned from Canada.
1830	Indian Removal Act passed and implemented by U.S. government.
1831-40	Ohio Shawnee Reservation emptied and residents removed to Kansas and Oklahoma
1840s	Thirty-eight communities became established in six states by groups from the remnants of Tecumseh's Warriors
1888	The Council of the Remnant band added "United" to make this band the Shawnee Nation United Remnant Band

The rest of the chronololgy is found in the previous section, "Known Locations." This does not account for the Canadian Shawnee, nor the other remnant groups known to exist, but deals primarily with those who signed the Greeneville Treaty and who lived on Ohio reservations. There were many other Shawnee communities in other states besides Ohio. Of all the chiefs who came and spoke, and all who sent words, the treaty was signed by only three known Shawnee leaders. Those who refused to sign were all from Ohio of course. The Shawnee in other locations had no say regarding the land in Ohio, and so were ignored by the U.S. government.

Foods and Herbs Used by the Shawnee
While East of the Mississippi River Prior to 1492

I have prepared listings of indigenous foods, herbs and seasonings, originally intending to share with my Shawnee sisters. But today everyone seems concerned about healthy diets, and it is known that at the time of discovery our People were very healthy indeed. Although there were many reasons for our good health at that time, I will list but a few: we had had no exposure to the devastating diseases of the Old World; we lived a strenuous life with many daily tasks that required strength and health, and our forms of play included running and swimming on an almost daily basis. Also, we ate a varied, nutritionally well-balanced diet which included the proper amount of roughage, and the food was either fresh or well-preserved and well-prepared. Finally, we ate what our bodies needed as fuel. While we enjoyed feasting and looked for opportunities to do so (at which time we ate tremendous amounts of food), normally we ate only what we needed, with little excess and little waste.

The predominant methods for preparing food were roasting, either over a spit or with food wrapped in corn husks and placed in the coals; steaming, using wet corn husks or mud; or baking in a similar manner sometimes using flat stones over fires to create both a grill and an oven underneath; and boiling. Through the ages and our migrations, the utensils we used changed and were modified according to what was available. Our women seldom used the stone matates and manos, preferring to use large tree stumps as mortars and long wooden sticks as pestles to pound our grains. Flat grinding stones were used for small quantities, for medicines or for grinding seasonings.

I tried to teach my Shawnee sisters about traditional foods, but even after several months I still found cole slaw, ham, broccoli and other such foods being served. Inquiring into this I discovered a great lack of knowledge about just what precisely *is* indigenous to America. Because of this I have listed many of the foods that originated here. Some spices were trade goods from Central and South American tribes, but still had a place in our daily life. It is estimated by the experts that between sixty-five and seventy percent of the known foods in the world today had their origins in America, although some experts disagree as to the actual origins of some foods and herbs. I have endeavored to leave the controversial items out, although by the time the second wave of explorers from the Old World came in the early 1500s we were using new things we had traded for with the first boatloads. Like all other people, we also love new things and often consider them good and exciting eating.

The men provided only the large meat items, as women were known to kill small animals such as rabbits very effectively with slings. We were also involved in fishing from time to time. Our women were responsible for preparing all the foods with seasonings and herbs. I am happy to report that I found no incidence of worms or grubs being in our diet, but I have included one recipe for "yellow-jacket soup." If you try it, please let me know how it turns out, as no one I know seems to want to try it.

We used many fruits in our meat dishes, especially in the winter when we had dried plums and berries which we added to our meat stews. Prior to the Aliens' coming to stay, we had *no apples, no oranges,* and *no peaches!* We did have sour little crabapples, and a small sour orange that people ate roasted and sweetened. We also had no wheat, barley, rye, or oats.

The women used different woods to cook over and well knew that each imparted a different flavor to the food. Hickory, maple, and wild cherry were just a few of the obvious ones used.

Our People had no dairy products — no eggs, milk, butter, cheese, sour cream, or yogurt. Turtle eggs were considered a delicacy; occasionally quail or grouse eggs would be found.

Fat in the diet came from several creatures, bear and buffalo being the choice ones,. Raccoon fat was common, but no hog fat was used until after the Pilgrims came. I am aware of wild boars in the south and southwest, but they are descendants of escaped hogs brought by the Spaniards. No true sheep or goats other than the mountain varieties existed here either. The buffalo was highly prized for his fat and he had several types, one of which was semiliquid. The Old People said it never became rancid. Raccoon fat was predominant as it was an animal which was eaten frequently. The bear was the most desired after the buffalo. Bear fat, even without the addition of herbs, is considered to have healing properties for some problems. A small amount, such as one teaspoonful or two, would be used to season large amounts of a stew or dish as it is powerful stuff. For more delicate dishes nut oils from pecans, peanuts, walnuts, and hickory nuts were used. We also pounded these nuts into nut butters which are delicious. A cure for rancid fat was to put several small pieces of box elder into the container of melted fat which would return it to palatability.

The grain we ate was corn. Once in a while we ate other available grain dishes such as wild rice, which was actually a type of grass seed. But corn was the only grain we cultivated, and we grew at least four varieties: flint or dent, a hard white corn; blue or deep red; variegated; and a soft, opaque, early-ripening white corn referred to as white shoe-peg corn. We used corn flour or very fine corn meal with corn starch in it for our baking needs. I have experimented with recipes and found if you leave out the Alien ingredients and substitute only indigenous foods, baked goods lose usually one-half inch in height and are more dense with fewer air bubbles. The taste is enhanced and any flavorings or seasonings can be enjoyed to a fuller degree.

Sweeteners were used very sparingly. There were no honey bees before the colonists brought them to pollinate the orchards they planted. We had bees here which produced very little honey, and that is why a honey tree was so highly prized that it was considered the private property of the finder. Maple syrup and maple sugar were standard sweeteners, along with corn cob syrup (such as the modern Karo Syrup). Certain fruits such as persimmons and pawpaws were very sweet, which was enhanced when they were dried naturally; a small one-inch piece of the dried fruit would be enough to sweeten a whole dish made to serve four adults. Children broke off pieces of theses dried fruits to eat as modern children eat candy or cookies today.

The life-style of the People did not lend itself to storing huge quantities of anything. Therefore, foods would normally be reduced to their smallest form by drying or dehydrating as much as possible, then stored in a clay, gourd, or basket container. Some fats were stored in skins, and meats were stored in rawhide parfleche folders. Once moisture is removed from foods they lose their appeal to insects and rodents. In addition to its moisture, meat also must have as much fat removed as possible to prevent mildew or mold from spoiling it. Food loses as much as three-fourths of its bulk when it dehydrates. The drying process helps the starches in food to convert to natural sugars, which are easier to digest and gives one more energy, besides making the food tastier.

There were several things used as leavening agents before commercial baking powders and baking sodas. The simplest way to duplicate the old leavens today is to use ashes from the first inch on the top of ashes from a fire that has at least a four-inch ash residue (if you go any deeper than the top inch you begin to get debris). Any wood will do. Ashes left from burning the bean pods of black-eyed peas were preferred; these impart a bluish tinge to the food with which they're mixed. Also the wetted, rolled leaves of box elder would be burned and then saved in their round ball forms and used one at a time, which was the choice of most good cooks.

Gravies and sauces were a specialty of Shawnee women. For thickeners, pounded dried pumpkins and squash could be used, as well as cornstarch and arrowroot.

Seasonings were many and delicious: sassafras root or powdered leaves, as is found in Creole dishes; the leaves, ground roots, or seeds, of at least ten different mustards; onions, garlic, and watercress; birch, sarsaparilla, and wintergreen and other mints. Add to those some flowers such as violets and nasturtiums, milkweed blooms, daylily buds, and many more. We had several pepper weeds, true spice bushes similar to allspice, and of course, salt which we made from salt licks or springs. While our territory in Ohio was not too far from one of the world's largest underground salt caves known, I have found no incidence of our trading the northern tribes for it, choosing to make our own instead. After its being brought here by the Aliens, the women would use coltsfoot leaf for salt, using it in the same manner as the box elder leaves, rolled and burned and carefully stored for later use. It is said the coltsfoot salt was highly prized as the most flavorful.

These lists are far from complete, and as we traveled from area to area, we learned about and adopted new foods. We viewed the world as our supermarket and all-purpose department stores. Everything we needed was there if we just searched it out. Following are a few recipes my friends and guests have greatly enjoyed. If you experiment with any new ideas from here I would love to hear about them.

Ohio Shawnee Foods

Corn
white: opaque, hard, early, and shoe-peg
flint, dent
blue
popcorn, red and black

Beans
string
snap
pole
butter
lima
sieva
kidney
black-eyed peas

Squash
acorn
butternut
turban
delicata
cushaw
pattypan

Fish
trout
catfish
bass
crappie
blue gill
salmon
sturgeon
pike
also: eels, crayfish, frogs and toads,
    turtles, mussels

Fowl
duck
turkey
goose
grouse
passenger pigeon
swan
crane
quail

Fruits and Berries
blueberries
huckleberries
blackberries
raspberries
strawberries
cranberries
bearberries
gooseberries
squawberries
currants
service berries
elderberries
hackberries
sumac berries
dewberries
wild red plum
cherries: choke, wild, black, and ground

pawpaws
May apples
persimmons
wild grapes (three types)
melons, orange flesh; watermelons, yel-
    low flesh
crabapples
haws: red, yellow, black

Nuts
hickory
black walnut
chestnuts
peanuts
chiquapins
butternuts
hazelnuts
filberts
acorns
pecans
pinenuts

Greens
marsh marigolds
yellow dock
poke salad
wild cabbage
pigweed
milkweed
wild lettuce
watercress
wild onions
wild garlic
wild mustards (thirteen varieties)
tubers
rue anemones
adder's tongue
violet leaves
Solomon's seal
trillium
spring beauty tubers
skunk cabbage
puff balls
lamb's quarter
curly dock
wood sorrel
shepherd's purse

purslane
broadleaf plantain
fiddlehead fern
cattail roots and pods

Seeds and Seed Pods
honey locust pods
redbud pods
primrose seeds
Kentucky coffee beans
yellow pond lily seeds
wild rice

Meats
buffalo (bison)
wapiti (elk)
deer
bear
antelope
pronghorn
beaver
raccoon
opossum
groundhog
squirrel
rabbit
panther
bobcat
wolf (if starving)
chipmunks (striped ground squirrels)
salamander

Vegetables
pumpkin
sweet potatoes, yams
potatoes
sun chokes
tomatoes
bell peppers
hog peanuts
husk tomatoes
chili peppers
wild carrots (Queen Anne's lace)
parsnips
beans

Sweet Flavorings
sassafras
maple syrup and sugar

wild honey (rare)
birch syrup
hickory syrup
butternut molasses
wild cherry syrup
berries and berry juice
bell peppers
watermelon syrup
corn cob syrup
husk tomatoes
fruits and juice
grapes and juice

Oils and Fats
bear fat and oil
buffalo fat and oil
hickory oil
black walnut oil
peanut oil
sunflower seed oil
pumpkin seed oil
hazelnut oil
raccoon fat
butternut oil

Seasonings
wild onions and garlic
wild alliums
wild ginger
mints (five varieties)
sage
sassafras
spice similar to allspice
pepper root (eight varieties)
mustard (over fifteen varieties)
wild rosemary

Miscellaneous
thickeners: arrowroot, pounded dry
    pumpkin, dried sassafras leaves
salt/ground or from water extraction
coltsfoot salt
mushrooms, shelf and morels
bird eggs
box elder syrup
Note: we ate much more, this is only a partial list.

Traditional Shawnee Recipes
from Dark Rain's Cooking Fire

Dried Hominy Dish
(Serves 4)

Dried hominy and bulk currants are easily found at Amish markets and most will ship to you if you live out of the area.

1 cup dried hominy

3 cups water

Combine water and hominy and bring to a rapid boil. Simmer at lowest possible heat, tightly covered, about twenty minutes. Remove from heat and let soak at least 45 minutes.

Add 1 cup coarsely chopped black walnuts or hickory nuts and 1 cup of dried currants or raisins. Season to taste with hickory flavoring or hickory salt. Cook on top of stove or in oven at 300 degrees until hominy is tender. It may be necessary to add more water. The hominy will never be mushy but al dente.

To make this a complete one-dish meal, jerky broken into bite-size pieces may be added instead of hickory salt or flavoring. Homemade jerky is best.

Note: this is a favorite dish and simple, good for bring-a-dish-parties. Usually there are *no* leftovers!

Sauteed Daylily or Milkweed Buds
Gather these early in the morning before they unfold. You should be able to see that they are one day away from unfolding into full bloom. There is no danger involved in eating those blooms, but they are sweeter-tasting if picked before unfolding. Wash and drain the buds; you might even soak them for a few minutes to make sure all insects are out. In a shallow, wide pan melt a small amount of butter or margarine. Add buds and lightly saute until blossoms are hot clear through (two or three minutes).

The buds are also delicious poached in herbed or spiced water, or in vegetable or meat broth. They should not be soggy but still maintain a bit of texture.

Scones, Shawnee-style
Modify standard recipe, leaving out flour, baking powder and/or baking soda, eggs, and milk. Substitute with cornmeal plus 2 tablespoons of corn starch for smoother product, or use plain cornmeal. Use water in place of milk, and don't worry about eggs — you really don't need them. Sweetener options include maple sugar and syrups (I personally don't care for strong maple flavors so I cheat and use dark brown sugar). Fruit juices can be for part of the water. Add 1 or 2 teaspoons of nutmeg (optional). Double the amount of vanilla — Shawnee are not stingy, even with flavors. Add dried currants or other dried berries such as dried strawberries, dried blueberries, dried black haws, dried cranberries, although the

cranberries add color, they are tasteless when dried. Add nuts if you prefer. (Raisins are okay in place of currants, but the currants are more subtle and less sweet.)

Adding cornmeal you have a reasonable cookie or biscuit dough consistency. Coat baking sheet with cornstarch to prevent sticking, and drop or hand-shape scones. Bake at 400 degrees about 20–25 minutes. (Ovens may vary.)

Pawpaw Pones

Combine about 2 cups cornmeal with pawpaw pulp for flavor and sweetness. Go slow — pawpaws are powerful! Usually much less than you think will be needed for sweetness and for flavor desired. Start with one fourth of a cup and add to taste. You may add about one-fourth cup of corn oil to maintain a soft interior when baked. Add nutmeg and/or allspice. Nuts or currants are optional. Drop by tablespoonfuls onto baking sheet coated with cornstarch sprinkled on it to prevent sticking. Bake at about 425 degrees from 10–17 minutes.

Baked Squash

Carefully cut the top off a large squash at least ten inches in diameter (turban squash work well), leaving the sides high and unpierced. Scoop out the seeds and fill cavity with cooked beans and onions seasoned with hickory flavorings. (Green beans work best, but kidney beans, butter beans or limas could be used. I use dried green beans that have been reconstituted in the same manner as any other dried beans. (Pintos and great northerns would be tasty in this dish even though they are not an indigenous food.) Place filled squash in a baking dish and bake for one hour at 375 to 425 degrees. When serving be sure you scrape part of the squash out with each serving.

Note: to dry green beans yourself, pick and wash, let air dry one day then thread on coarse thread with crewel needle until you have about a four-foot strand. Triple the amount of thread, and hang where air can circulate around it, over or in front of stairwells, or over gas-fueled hot water heaters. After the second day you should check it twice a day and adjust the beans as they shrink and dry. When they are totally dry (four to ten days, depending on humidity in air and temperature) store in airtight containers or hang with a dust protector. The beans sweeten while drying, giving them better flavor and easier digestibility when reconstituted. Reconstituted green beans are chewy, and they tend to droop as they dry, which is how they acquired the name "leather breeches" from the Dutch.

Baked Pumpkin

Cut the top off a pumpkin about 10 to 12 inches in diameter, and scoop out the seeds. Be most careful not to pierce the sides clear through. Score the inside of the pumpkin with a fork or sharp knife blade, at least half an inch deep, again being most careful not to pierce the sides clear through. Fill with old-fashioned, hot, cooked vanilla pudding to which you have added two teaspoons of real vanilla extract (don't use imitation); add 1 teaspoon nutmeg, and 1 cup of dried currants or dried blueberries if desired. If you use fresh blueberries you will have blue pudding. Bake from one to one and a half hours at 400 degrees, or until the pumpkin is tender when tested gently with a fork. Note: If you pierce the sideskins it will wilt and be a big mess!

Buffalo Stew

Cube buffalo meat into bite-size pieces, add quartered onions, cubed potatoes, carrots, beans, squash, or corn if you like. Add fresh pepper, salt, and bay leaf. Cover with water to about three inches above the ingredients. Bring to a boil. Reduce heat and slow simmer about two hours. Buffalo should be very tender. Proportions per person: three-fourths cup of meat, one large potato, one large carrot, one large or two medium onions, one half-cup of each other vegetable, no more than three bay leaves (which you should remove before serving). Hickory, maple, dried pears, or nuts add interest to this dish. The meat should taste a bit like corned beef and will possibly turn red. This is normal for buffalo. Adding bell peppers will change the entire flavor.

Baked Small Fowl

Fill cavity with wild rice mixed with one small medium-hot pepper, diced into eighth-inch pieces. Bake at 325 degrees until tender, then coat the bird with any type fruit preserves mixed with half teaspoon dry hot mustard as a glaze. Return to oven for 15 minutes, the last 3 on broil. Serve. Works great with Cornish hens since passenger pigeons are hard to find. Chickens or prairie chickens and grouse also work well. Ducks and geese are too greasy to fix this way unless you bake them first, slice the meat, cover with the glaze, and reheat.

Meat Sauce

(Grape jelly and dry mustard are traditional; horseradish is an Alien import.) Mix concord grape jelly and spicy brown mustard, heat and pour or use as a meat dip. If this seems too tame, add the dry hot mustard or dry horseradish in tiny increments to taste.

Rich Gravy

For best taste use the brownest part of the meat drippings, scrape them into your saucepan. Use corn starch for thickener, not flour. Season with one-fourth cup of dried mint leaves, crushed. Use more to taste. I use mostly spearmint leaves, but peppermint works just as well. Fresh coarse cracked pepper and two crumbled bay leaves will enhance the flavor. This should be used with beef, buffalo, or lamb. I have never tried it on fowl, and I don't cook pork.

Baked Sweet Potatoes

Wrap sweet potatoes in aluminum foil and bake at 425 degrees until tender, one and a half to two and a half hours . Remove from oven and open without removing the foil. Make a slit from end to end in each potato. Gently stab interior of potato with fork or knife, being careful not to go through the skin. Add butter pats one-sixteenth to one-eighth inch thick along entire length of slit. Sprinkle generously with fresh ground nutmeg and two heaping teaspoonfuls of dark brown sugar along slit. Reclose foil, pressing the sweet potato shut. Let stand for the flavors to blend for at least one half hour before serving.

Jerky

Yield: 1 pound of meat yields 4 ounces of jerky.

Use a whole round, tip round, steamboat round, or bottom round roast. (These are best purchased from a hotel or restaurant purveyor or wholesale meat supplier.) If you are using beef you need not worry about the grades such as good, choice, or prime: good old 'utility' grade or 'cow' grade will work just as well. If you are using buffalo meat it will have a more subtle flavor and a bit of sweetness unless you use lots of spices and herbs. I will describe the process first, then I will give you optional spice recipes.

By purchasing the types of meat described above you will find you have a large chunk weighing from 16 to 30 pounds. Ask the butcher — sweetly — to slice this for you while it is still semi-frozen, into slabs one-eighth inch thick. They may charge you ten cents more per pound, but trust me, it is worth every penny. If you must slice it yourself, an electric knife is the best tool to use. I have found one-fourth inch slices too thick for easy chewing. Leave the fat on it as it will become the tastiest part. Have the butcher cut the meat *with* the grain so that if you pull a strand of meat off it will come off like string cheese. If you cut it across the grain the jerky will be very breakable but lack the chewiness good jerky is noted for.

Note: the thinner the pieces of meat are before drying, the quicker they will become tender when you soak and cook them. Drying the meat intensifies the flavors, so don't overdo and don't depend on your sense of taste as you prepare the marinade.

Rub each piece of meat with the seasonings and spices. You must rub the meat with a *fresh* garlic clove — the dried powder does not permeate the meat.

Sprinkle whatever spices or flavorings you will be using on the bottom of a large crock or pot (I use one that has a five-gallon capacity). Sprinkle the meat slices on both sides with the seasoning mixture, and layer them in the pot. After every inch or so layer of meat add some moisture (standard recipes use soy sauce but it is not mandatory) to bring the fluid content up to cover the level of the meat in the pot. Continue in this manner until all the meat is in the pot, again topping it off with liquid and spices. Set in a cool area, 50 degrees or less, and let marinate at least 12 hours (48 hours is ideal). Check the meat from time to time and either add more soy sauce or water, as the meat will absorb it. When the marination is done, take the meat out one piece at a time, pat dry with paper or terry towels, and lay with sides touching on a screen wire or drying rack. (If you have a gas oven, the meat can be placed on the racks in the oven, being sure to prop open the door with a wooden spoon or such so the moisture has an escape route; the heat from the pilot light is all that is needed. In an electric oven set at warm, no hotter than 150–175 degrees, again leaving the door propped open.)

The time is a delicate thing to gauge: for chewier jerky, take it out when it is still somewhat bendable; for cooking by breaking it into pieces or pounding for pemmican, dry it until it is brittle. To test a piece, take it out of the oven and let it cool before handling, because it will fool you when it is hot by still being pliable, but when it is cool it may be brittle. It generally takes my jerky from 6 to 9 hours to dry, depending on the humidity of the day, the house, and other variables. I do not recommend upping the temperature gauge on the oven as it causes a very hard product, and the jerky may scorch. A commercially produced dehydrator with a fan is great, but do watch your first two or three batches closely until you are familiar with the gadget.

Suggested spices and seasonings for jerky (per each 3 pounds of meat):

2 tablespoons soy sauce

1/4 teaspoon salt (hickory, onion, garlic, or celery)

2 drops hot pepper sauce, or to taste

ground pepper to taste

1 fresh garlic clove, minced

lemon pepper or paprika

Variations for salt watchers: Substitute fresh garlic, onion powder, or smoke flavoring for the salt Mix 1/4 teaspoon cider vinegar with water in exchange for the soy sauce (this gives the marinade the moisture it needs and a tenderizer-preservative; the vinegar flavor evaporates during the marinating time).

Traditional Yellow Jacket Soup

Find ground-dwelling yellow jackets, either early in the morning or late afternoon. Gather the whole comb and place over fire or on a stove with the right side up to loosen the grubs. Remove all the uncovered grubs. Place comb over the fire or stove upside down until the paper-like covering parches. Remove the comb from the heat, pick out the yellowjackets, and place in the oven to brown. Make soup by boiling the browned yellowjackets in a pot of water with salt and grease added, if you like. Prepare the soup as soon as the yellow jackets are parched.

Sassafras Jelly

Put 2 cups of strong sassafras tea in a pan. Add one package of powdered pectin and bring to a low boil. Add 3 cups strained honey and 12 tablespoons of sassafras root bark that has been grated to a fine powder. Simmer 6 minutes. Put in hot jelly glasses and seal.

Corn Cob Syrup or Jelly

Fill a large pot with dried corn cobs. Cover with water and boil until water is half gone; add more water and continue boiling; continue adding water as needed, taking care to keep the corn cobs from scorching. This procedure may take a full day or more. Add crabapple juice or pectin for jelly. A five-gallon pot of corn cobs yields about half-gallon of syrup. Using fresh cobs, not dried keeps the syrup from being as naturally sweet. This is the same thing as Karo Syrup. For brown syrup with more robust flavor allow it to scorch slightly.

Shawnee Beverages

Note: Please do not try to make any of these unless a recipe is included. Collecting the ingredients requires careful instruction to keep from gathering tainted plants or plants at improper times. Many known plants may not be mentioned as their purpose is primarily medicinal.

Roasted Acorn Shell (Quercus) Tea — Crush acorns with stones or hammer, roast to deepest color. Steep in boiling water for wholesome, coffee-like beverage (1 teaspoonful per cup of hot water, boil gently for at least fifteen minutes).

Barberry (barberis canadensis) — All but flowers and roots are edible. Steep crushed leaves in boiling water 15 minutes; also, an acidic lemonade pretender can be made by diluting the berry juice, cooking it 15 minutes, and sweetening.

Bergamot (Monarda didyma) Red Bee Balm, or Oswego, Tea — Pink or lilac colored blooms are the wild bergamot; soothes throats and settles stomachs. Use whole plant minus roots, cover with two quarts boiling water, cover and steep 15 minutes. Individual serving: 3 leaves per cup of water. Note: this contains antiseptic thymol, so use *sparingly!*

Birch (Betula) — Tap the same way as maples in early spring; makes teas, medicinals, beer, nonalcoholic like rootbeer.

Blackberry (Rubus) Tea — from leaves, stops diarrhea. Steep several leaves for five minutes in boiling water. Juice also makes an excellent drink. (Raspberry Tea — Same as blackberry.)

Birch, black cherry, and sweet (Betula lenta) — Twigs and bark are a source of artificial wintergreen oil. Cover fresh or dried bark chips with enough boiling water to steep in a covered cup or pot, 15 minutes.

Elderberry (Sambucus canadensis) — Use flowers and berries separately, as flowers have vanilla flavor, and berries have a strong berry flavor. Boil berry juice into syrups or concentrates for drinks hot or cold. Cover one dried flower per cup of boiling water, steep 10 minutes.

Goldenrod (Solidago) — Air dry flowers and leaves. Add two teaspoons dried leaves and/or flowers to small pot of boiling water; cover, boil 15 minutes

Grape (Vitis) — Clear, watery sap obtained by cutting vine, which holds a considerable amount of fluid. Crush 1/4 cup grapes, cover with boiling water, steep 10 minutes

Maple (Acer) — Tap for sap in early spring, boil down to concentrate flavor.

Mints (Mentha) — Fresh or dry leaves, this includes peppermint, spearmint, pennyroyal, and catnip. One teaspoon fresh or dried leaves in cup of boiling water, steep 10 minutes

Persimmon (Diospyros virginiana) — Dried leaves similar to sassafras or crushed fruits added to other fruits in drinks. One teaspoon in cup of boiling water, steep 10 minutes

Sassafras (Sassafras albidum) — Roots, leaves, bark. Two or 3 crushed leaves per cup boiling water, steep 10 minutes or, one heaping tablespoon bark or root chips in two cups boiling water, simmer thirty minutes. Or, 4 sassafras roots, 2 inches long each, in pan with 6 cups water. Bring to a boil, reduce heat, simmer 15 minutes, turn off heat and let steep 10 more minutes, strain and serve. Sweeten if desired.

Spicebush, Wild Allspice, Feverbush (Lindera benzoin) — Leaves, twigs, bark. Three or 5 fresh leaves covered with one cup boiling water; steep 10 minutes. Or, one heaping tablespoon roots and bark to 2 cups boiling water, simmer 30 minutes.

Sumac (Rhus glabra and Rhus Typhina) — Red seed cones can be used even in winter, best to harvest from late August through September; tastes like raspberry lemonade. Bruise one cup berries by removing the berries from the pod and rubbing gently between the palms of the hands. Soak in warm or room-temperature water for 15 minutes. Strain, sweeten, serve.

Sweet Fern or Meadow Fern (Comptonia peregina) — Harvest in spring and dry. One teaspoon dried grass in cup of boiling water, steep 10 minutes.

Note: There were many others beverages used, but some discretion was necessary, and persons preparing must have knowledge of herbs. By the time the Shawnee left Ohio, amounts of herbs and plants used in beverages had been greatly increased.

Often, some plants or fruits will be listed as poisonous or toxic; cooking usually cancels out those properties but not always. In some instances the seeds were the culprits, as in wild cherries and elderberries. When using these, use only the juice and throw out the seeds. Other plants and foods that the Shawnee used are currently listed as harmful, toxic, or poisonous. Usually boiling for ten minutes neutralizes most toxicity, but for others, changing the water three times allows the plant to be used for a nutritional food without harmful effects, such as acorns and buckeyes. I have also *not* included hundreds of medicinal teas, as I wish this to be purely a pleasant experience with no bad side effects. If you are in doubt about any of these, do not try them. I have not tried the acorn shell tea nor the ferns. The others I can honestly call some of my favorites.

Current Tribal Structure of the Shawnee Nation
United Remnant Band

The Principal Chief serves for life unless the council determines he is extremely unfit, in which case, for the good of the tribe, they may vote him out. He is usually replaced with one of his sons, if he is deemed fit. The Principal Chief leads the People where and how they choose to go. He may suggest, explain, educate, and otherwise attempt to convince the People on what he believes is necessary, but he can *never* demand it. The People must sanction it and willingly participate in any action proposed by the chief, or they may in the long run be dissatisfied and remove the chief for being a bad leader. The Principal Chief heads the tribe just as the President heads the government, except he has more personal contact with the People and carries more clout. Tribal business, financial business, political business, inter tribal business, international business, traditional, religious and ceremonial matters all fall under his direct attention and guidance.

Second in authority is the Nation's Mother, the embodiment of the old traditional women's peace chief. She is the chief negotiator and peace keeper.

The Vice-chief is privy to all tribal business and is capable of taking over should something happen to the Principal Chief. Currently, the Vice-chief is also the tribal treasurer and the youth director. The Vice-chairman is the main organizer of the tribe's public presentations, festivals, and other such events.

As an administrative unit, the Principal Chief, Vice-Chief, and Nation's Mother act to handle the most serious problems involving tribal membership and business matters resulting from council decisions, and in emergencies, when council is not in session.

The United Remnant Band of the Great Shawnee Nation has twelve clans, each with a male and female head referred to as Clan Chiefs and Clan Mothers. These leaders have many functions. They serve as the first line of counselors to their clan members in personal conflicts and problems, such as domestic relations concerning husbands and wives, children and parents, relatives, and friends. They also serve the clan members as liaisons to the council, presenting the sentiments and wishes of their clan members on matters of business and policy. Politically they function similarly to a U.S. Senator, and as a president's cabinet, as they advise the Chief and Council as well as vote.

There currently is no great need for the traditional warriors, but there is still a War Chief, and heads of different divisions of warrior societies, including a women's warrior society. In modern times these individuals are in charge of security, as well as supplementing other civil service positions, being trained in emergency techniques and skills such as first-aid, CPR, fire fighting, and crowd control. Many tribal members are veterans of the armed services, and others are specialists and instructors in martial arts, wilderness survival, hunting and fishing guides, and other areas that encompass the old, traditional attributes of warriors. These men and women look out for the welfare of the elderly, the children, and those needing special assistance. They also supply much of the muscle needed to create and maintain the community, working hard and usually practicing invisibility to ensure the People's security in all ways.

The Temple Woman is in charge of preparing the Great House for ceremonies, assisting in the ceremonies, and teaching the religion and supplementing the spiritual needs of the People.

Besides the set Council, there are elders. The elders must be at least sixty-five years old, and there is no set number, as each one is allowed to sit on Council. But although there is no set number of elders, they have a maximum of four voting members on Council. This is the structure of the traditional and governing Council, whose meetings are closed.

Modern-day additions have been added to insure good communications and understanding, since the People do not live in a single community. They are as follows:

1. There is an organization within the structure of the tribe called Moon Society, which is for the non-Shawnee spouses of the members and a few very special People who are friends of the tribe, so they will feel a part of the tribe, not alienated. They have a representative at Council who may speak for them but who does not have a vote. They are not on the "enrollment list." They are listed in accompanying documents, and for political reasons are never included as official members of the tribe, which is a concession to interacting with the government, but is not Shawnee tradition, which we deeply regret.

2. Recently the youth have elected two representatives who, like the Moon Society, appear and speak in Council but have no vote.

There are a minimum of thirty Council members, more when the youth are present, with twenty-nine having a vote.

There are two types of Councils, Open Council and Closed Council. The Open Council is open for each and every tribal member to speak his or her mind if he or she so desires. Each is given the exact same opportunity and courtesy as the next. After they finish speaking there is a minute or so of silence to give them an opportunity to say something they may have forgotten before the next person begins speaking. This courtesy is extended even to the children, should they have something they wish to bring to the attention of the tribe and the official Council members.

The Open Council is advised of the business matters the Closed Council will be dealing with. After Open Council, then the Closed Council begins where the actual decisions and voting take place. After the Closed Council has concluded their business they then must report back to the General Tribal membership in another Open Council what decisions have been made and how things will proceed from there.

Each Council member has one vote. It is possible for a person to hold more than one Council position, but he or she has only one vote, no matter how many positions they are filling.

There are adoptions which should be mentioned as they are sometimes misunderstood. Again because of interacting with the U.S. government the old traditional style of adopting individuals into the tribe and their being totally accepted as tribal members is not possible at this time; again this is regrettable, and not traditional. There is a tribal adoption that must be a unanimous decision by Council and ratified by the tribal members, but this is reserved for People of some Shawnee provable blood. Then there are personal adoptions, such as this writer adopting a young woman who had lost her mother. In family matters, practice and our hearts, we are mother and daughter and each treats the other as though they are birth related. This in no way changes her status concerning the tribe, nor does it make her eligible for the writer's Council position by hereditary right, that is still a right retained for my birth daughter, if Council deems her acceptable. It seems peculiar that adoptions by Indian People should be held to a different standard than the adoptions performed by the Aliens. But this seems to be just another example of holding the indigenous People to different rules, lessening their rights as humans who are equal to other peoples of the world including the Aliens.

Tribal Council's Current Structure Chart

Voting Members
> Principal Chief
> Chief's Man (body guard and messenger)
> Sub-Chief (old term was Pocili)
> Nation's Mother
> War Chief
> Clan Chiefs of each of the Twelve Clans
> Clan Mothers of each of the Twelve Clans
> Temple Woman
> Elders
> Village Chief

Non-voting Members
> Moon Society
> Youth Representatives
> Allied Tribes Representatives

Treaties

There were 349 treaties between the United States government and only 54 of the more than 480 American Indian nations through 1871, at which time Congress declared there would be no more treaties made. Many volumes would be necessary in order to incorporate all of these treaties. I have chosen to only list the Nations and the number of various treaties the government made with each. Remember that prior to the U.S. government, treaties were also made with these nations by the British, French, Dutch, Swedes, and Spanish. There were other countries who had very fleeting experiences and also had treaties, such as Russia, and at there was at least one Portuguese treaty. Treaties involved only specified tribal nations, not American Indians in general.

Research indicates the single consistency of all these treaties came from the exercising of the Alien governments in taking the tribal nations' lands. No other provision of the treaties was ever honored as per the treaty negotiations. Not one treaty was ever executed fully.

From time to time the government has been brought to court by various tribal nations to adequately settle and pay up. During an almost forty-year span from the 1930s to the early 1970s the government searched old records and even oral traditions of the tribes in an effort to sort out and validate the claims against them. This was to have been the 'final' settlement of claims. Even then the tribal nations were not allowed to chose their own attorneys but did have to pay the ones chosen for them by the government.

After forty years of investigations and preparations by these law firms, some small settlements were made. But again, by the time the law firms were paid, the tribal nations' citizens received pennies on the dollar for their share of the settlements. As more American Indians become better educated and go into the practice of law, perhaps some day in the future such will not be the case.

Greeneville Treaty

It is important to note at this time some of the interesting details of the Greeneville Treaty. First, at that time the town was called "Greene Ville" in two words. The third "e" has been dropped and the name merged into one word for the current name of the town.

Treaties took many weeks of preparation, and this one took months from the time General Anthony Wayne defeated the Indian confederacy at the Battle of Fallen Timbers, August 20, 1794. This defeat was the most crushing the Indians had ever received, costing them and their British allies several hundred casualties, including eight Wyandotte chiefs. The Indians started arriving at Greeneville for negotiations the first week of June, 1795. The Councils then began in earnest, even though there had already been some Indian groups who had visited General Wayne, but did not return for the formal Council negotiations.

The wording may be fancy but the plain truth is that Wayne insisted that the principal chiefs, their sachems and war chiefs, and all the lesser chiefs possible come into Fort Greene Ville first. These Indian leaders were literally held hostage and not allowed to leave to return to their villages, but General Wayne insisted that the chiefs were his "guests." Any business they needed to conduct with their own People was done through couriers if at all. The chiefs were held until all their lesser chiefs came in to negotiate and "accept" the terms of the treaty.

Many flowery speeches were given during those months that the chiefs were held hostage, words of good will, and there were many promises of good treatment of the Indians by the Americans. However, it was at these negotiations that the chiefs first heard of land being ceded, relinquished by treaty. Prior to the negotiations, the Chiefs thought they were accepting the new boundary terms for the Aliens to come and live in the territory with them, instead of being held at bay at the Ohio River. An insignificant and invalid treaty had been brought forth, the Muskingum Treaty, that supposedly spelled out some of the land transfer. Land not belonging to some of the chiefs who signed that document was supposedly given up. Wayne referred to treaties the Indians had supposedly made to cede land to the British, but none of the Indians were aware of these treaties. Much time was spent in heated discussion of these points, to no avail. These treaties included the Muskingum Treaty, a treaty with St. Clair, and a treaty with Harmar. None of the chiefs present were aware of these treaties and certainly not the supposed terms of them.

A treaty was signed by some of the chiefs April, 1795, then another August 3, 1795 of which there were at least two different versions, then another treaty signed at Greeneville July 22, 1814. The 1814 Treaty claimed to be the last word, making null and void all other treaties between the government and the Indians. Each version was more all-encompassing and sweeping, and took more freedom and land from the Indian People until there was nothing left but the small reservation areas.

The 1814 Treaty stated the People were to be allowed to hunt and fish in the territory they just gave up exclusive claim to which these rights were not to be denied or disturbed by the treaty, the Aliens were not to build their houses on reserved land, and many more generous-sounding terms were presented, but it was only three more years before it was decreed that all Ohio Indians had to live on the reservations and depend for sustenance on trading with the white traders and what they could grow themselves.

Many times General Wayne proposed that the People give up the land to show their good faith to the U.S. government, and to further show good will, "repay" the government for the expense of the previous warfare. That is something it had never asked of a conquered people before or since: it was a little gesture reserved for the Indians. This dreadful and unfair treaty gave the American Aliens more than half of the Ohio territory and about one-fourth of Indiana. It is considered the heart and spirit-breaker of the Ohio Valley Native People.

Treaties Between the United States Government and Native Peoples

Apalachicola	2	Mohawk	1
Caddoe	1	Muscogee	2
Omaha	2	Oneida	1
Cherokee	18	Osage, Great and Little	7
Chickasaw	8	Ottoway	19
Chippewa	21	Ottoe	5
Choctaw	11	Pawnee	6
Commanche	1	Peoria	2
Creek	12	Piankeshaw	8
Crow	1	Poncarar	1
Delaware	16	Poncar	1
Eel River	16	Potawatomi	38
Florida	7	Quapaw	4
Fox	10	Ricara	1
Hunkpapa	1	Sac	12
Illinoi	1	Seminole	2
Ioway	5	Seneca	12
Kanza	3	The Seven Nations of Canada	1
Kaskaskia	6	*Shawnee*	*14*
Kickapoo	11	Sioux	10
Maha	2	The Six Nations of New York	4
Mandan	1	Teton	2
Menominee	6	Wea	8
Miami	10	Winnebago	6
Minnetaree	1	Wyandot	14
Missouri	4	Yancton	3
		TOTAL	**349**

Identification of Those Who Contributed
Oral Traditions

Much of the information concerning the Oklahoma Shawnee came from Erminie Wheeler Voegelin's papers and field notebooks. The information was considered to be correct at that time. There is great evidence that the Shawnee have been in the process of regaining their lost knowledge for some time and that their religious ceremonies and the other aspects of their culture may have changed significantly since that time, and certainly has changed several times since 1492. As an example, the Loyal Shawnee are very proud that they have certain ceremonies, although there is some inference in Erminie's work that their religion is no longer complete. Rather than some ceremonies having been performed continuously, because of the federal laws against their performance, it is known that many years went by without the People renewing them. Then, on two separate occasions two elders were given visions that caused them to reintroduce these two ceremonies according to the new directions given these elders by Creator in their visions. These ceremonies differ somewhat, though not too greatly, from those of other divisions of Shawnee who did not cease performing the ceremonies and thus the latter have experienced the modifications that come from evolution rather than having had to totally recreate the ceremonies. While all religious ceremonies should maintain every particular without any change whatsoever, this is not possible in the human world we all live in. For example the Bread Dance ceremony has indeed changed, if in no other way than the recipe used to make the bread. The ancestors certainly did not use wheat, nor yeast, nor gas fired or electric ovens. The People's dress has changed considerably from ancient traditional ceremonial, and even daily attire, primarily because of the Aliens' Christian influence as well as the fact that deer skins are no longer plentiful. This is said merely to point out that there are, of course, going to be some variants in the different Shawnee divisions, and what was true sixty-five years ago, may not have been true one hundred sixty-five years ago, and may not be true now, it is none the less, considered good valid information that should not be apologized for today. The People have continued to evolve and may have modified things to suit today's needs, capabilities and new directives they may have received from Creator.

The elders from the Oklahoma Divisions of Shawnee gave their interviews to Erminie Wheeler Voegelin, an anthropologist, primarily between the years of 1932-38. Later in 1938 more information was given that included the Great Laws. A third stage of interviewing was conducted in the late 1950s and early 1960s for linguistics purposes, done by Charles F. "Carl" Voegelin, Erminie's former husband. Interviews of these Oklahoma Shawnees plus others who had been introduced to the Voegelins by the original interviewees, continued on a scattered basis through the 1970s. The information concerning some of those interviewed is not as complete as it is for others. All details available to this writer have been included to help positively identify these elders.

Pictures of Jennie Segar can be found in the *Handbook of North American Indians*, Vol. 15, p. 633, figure 7. The Smithsonian Institution also has pictures of interviewees James Clark, Fannie Washington, Frank Doherty, Billy Williams, and, an Absentee Shawnee named Joe Billy, who gave information to anthropologist-linguist Truman Michelson in 1911.

Primary Oklahoma interviewees according to sept or band are:

• Kispoko Division —
Billy Williams, Kispoko and Creek blood, age 65.
Mary Williams, Billy Williams' daughter, age 27.
James Clark, Kispoko Shawnee-Eyuchi-White blood, age 63, deceased 1939.
Jennie Segar, Kispoko-Thawakila Shawnee-white blood, age 78 (?), deceased 1939.

These elders all lived in central Oklahoma between Norman and Shawnee, and most were of the Absentee Shawnee. Jennie Segar spoke no English; Thomas Wildcat Alford served as interpreter.

• Pekowi-Piqua Division —
Nancy "Dora" Skye, Pekowi-Chalakaatha Shawnee-White Blood, age 60, deceased 1938. She lived near Miami, in northeastern Oklahoma, and was an Eastern Shawnee.
Thomas Wildcat Alford, Pekowi-Thawakila Shawnee- White blood, age 74, deceased in 1938, lived near Shawnee in Central Oklahoma.

Both were Absentee Shawnee, both spoke both English and Shawnee.

• Thawakila Division —
James Clark, information above
Jennie Segar, information above

Chalakaatha — Modern Mekoce Divisions

These septs are represented by the Loyal-Cherokee Shawnee, and at the time of the interviews were not performing their religious ceremonies with regularity; therefore, information for the division the was scant. Until the 1937 Wheeler Act many appeared on more than one roll at a time, causing much confusion. Frank Doherty, of Mekoce-Kispoko Shawnee-white blood, aged 73, belonged to the White Oak subgroup of the Loyal-Cherokee Shawnee. He lived near Shawnee, Oklahoma, on an allotment belonging to his third wife, an Absentee Shawnee. Doherty spoke both English and Shawnee. (Old Mekoce Division James Clark stated that it was believed the old Mekoce traditions ceased being practiced around 1800.) Other elders whose stories were used include

Joe Billy — Absentee
Carrie Blue Jacket — Eastern
Irene Clark, wife of Jim Clark — Absentee
Henry Turkeyfoot — the last full-blood Eastern
Old Lady Washington —an Eastern who lived with the Absentee

Others mentioned who are indirectly quoted include Willie Skye, Charlie Switch, Solo Washington, Little Charlie, and Switch Little Axe. Also, Mrs. Nolan, Rachel Brown, Big Jim, Jacob Tomahawk, John Logan, John Mohawk, John Snake, and Jim Squier.

Non-Oklahoma Shawnee Oral Tradition Givers

Chief Hawk Pope of the Shawnee Nation, United Remnant Band of Ohio, Kispoko sept, aged 52 in 1994, living near central Ohio and the tribal lands called Shawandasse.

Yahma Walter Shepherd, also of the Shawnee Nation, U.R.B.-Ohio, aged 38, Mekoce sept, living near Parkersburg, West Virginia.

Black Wolf Paul Harmon, Shawnee Nation-U.R.B.-Ohio, aged 34, Mekoce-Kispoko Divisions, living near Lyndhurst, Virginia.

Janet Reed, near Mason, West Virginia, friend and Shawnee researcher and of Shawnee descent.

Sun Spirit Marlene Lowe, Shawnee Nation-U.R.B.-Ohio, aged 60, Pikowe Sept, living near Urbana, Ohio.

Specific Oral Traditions and Those Who Gave Them

Thomas Wildcat Alford — Traditional foods, preparations, preservation, recipes.

Joe Billy — Sweat house construction, purpose, procedures.

Carrie Bluejacket — Sweat bath; ball game; deer hide curing and uses.

Jennie Segar — Foods, recipes, preparation, and preservation; women's agricultural activities; uses of bushel gourds, hickory nut oil. Also, using brains to tan deer hides; gathering, curing, and use of herbs; Tecumseh's premonition of his death, his knowledge of ceremony against him, his knowledge of his People's suffering, his feeling for justice and mercy; bundle beginnings; education and precepts.

Jim Clark — The Great Shawnee Laws; tribal structure — women chiefs, counselors, positions, responsibilities; types of doctoring including sweat doctoring, medicines; fire and tobacco as witnesses; babies; making salt; pottery information; Mexican-Shawnee Chihuahua 1852; Treaty information; details of relationship and legal transactions between Cherokee and Shawnee; Sam Houston, Texas and Mexico.

Irene Clark — Story of Cyclone person; foods, planting, preservation, preparation; tobacco witness; never be stingy; women's rules given after (flood) second creation; information on babies, Kohkumthena's keeping babies with her in clouds, other stories of babies' first four years, woman's typical day back in Ohio; man's typical day back in Ohio; Tukabahchee Creek information; Law of Indians called Kweteletiiwena; Florida Creation stories; traditional birthing and midwife information.

Frank Doherty — Warrior Meal; women warriors; invisibility; Doll Dance for Rain; principal chiefs clans or septs; sacred bundle information; hide-tanning, food preparations, recipes; ceremonies, no metates or manos; Cherokee-Shawnee land and entitlements transaction details; naming, Shawnee way of speaking to babies; attempts to have sacred bundle bought and stolen; original paints; use of slings; Grandmother Kohkumthena's grandson Roundsides; murder, stars, animals with four lives, the original twelve children; migration of Shawnees; objections to injuring trees; trees to be considered our grandfa-

269

thers; Walam Olum info Creation, Deluge, Migrations, Chiefs, corn preservation.

Nancy French — Well-versed on Tukabahchee Creek-Shawnee relationship, was part Creek, received annual allottment from Creek; went to their annual Green Corn Busk Dance when she was seven, she was ninety-two years old at time of interview in 1935; she had seen the copper plates Shawnees gave Creeks as a gift in 1786; information on corn varieties, women's chores, eating and cleaning up before dark; oldest traditions from oldest source; women's typical day in Ohio, man's typical day in Ohio pre-reservation.

Paul Black Wolf Harmon — West Virginia locations of Shawnee villages before and after 1840, history of minor war chief Black Wolf, McDowell County Shawnee history.

Hawk Pope — Migration information, Origination stories, Florida information; information of Tecumseh and his warriors and followers, their whereabouts in the aftermath of the War of 1812; location of hidden Shawnee communities of six states and Canada, (validated by difficult-to-obtain government documents); religious teachings, ceremonial teachings, celebration teachings, language, cultural details, clarified contradicting information.

Yahma Walter Sheperd — Information concerning West Virginia Shawnee communities and Mekujay communities and Shawnee speakers of West Virginia, and southern Ohio, and Kanawa and Ohio River communities.

Nancy Dora Skye — Foods, planting, preparations, preservation; hide tanning; herbs, forms of doctoring including sweat doctors; use of wooden pestle for cracking and refining corn; stones-rocks and trees are grandfathers.

Henry Turkeyfoot — Foods, planting, preparations. preservation, deer and other animals that have four lives, hunting etiquet.

Billy Williams — Tobacco and Fire as witnesses, messengers to Creator; religious details.

Mary Williams — Foods planting, fertilizer use, preparations, preservation, recipes, layout and directions of planting gardens; medicine, doctoring, traditional teachings; tanning, star and general astrological knowledge; much miscellaneous information.

Note: each informant offered much more information than I have been able to utilize in this book, including much language information. In the future I may be able to utilize more of this information, especially the language.

Shawnee Language

ordered obtained by
George Washington, General

compiled in Ohio by
General Richard Butler 1787-1788

at request of
Marquis de La Fayette
as a gift for the Empress of Russia

SHAWANO   ENGLISH

MONNITTO .... God or a diety
WOSSA MONNITTO .... Good god or diety
MISSI MONNITTO .... Great god
MOTCHIE MONNITTO .... Evil spirit or devil
MONNITTOKIE .... Snakes, worms, etc.
MONNITTOLETHAKIE .... Insects
LINNIE .... A man, or an Indian man
MECHTACOOSIA .... An American
TOTIE .... A Frenchman
SPANIE .... A Spaniard
LINNIEKIE OR LENNAWEKIE .... Men, Indianas, etc.
WOSSA-LENNIE .... A good man
MOTCHIE-LENNIE .... A bad man
MOTCHIE-LENNAWI .... Bad men
KEE MOTCHIE LINNAWEWIANNE .... You are a bad man
LENNOWE .... Indians, generally
OKIMA .... A king, a headman
OKIMAKIE .... Kings
MEKICKILECHKIE .... Great or principal man
NENOCHTOO .... A captain or chief warrior
NOTTOOPOLWITTA .... A warrior
NOTTOPOLWIE .... Going to war
NIE-NOTTOOPOLWIE .... I am going to war
LEPIDOWA .... Wise, sagacious
LEPWOACHKIE .... Wise men, counselors, etc.
POSHITOTHA .... An old man
POSHITOTHAKIE .... Old men
KECHTALINNIE or KECHTALENNAWE .... The first man, or ancient men
SECHCOMMIKA .... Old, or long since
MOIOCKIE .... Lately, or not long since
INNUCKIE .... Now, at this time
MIANIE .... Young, youthful
MIANIE LINNIE .... A young man
MIANIE LINNIEKIE .... Young men
HOLLAWIE .... Hunting
HOLLAWITTA .... A hunter
HOLLAWICHKIE .... Hunters
NIE HOLLAWIE .... I hunt
KEE HOLLAWIE .... You hunt
HOLLAWEEKIE .... They hunt

271

?? TA HOLLAWIACHIE .... The hunting camp or grounds
ICHQUE OR ICHQUEWA .... A woman
ICHQUEKIE OR ICHQUEWAKIE .... Women
WOSSA ICHQUE .... A good woman
MOTCHIE ICHQUE .... A bad or ugly woman
MIANIE ICHQUE .... A young woman
MICKIEPWETHETHA .... An old woman
WOSSA .... Good
MOTCHIE OR MOTCHATHIE .... Bad
WILLITHIE .... Handsome or comely
SCIHOTTEE.. Pretty
OPPELLOOTHA .... An infant or young child
OPPELLOOTHAKIE.. Infants, little children
SKILLAWETHETHA .... A little or young boy
SQUETHETHA .... A little or young girl
MICKIEPWETHETHAKIE .... Old women
OLAMI-WOSSA .... Very good superlative
ALALLICA WOSSA .... Excellent, or extraordinary
AH! *sounded long from the stomach* .... Yes
SKEALLA OR SKEALLIE .... Yes also
ALLAH sounded long or tedious .... So-so, or it may be so
IENIE OR IENIEKELAH .... That's it, or that's right
KEPPAHE .... I am willing, or I am contented
MOTTAH .... No
MOTTAYECHIWE .... No positively
MOTTAHWIEAHE .... Nothing at all
MOTTALAQUA .... None or none at all
ISHETTEHE .... Thought, or to think
NIE-TISHETTEHE or ISHETTEHEIA .... I think
KEE-TISHETTEHE .... You think
A, KEE-TISHETTEHE .... Do you think
SWE-KEETISHETTEHE .... What do you think
MUCKHSWEISHAETTEPIalso means .... What do you think
MOTTA WEEAHE NIETISHETTCHE .... I think nothing at all
MISOI OR MESSAWIE .... Big or large
KENHAWIE OR KENWHAIE... Long
PELLAWIE .... Far or afar off
MOITCHQUATHIE .... Small
CHUCKIE or CHUCKIATHIE
   or CHUCKILOSHUTHIE .... Little or diminutive
MOICHQUATHIE .... Short
EENEE ELICKHE .... So long or that long
EENEE-ELLICKELLO .... That large or that size
EENEE-ELLICKICHQUAKIE... So big
KITTESKIE .... Exactly
KENNOCHQUE MOLSPIE
   or MOLSPIETHIE .... Tall
MOLSPEETHEETHIE .... Short or low in stature
MITHOCHQUIE .... Lusty, corpulent
MITHOCHQUIE LINNIE .... A lusty, corpulent man
WANNITHO .... Drunk or drunkenness
WANNITHOTTA .... A drunkard
WANNITHOTAHKIE .... Drunkards
WEELOOTHIE .... Sober or sobriety
WEELOOTHICHKIE .... Sober people, people not fond of drink

OPPIWANNITHO .... Get sober or often being drunk
NIT-OPPIWANNITHO .... I am got sober
KIT-OPPIWANNITHO .... You are got sober
WIOKOWE .... Anagry or enraged
WIOKOWETTA .... An angry or enraged person
WOSSITTEHE .... Good-hearted — well meaning person
WOSSITTEHEEHIKIE .... Well-disposed people
MOTCHITTEHE .... Evil thinking
MOTCHITTEHETHIE .... An evil-thinker
MOTCHITTEHECHKIE .... Ill-disposed, evil-minded
_____ .... People
WANNIE .... Lost, to be lost
WANHTOO .... Lost, to lose
WANNINE .... Lost, or deranged in mind
WANNISUCKA .... An idiot, fool, or crazy person
CHIPPOMMIE .... An apparition, ghost or spector
NOOTHA .... Father
MISSUMTHA .... Grandfather
NIEKEA, OR NIEKEAHE .... Mother (actually "my" mother)
((Nie=my , kea = geah =mother))
NOOCH, COOM, THA
   or NOOCHCOOMTHAHE .... Grandmother
SHEETHA .... Uncle
NIE-LOQUOLTHA .... My nephew
THETHA .... Older brother
THEEMETHA .... Younger brother or sister
MEETHA .... Elder sister
WESSIA or WE, SOI, ANNA .... Husband
WEEWALLIE or WEEWA .... A wife
NIEWA OR NIE HA, CANNIMIE .... My wife
NEECHA, OR NEECHAN .... A child or my child=
NEECHANNAKIE
   or NEE, CHA, NI, NA, HIE .... Children or my children
USSALLITTA .... Marry or marriage
USSALLITTOMMO .... Married
NEELIMO .... Cousin, or Brother or Sister-In Law
WOSSOLLACRITTIE ?? .... A hole
MISSOLLACRITTIE .... A large hole
MOTCHQUALLACRITTIE .... A small hole
MOTCH,QUALLA,COT,TOO,THIE .... A very small hole
WAWA,WI AKIE .... Anything round, a ring or circle
WA,WI,OCH,TOE,HIE .... A whirlpool
TE,TEP,THI,TE .... A wheel, carriage, or thing that turns
QUOSHTOE, KIE .... A cataract or waterfall
KISSHICH, TON, NIE .... Swiftness, a rapid current or stream
NOO, LE .... Still, calm, quiet, not turbid
NOO, LECH, TON, NIE
   or NOO, LECH, TOE, KIE .... Still, calm, or smooth water
MIS, SICH, CON, NE .... Wind, breezes, etc.
OLAMI-MIS,SICH,CON,NE .... Very windy, tempestuous,boisterous
WEA, PSI .... Cold
THOU, CUT, CHIE .... Frost
COUSHINNOKIE .... A person frozen or frostbitten
THO, OUT, TIN, NIE .... Frozen water
KEE, POT, TIN, NIE .... Frozen up or frozen over

COO, NE or KOO, NE .... Snow
KIM, MEI, WA, NIE .... Rain
NIMPS-KIE .... Lightning
NIMPH-KEE-WAN-NIE ....Thunder
KEESHA, THWA .... The sun
KEESHTHWA .... The moon
LECOE, HIE .... The stars
OCH, QUOT, TI, TE .... Clear and hot sunshine
POSH, QUOT, TE .... Cloudy and sultry
WAP, PO, NE .... Daylight
SE, PAW, IE .... Early in the morning
QUOL, LOCH, WAP, PAKIE .... Early tomorrow morning
KEES, QUA .... A day
NIH-KEES, QUA .... Today
OO,LA,QUEE,THIE or LA, QUEE, THI, KIE .... The evening
TEPEEH, KIE .... Night
PEPE, KI, CHA .... Dark
POEK, SHIM, MO .... Sunset
LAW, ACHQUE
    or LA, WACH, QUE, THI, KIE .... Midday or meridian
KUCH, CUT, TOO .... A year
QUIT, TIE KEESH, THWA .... One moon or lunar month
IN, NIEC, KIE .... Now
SCON, NOOC, KIE .... Immediately
MOI, OCH, QUOTCH .... Hereafter
OT, TEIE, KA .... Some other time
YECH, KIE .... Formerly, time past, before now
SECH, COM, MI, KA .... Long since or long ago
EE, NIE, LA, QUA .... About that time or so long ago
PELLA, WIE .... Far away or far off
MOL, CA, HE .... At a great distance off
MUC, KA, CHIN, NA, HE .... Near at thand
MA, LA, QUA, HE .... Close by or very near
MA,WI, E, CHIE .... This side,that side, or this or that way
OO, TOTH, HA
    or OO, LOTH, A, WI, ET, TI, CA .... This way or nearer to
AL-LI-KA ....Farther off or beyond, more far
IN-NIEC-HIE ???? -KASHI-KIE .... This day
WAP-PA-HIE .... Tomorrow
AL-LI-KA-WAP-PA-KIE .... The day after tomorrow
OO'LA-COO .... Yesterday
AL-LI-KA-OO-LA-COO
    or NIE-NEESH-A-HOO ....The day before yesterday
PUC-HA-CHIE .... To go away
NIH-PUC-KA-CHIE .... I am going away
PUC-KA-CHIE-LOO .... Go away or be gone
ME'CHI'E-PUC-KA-CHIE .... Gone away
PE-A-LOO .... Come herd
PEA-WA .... Arrived or come
OO-TOTH-HA-LOO ....Come this way or come nearer
WISSA-OO-TOTH-HA-WA .... Wants to come this way
OO-TOTH-HE-WA .... Coming this way or coming nearer
WIS-SA-PUC-KA-CHIE .... Wants to go away
NIE-WIS-A-PUC-KA-CHIE .... I want to go away
KEE-WIS,A,PUC,KA,CHIE.. Do you want to go away

IL'SKIMMA	Scolding
NIE-ILSKIM,MI,QUA	They scolded me
ILSKIL,LA,WE	Wrangling
PUC,KA,CHIEH,EA,TIP,PE	Disputing
WALLESKAWE	Yoaking (sic), joking
KEE-WAL,LES,KA,WE,	You joke
OP,PAL,LE,LIE	Making diversion (sic), ridicule
NIE-OP,PAL,LE,LE,MI,QUA	They made derision of me
NUTCH HITTIE	To fight
NUTCH, HIT,TIE,KIE	Fighting, or the fight
WIP,A-NUTCH,HIWE	Wanting to fight
WIS,SA,CUT,TA,WIE	Strong
MOT,TA-WIS,SA,CUT,TA,WIE	Not strong
SHE,EPEN,NIE	Hard
SCON,NO,THIE OR SPIN,NO,THIE	Soft, maleable
KISH,A,NOT,TI,TIE	Hard to obtain, dear
WETE,THEC,THIE	Easily obtained, cheap
TOL,WAT,TIE or TOL,WAT,HIPE	Gaming, gambling, play
WAN,NI,MIE	Cheating, deceiving
KEE-WAN,NI,MIE	You cheated me
NIE-WAN,NI,MI,QUA	They cheated or deceived me
WIE,CON,NIE OR WEE,CON,WIE	Sweet, pleasant tasting
WEE,THUC,KON,WIE	Bitter, ill tasting
WEE,THUC,KIP,PIE	Spirits or bitter water
ISSHIP,PIT,TE	Salt or sour tasted
UL,LOCK,QUIE	Fat, in good order or condition
UPH,CUT,TE	Lean, poor, starved
SKIN,WIE	New, fresh, also raw
KISH,ETTE	Boiled, roasted, fit for us
KEE,SHE,THO	Warm
TIC,KUN,WIE NIPPIE	Cool water, a cool spring
TIC,KUN,NI,KIE	Cool springs
THEE,PEE	A river or large creek
THEE,PEE,KEE	Rivers, creeks
THEE,PO,WE,THIE	Rivulets, runs, small streams
MIS,SI?,WAT,CHI,WIE	A mountain
WAT,CHI,WIE	A hill
WAT,CHI,WACH,KIE	Hilly mountains
A,WA,THIE	Over or beyond the hill
LWE,WA,MIC,KIE	A vale, or level land below a hill
TOUH,SCUT,TE	A plain
TOUH,SCUT,TE,KIE	Plains, clear open land
KIT,TE,KA or KIT,TE,KA,NA	A cornfield
KIT,TI,KA,NI,KIE	Cornfields
WOCH,KA,HO,WE	A fence or fort, fortress
MOO,MOO,LICH,KA	A saline place used by wild beasts to lick
MOO,MOO,LICH,KA,NI,KIE	Licks or saline places
WIS,H'OPIP,PI,KIE	Salt springs
WIS,KO,OPIP,PIE	Salt made at a saline or salt spring
NIP,PIE-PIM,MIE	Salt, literally the oil or fat of water
NIP,PIE	Water
PIM,MIE	Oil or fat
SEOCH,HON,NIE	Wet
MUCH,QUOM,ME	Ice
MUCH,QUOM,ME-PEM,HOE,QUIE,KIE	Ice driving on a river

SCUT,TE .... Fire
NIP,PO,THO .... Burned, person burned, destroyed by fire
SA,COO,THA .... Houses, woods consumed by fire
THUCK,TA,NA .... Conflagration, blazing
OO,TEEH,QUA .... Wood, firewood
PEE,LESKIE .... The woods, forest
PEE,LES,KEC,KIE or PEELES,KI,TUS,SCY .... In the woods
PEE,QUA .... Brush, underwood, high weeds
PEE,QUA,KIE .... Thickety, brushy
PECK,WEE .... Ashes
METH,TIEK,QUEE .... A tree
METH,TI,QUOT,KIE .... Trees
PEC,KI,MEESIE .... Cherry trees
PUC,KA,NIE,NEESIE .... Nut trees
PUC,KAN .... Nut
PUC,KA,NIE .... Nuts
SOO,SOO,WI,MIE .... Chestnuts
MIS,SIM,MI,NO,KIE-MAIS,IE .... Apple trees, fruit trees generally
MIS,SIM,MI,NO,KIE .... Apples, pears, etc.
POCH,KI,MO .... A plumb (sic), plum
POCH,KI,MO,KIE .... Plums
POCH,KI,MO-MEESIE .... Plum trees
WEE,THI,A-POCH,KI,MA .... Peaches (literally hairy plums)
   (weethi,a is hair therefore peaches are so called from being hairy)
OHSEE,MIEPAPPAS, (sic) PAWPAWS .... a wild fruit, shaped like pears
OHSEE,MIE-MEESIE .... Pawpaw trees
SECK,QUA .... Turpentine wax
SECKQUA MEESIE .... Turpentine tree, the pine
TOC,QUA MEENOCKIE .... Tree berries, the mulberry

Shown on the next two pages are samples of the original handwritten records of the Shawnee language done in 1787–88.

Shawano	English
Monrietto	God, or a Deity
Wessa–Monrietto	Good God or Deity
Mifsi–Monrietto	Great God
Moschie–Monrietto	Devil or Evil Spirit
Monnittokie	Reptiles, worms &c
Monnittolethakie	Insects
Linnie	A man, or an Indian man
Mechlacoffia	An Englishman, or rather a Virginian
Tofie	A Frenchman
Spanie	A Spaniard
Linniekie or Lennawekie	Men, Indians &c
Wofsadinnie	A good man
Wofsa–Linniekie	Goodmen
Moschie–Linnie	A bad man
Moschie–Lennawie	Bad men
Kee–moschie,linnawewiannie	You are bad men
Lennawe	Indians generally
Okima	A King, a head man
Okimakie	Kings, &c
Mekichilechkie	Great, or principal men
Nenochloo	A Captain, or Chief Warrior
Nottoopolwitta	A Warrior
Nottoopolwichkie	Warriors
Nottoopolwie	Going to War
Nee–Nottoopolwie	I am going to war
Lepedowa	Wise, Sagacious &c
Lepewoachkie	Wise men, Counsellors &c
Bofkelotha	An old man
Pokelothakie	Old men
Kechtalinnie, or Kech,talen,nawe	The first man, or Ancient men
Sech,commeka	Old or long since
Moiockie	Lately or not long since
Innuekie	Now, at this time
Mianie	Young, youthful
Mianie–Linnie	A young man
Mianie–Linniekie	Young men
Bollawie	Hunting
Bollawitta	A hunter
Bollawichkie	Hunters
Nee–Bollawie	I hunt
Kee–Bollawie	You hunt
Bollawekie	They hunt
Te–Bollawiwachie	The hunting camps or grounds
Sequie or Sequewa	A Woman
Sequiekie or Sequewakie	Women
Wofsa–Sequie	A good Woman

Shawano	English
Cathera. mequoohie. (Cathera is black)	Blackberries or the dried berries
Otheheemie (Othehe is heart)	Strawberries, litterally heart berries
Thabomee	The full grapes, or the purple grapes
Pethie, sochtomie	The little black tart grape
Tamee	Maiz, Coon or Indian Corn
Caws, guie	Wheat, Rye, Barley, Small grain generally
Tamequa	The Cob of the corn
Iqualetqua	The corn stalk
Nsseqummie	The corn after in the milky state, scraped off the cob dried & boiled
Methequate	Hommony, Corn pounded & boiled
Tochutha or Tochythana	Bread made of corn meal
Toochthana	Meal made of Corn
Caws, guie, toochthana	Wheat flour
Caws, guie Toochuthia	Bread made of Wheat flour
Mescoohie, thapei	Beans, Peas &c
Rennickie	The wild hoppnies, Pottatoes &c
Misiohie	Cabage, leaves & greens, called &c
Wotsiohia, chehie	Cucumbers
He teemie, cuohie	Mushmellons
Pthi, tomme, hie	Watermellons
Wappicoe	Pumpkins
Cuto, picoo	Squashes, Simlins &c
Thulthi, tommie, hie	A Sugar camp, or place for making Sugar
Mennethie	An Island
Monnethie, hie	Islands
Lewamikie	A bend or curve in a River
Tulthie wa wamikie	The fork of a river or road
Poolgue, wamikie	A bend out from the main land forming an Island in high water
Meawie	A Road
Messewa	A Horse
Messewahie	Horses
Meekillie = Messewa	A Colt
Squethima. Messewa	A Mare
Mochcootalutha. Messewa	A Colt & young horse
Meekillie = Methotha	A Bull
Methotho	Neat Cattle
Tsppelloo Methotho	Buffaloe
Meth, thohie	Buffaloe or cattle generally
Noo, fascutha	A Cow, a Caws, mare or Ewe &c
Squethimo	A Brute female, of almost any kind
Merotha	A Sheep
Mekethakie	Sheep
Kooshho	A Hog
Kooshhakie	Hogs, Swine &c
Pifsick, hie	A Deer
Pifsick, theehie	Deer
Sappe	A Buck

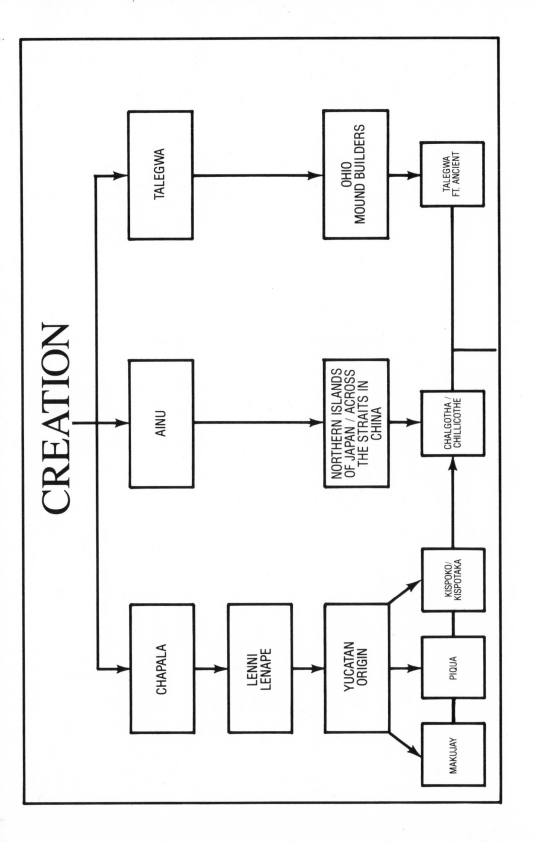

CREATION

Facing page —
A map from *Enquiry Into the Causes of Alienation*

A B C D — lands granted by the Indian Walking-Sale, as walked out by W. Pearson, containing 330,000 acres.

A E F G — land of the same grant according to the Proprietaries Claim, containing about 1,000,000 acres.

H I K L — bounds of the grant made by the Six Nations in 1749, containing about 1,500,000 acres.

H M N O — land requested by Teddyuscung for a settlement for the People, containing about 2,000,000 acres.

L H P Q R S — bound of the Purchase of 1754, containing about 7,000,000 acres.

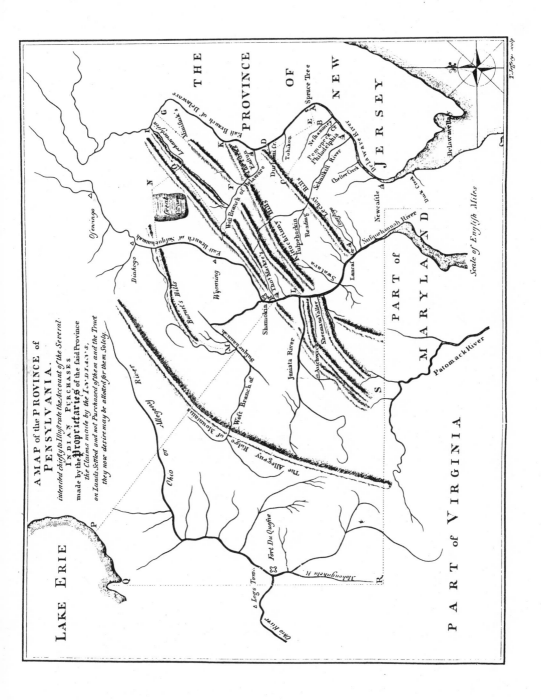

A MAP of the PROVINCE of
PENSYLVANIA.
intended chiefly to Illustrate the Account of the Several
INDIAN PURCHASES
made by the Proprietaries of the said Province
the Claims made by the INDIANS,
on Lands Settled and not Purchased of them and the Tract
they now desire may be allotted for them, Solely.

LAKE ERIE

THE PROVINCE OF NEW JERSEY

PART of MARYLAND

PART of VIRGINIA

Scale of English Miles

T. Jefferys sculp

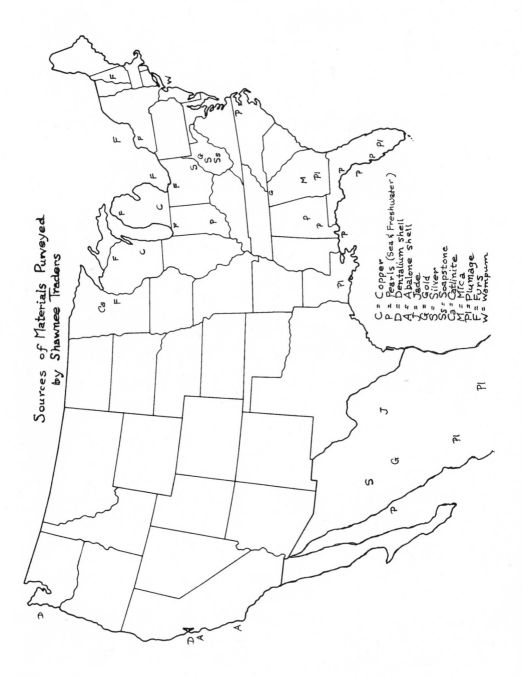

Sources of Materials Purveyed
by Shawnee Traders

C = Copper
P = Pearls (Sea & Freshwater)
D = Dentalium shell
A = Abalone shell
J = Jade
G = Gold
S = Silver
Ss = Soapstone
Ca = Catlinite
M = Mica
Pl = Plumage
F = Furs
W = Wampum

Shawnee Reservations 1818-1831

Shawnee Nation United Remnant Band Urbana, OK

Eastern Shawnee Seneca, MO

Loyal Shawnee Tahlequah, OK

Absentee Shawnee Shawnee, OK

LAST SHAWNEE RESERVATIONS IN OHIO (1818-1831) and

PRESENT-DAY Shawnee Tribes and Bands

KNOWN LOCATIONS
OF SHAWNEES
1539 - 1700

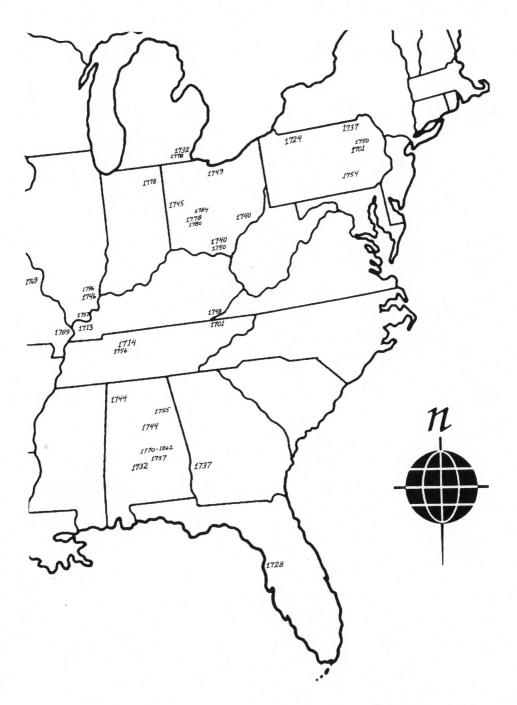

NEWLY REPORTED LOCATIONS
OF SHAWNEES
1700 - 1800

②

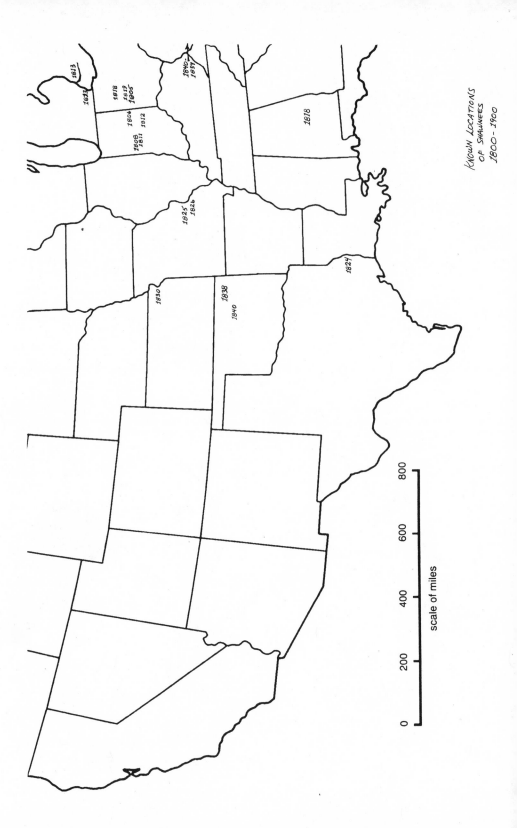

KNOWN LOCATIONS
OF SHAWNEES
1800-1900

1813

1833
1818
1819
1805
1806
1812
1808
1811

1840-
1859

1818

1825
1826

1830

1838

1840

1824

scale of miles

0   200   400   600   800

Land and sea voyagers
meet near Etowah (Georgia)

Ohio

MEXICO

Gulf of
Mexico

Lake Chapala

Shano

Old Cuna
Home —
place of
Embarkation

>······> Walking routes

→ → → Boat route

Map of Migration of the People
from Mexico in the 10th Century

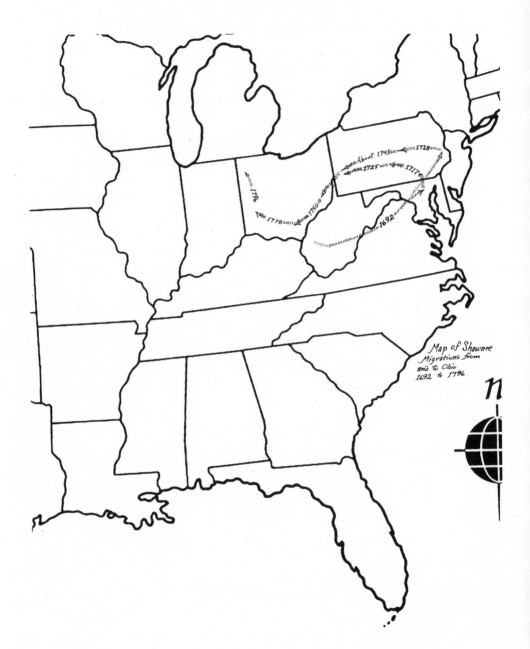

About 1743   1728

1725   1717

1796

1778   1750

1692

Map of Shawnee
Migrations from
and to Ohio
1692 to 1796

n

Locations of Special Interest:
What they were called and where to find them today

Shawnee Village Locations

1. **Chillacaathee, 1773**—North of a large plain adjacent to a branch of Paint Creek; cultivated corn fields on the plain, erected log houses. This was the chief town of the Shawnee; Chief Othaawaapaalethee (Yellow Hawk) lived there.

2. **Chillicothee Town, 1772**—Est. by Chalakaatha division. On branch of Paint Creek, a western tributary of Scioto River near Frankfort, OH.

3. **Chillicothe, 1774–80**—(Also called Old Chillicothe, Old Town) Had council house and small fort, cultivated 300 acres of corn. Three miles north of Xenia, OH, on Rte 68 (present-day Oldtown). ("New Town," 1774—Shawnee Chalakathaa division moved from Scioto location to the Oldtown location. The identity of this New/Old Town changed several times. In 1756 called Peckuwe (Pequa) and was inhabited by Pekowi division Shawnee. In 1768 Kispoko Shawnee from Scioto region removed to Pequa. By 1770 the town was predominantly Chalakathaa and became known as Chillicothe.)

4. **Chillicothe, 1780–82**—(Also called Standing Stone Village) Est. by those burned out from Chillicothe in Greene Co., OH (above). Seventeen miles south of present-day Piqua, OH. (Piqua is on I-75, about 25 miles north of I-70.)

5. **Girty's Chillicothe, 1783–90**—On lower St. Mary's River, about one mile northwest of city of St. Mary's, OH, near Lake St. Mary's.

6. **Chillicothe, 1788**—Shawnees from the White River in Indiana returned to found this one on the Maumee River a few miles east of Fort Miami, across the river from Fort Meigs at Toledo, OH, and several miles downstream.

*7. **Chillicothe, 1787**—Northwest of Cape Girardeau on White Water River, Missouri, a tributary of the Mississippi, about 65 miles north of the junction of Mississippi and Ohio Rivers.

8. **Pickaweeki, 1772**—(Also called Pecowick) Est. by Pekowi division. On Deer Creek, a western tributary of the Scioto River, six miles up from the mouth of the creek. Matthew Elliott had a trading house there.

9. **New Pickaway Town, 1777–80**—Est. by Pekowi division, later called New Boston; four and a half miles west of Springfield, OH, on northwest bank of middle Mad River, called Pickaway Fork of Great Miami River. Contained a fort, cultivated 800 acres of corn.

10. **Upper Piccawa, 1780–82**—(Also called Pecaway/Piqua Town) Est. by Pekowi Shawnees from New Boston, three miles north of present Piqua, OH, on west side of Great Miami River; was burned by George Rogers Clark.

11. **Pickaway Town, 1782–86**—Est. by Pekowi Shawnee. On west bank of upper Mad River at present West Liberty, OH. Established after Clark burned Upper Piccawa Town on the Great Miami; this one burned by Logan.

12. **Blue Jacket's Town, 1772**—Est. possibly by Mekoce division. Three miles northwest of Pickaweeki (#8 above) on east bank of Deer Creek, nine miles up from its mouth, north of a large plain. Was residence of War Chief Blue Jacket and Headman (Chief) Kiahahinottisthee, also known as Hardman.

13. **Blue Jacket's Town, 1778–86**—Located at present-day Bellfountaine, Logan Co., OH, burned by Logan Oct. 1786. (In 1788 Blue Jacket had a fine plantation well stocked with cattle on the Upper Maumee River.)

14. **Kishapookee, 1772**—(Also called Kispoko Town.) Est. by Kispoko division. Twenty miles north by northeast of Chillacaathee, west side of Scioto, south of Darby Creek, 11 miles north of mouth of Deer Creek, a mile above the mouth of a creek emptying into the Scioto from the west-the trader at this town was Col. Richard Butler, brother to William Butler.

15. **Wockachalli, 1772**—(Also called Crooked Nose's Place.) Three miles northwest of Chillicothe Town on east branch of Paint Creek, middle course; residence of trader Alexander McKee and his Shawnee family.

16. **Cornstalk's Town, 1772**—Est. by Mekoce division. On north bank of Scippo Creek which empties into Scioto River, village was four miles south of Circleville, Pickaway Co., OH, just east off Rte. 23 on Pickaway Plains, twenty miles northeast of present Chillicothe, OH; town was opposite that of his sister, Grenadier Squaw's Town (below).

17. **Grenadier Squaw's Town, 1772**—(Also called the Burning Grounds.) Est. by Mekoce division. Same location as Cornstalk's Town, but on south bank of Scippo Creek; this town was much larger than Cornstalk's. (Note: Nonhalemah, the Grenadier Squaw, was a war chief, born c. 1720 in Oldtown, MD. Her grounds were used for burning prisoners at the stake.)

18. **Maguiechaik Town, 1772**—Est. by Mekoce division on west bank of Scioto River at north side of mouth of Darby Creek.

19. **Packshenose, 1772**—(Also called Puckshenoses.) On middle course of Darby Creek. Est. by Packshenose, a Shawnee chief removed from the Susquehanna River to Ohio in 1758.

20. **Mamacamink Town, 1772**—On middle course of Darby Creek upstream a few miles northwest from Packshenose, probably a Shawnee town, but there are no previous references to it.

21. **Old Shawnee Town** (ancient Shawanese)—Probably refers to Lower Shawnee town, at mouth of Scioto on its west bank; abandoned in 1758.

22. **Sam Jamison's, 1772**—On east bank of Scioto at mouth of Walnut Creek, thirteen miles north of Kishapookee Town/Kispoko Town.

23. **Pluggy's Town, 1772**—Est. by mixed tribes: Mingo, Seneca, Six Nations from Cross Creeks on Ohio River, and others. On Olentangy River, at or near Delaware, Delaware Co., OH.

24. **Salt Lick Town, 1772**—(Also called Secaium Town.) Town was Shawnee until 1774, then became Mingo. West of junction of Scioto and Olentangy Rivers near Columbus, OH, 30 miles north of Kishapookee Town. In 1735 Senecas camped there. Later determinations say location is at junction of Scioto and Little Scioto Rivers, 45 miles north of Columbus.

25. **Will's Town, 1777–82**—Probably on Great Miami River north of Piqua, OH. Burned by George Rogers Clark 1782.

26. **Wakatomica**—(Also called Capitol Indian Town or Shawnee Town; was another Burning Ground.) On west bank of Upper Mad River, two miles below Zanesfield, OH. From 1777–86 occupied by Shawnees from Wakatumaki on the Muskingum which was destroyed in 1774; was considered main town of Shawnees of Upper Mad River. Cherokees-burned it in Oct. 1786.

27. **Mackachack, 1777–86**—(Also called Micochekay, Michacheck, Macuchca, Maycockey Town, Mackacheek, Major Jack.) A Mekoce Shawnee town on Mackchack Creek, one mile up this creek from its junction at Mad River, east of and a little below West Liberty, OH. Consisted of two settlements, one on east side of Mackachack Creek, and one on west side of Mackachack Creek. Was home of trader Matthew Elliott.

28. **McKee's Town, 1778–86**—(Also called Kispikuki, Kismagogee.) Kispoko town on McKee's Creek, two and a half miles southeast of Bellefountaine and 4 miles west of Zanesfield, OH. Residence of British agent and trader Alexander McKee and his Shawnee family.

29. **Villages near Greeneville, Darke Co., OH**—Some Indian villages near Greeneville, 22 miles west of Piqua, OH. No actual documents exist to prove these were Shawnee but are presumed so by the fact that at some time after the turn of the century (1800) Tenskwatawa had his headquarters there.

30. **Cluster of nine villages**—About 30 miles northeast of Piqua, OH, on the headwaters of the Great Miami and Mad Rivers. From 1777–86 these towns were inhabited chiefly by Shawnees, Delawares, Mingos, and Cherokees. (Note: In 1786 ten towns were destroyed.)

31. **Mekoce village (name undetermined), 1791**—On the Maumee River, in vicinity of Grand Glaize which is now known as Defiance, OH.

32. **Pigeon Town**—On a tributary of the Upper Great Miami River. Howe states it was Shawnee, on Mad River three miles northwest of West Liberty, OH; Butterfield places it

on the west side of Mad River, three miles norhtwest of Mackaachack.

33. **Waupaughkoneta**—Small town on east side of Upper Mad River, two miles south of West Liberty. Est. 1778, destroyed in Oct. 1786.

34. **Wapakoneta**—At present-day Wapakoneta, OH, west of I-75 north. Last Shawnee reservation in Ohio, last Loyals left 1836 or 1838. (An earlier Wapakoneta was on Mad River during the Revolutionary War.)

35. **Loramier's Store**—A trading depot and encampment place for Indians, destroyed in 1782. At Fort Loramie, OH.

36. **Camp at salt spring**—Where Shawnees made salt; at head of Beaver Creek where it flows into lower Scioto from the east.

37. **Camp on east bank of Scioto**—At mouth of Sam Jamison's Creek, thirteen miles above Kispoko Town.

38. **Shawnee towns**—Several located in Logan Co. before and after signing of the Greeneville Treaty.

39. **Sinhioto, 1738**—A lower Shawnee town on east bank Scioto at the mouth at Ohio River.

Places

Cuyahoga River—Earlier called White River, its horseshoe-shaped course enters Lake Erie near Cleveland. In 1742, tribes of that area included Seneca, Cayugas, Oneidas, Onandagas, and Mohawks. Also Loups, Moraignans, Ottawas, Abenakis of St. Francis, and Saulteux Chippewas of lower end of Lake Ontario.

Fort Duquesne—Built at the Forks of the Ohio, present-day Pittsburgh, PA.

Coshocton (Conchake)—At forks of Muskingum River, at Coshocton, OH.

Kekionga (Kishkagon)—At current Fort Wayne, IN.

Logtown—On Ohio River near Pennsylvania-Ohio border near Ambridge, PA.

Falls of the Ohio—In Indiana, on the Ohio River, between present Louisville, KY, and Clarksville, IN, at first exit off I-65 north of Ohio River.

Battles

Battle of Point Pleasant, Oct. 10, 1774—(Ohio River at mouth of Kanawa River) Predominantly Shawnee force of 800–1000 Indians fought from dawn till noon an equal white force; no clear victory, but Indians were demoralized. Participating Shawnee chiefs included

Cornstalk, Blue Jacket, Black Hoof, Red Hawk, Captain Dickenson, Elinipsico, and Scoppathus; also, Wyandot chief Chiyawee. Blue Jacket and Black Hoof signed the Greeneville Treaty. Cornstalk, his son Elinipsico, and Red Hawk were murdered at Fort Randolph in November of 1777, at mouth of the Kanawa River.

St. Clair's Defeat, Nov. 4, 1791—At Saint Mary's, an assault against the Miamis led by Little Turtle and their allies, it was the most spectacular defeat of any and all of the white armies. The three principal leaders were Little Turtle (Miami), Blue Jacket (Shawnee), and Buckongahelas (Delaware). By 1792 large towns of these mixed tribes were located at the Glaize, (Auglaize River), and included the aforementioned "big three" and Nanticoke, Conoy (Piscataway), Mingo, Cherokee, Creek, and a number of white captives.

Battle of Fallen Timbers, Aug. 20, 1794—(Maumee River, about 10 miles from Toledo, OH, near I-75.) Battle lasted several days, the ultimate result of the conflict being the signing of the Greeneville Treaty the next year. Approximately one hundred Indians killed, including eight Wyandotte chiefs; 33 white American casualties. Ratio of injuries to deaths was 3:1 for both camps.

Battle of Tippecanoe, Nov. 7, 1811—(Near present-day Battle Ground, IN.) Battle occurred while Tecumseh was on a southern trip to enlist those nations into a political unit to deal with the American government. Site was within three-fourths of a mile of Prophet's Town II, where Tecumseh's brother preached return to traditional Indian religion and customs, to break dependency on American goods. Had been home of Tecumseh and his family since the signing of the Greeneville Treaty sixteen years prior. During Tecumseh's absence Governor Harrison trespassed over sixty miles into territory belonging to the Potowatomi and Miami, where Prophet's Town lay, thus goading the Prophet into an attack. Indian forces were defeated, Prophet's Town was destroyed, 38 warriors died.

Battle of the Thames, Oct. 5, 1813—(Tecumseh's last battle.) Thirty miles north of Chatham, Ontario, one mile below Moravian Town near present-day Bothwell. The Canadians consider Tecumseh a national hero and the battlefield is now a state park.

Chief George "Buck" Captain, Eastern Shawnee Tribe of Oklahoma

Chief J. Hawk Pope of the Shawnee Nation, United Remnant Band, Ohio.

Erminie Voegelin, anthropologist and Shawnee researcher.

Charles "Carl" Voegelin, linguist.